This is Tanzania

ADRIAN STRAIN

DEDICATION

This collection of writings is dedicated to the late Mr Philibert Ngairo of Kiangu, Mtwara without whose help and advice we would have left without understanding much of life in Tanzania

CONTENTS

ACKNOWLEDGMENTS

To Voluntary Services Overseas for arranging my placement,
To Mtwara Teachers College for accommodating us and
to the many friends we made who have provided me unknowingly with all
the material for this book.

This is Tanzania

Introduction

In 2010, my wife Caroline and I set off for a year in Tanzania. I was to support tutors at a teaching college; Caroline was joining me for the experience of a lifetime. What follows are some idle rambling diary entries written over a period of three years and covering the time we spent in Mtwara, Tanzania. It covers the heady and stressful time we spent settling into our new home, meeting our new neighbours and learning how to go about daily life in a new and very strange culture. It covers the huge number of misunderstandings caused by cultural differences and the wide range of strong characters who thrive in the face of a level of adversity few Europeans have ever experienced.

It is not a travelogue for we saw very little of Tanzania. It is not a political journal for my views are rarely supported by data. But it tries to be a series of observations seen through the lens of a very ordinary couple in an extraordinary place.

Part One

October 2010 – May 2011

Getting ready for the big day

No matter how many times I suggest to Caroline that we should start packing or at least practise packing, she says, "No, we just need to be patient." I'm so excited.

We have almost completed the schedule of vaccinations; we have the anti-malarial tablets ready; we have bought our medical kits and have started lists mental and real of all those items we think we might need. We have still to cancel telephones, car insurance and explain hundreds of things about the house which Sarah needs to know.

Our tickets are ready apparently. We have Charity tickets with BA and with a baggage allowance of 46kg each. Apart from some extra boxers and a pair of goggles I'm not sure how we're going to use that weight allowance. A previous volunteer advised us that we could and perhaps should buy much of our stuff out there - better for us and better for the local economy, so apart from footwear, essential luxuries and a steel knife sharpener which might come in very handy, we're planning to travel fairly light.

Sunday 3 October

Well we're here

We're here. It's hot. And the people are very welcoming. We have spent the last two days with a mixed group of Dutch, Kenyan and British volunteers, learning more about Tanzania - one minute the strategic plan and the MDGs, the next, how to use a dalalala safely. All very useful, some of it more interesting than others.

I'm trying very hard to eat only cooked food - peel, cook it or forget it, some friend advised before we left and I'm trying to adhere to that MO. No problems so far, but the rats looking over us, as we ate last night and the long, long hair in Caroline's rice and fish today, make every mouthful a new adventure.

We've worked out already that we will not live well on the allowance we have, but everyone - absolutely everyone - speaks so warmly of Mtwara, the College, the accommodation, the beach and the people that I can't wait to get there, but first, we leave for Morrogorro on Saturday to learn Kiswahili. Already, I feel a huge deficiency in my understanding of Tanzanian culture because I have no knowledge whatsoever of the language. The simplest greeting leaves me baffled. I'm reading about the skirmishes and conquests of the Europeans in Africa in the nineteenth century and it helps, but to be able to say "hujambo" in precisely the right tone would help a lot more.

Monday 11 October

We're staying at a small convent in Morrogorro. It feels a little like how I imagine Paradise to be with a CD player. We were woken to the sound of African choirs singing. It was actually filming being done for a Christian DVD but in those waking moments it created a strange atmosphere.

On a walk up the hillside, past a teachers' training college, we passed huts made of clay and crooked timbers, women washing clothes in a bucket, children were feeding pigs in a wooden sty. The water here is fed from a spring further up the hillside; local people were keen for us not to climb past the source as there has been typhoid in the town and they want to keep their water supply pure and safe from poison.

Ninanupenda kujifunza Kiswahili!

After one day I can conjugate verbs, count, greet people and sustain a simple conversation. It is so liberating, certainly the most productive day since I arrived in Africa, just eight days ago. Greetings are very important in Swahili culture and we spent an hour or so learning the many and varied ways of asking the same question about one's family, children, job, journey or spouse. One important greeting is to an older person. No matter their status or gender, if they are older than you, you must greet them once with "shikamoo". The reply is always given, "maharaba". It matters not whether your assessment of their age is wrong, you cannot cause offence by offering shikamoo to someone younger than yourself. It will be taken as a humorous mistake as it is invariably a compliment because age is synonymous with wisdom. In most parts of the developed world our western culture values youth above all other qualities. We associate youth with dynamism, vibrancy, creativity and fecundity. Experience, understanding and wisdom are subordinate to these greater life-giving attributes. As a result we must never intimate that a woman is older than she is. Once she has turned thirty it is considered on the fringes of good manners to allude to her age at all. Our Tanzanian teachers thought this hilarious.

Friday, 15 October 2010

Today we're preparing to cook our first meal. Starting with the vocabulary and the protocol for the market, we learn how to ask for onions, rice, limes, garlic, tomatoes and everything we'll need for a spicy pilau rice with green peas. I have to go to the market and say: "ninaombe kununua malimau tatu na nlimu tanu?" That's three lemons and five limes to non-kiswahili speakers. I'm going to ask the young lad who charged me 700 shillings for an old dry orange. I also have to find out the price for a kilo of green peas – that's "bei gani njegere kilo moja?" We'll be cooking the rice in coconut milk having creamed the coconut on an ingenious blade attached to a folding wooden stool. The creamed coconut is then strained by hand. No water is used, partly to enhance flavour, but also of course because the water is not clean. The rice is cooked on a charcoal stove or jiko. We'll buy a stove for about 3000 shillings.

As aside on matters of language, students of Kiswahili soon become aware just what a melange of Arabic, bantu and European words is the language of Tanzania. Some of us have taken to spotting the more humorous ones. You might need to know, for instance, that deep fried potatoes are called "chipsi", or a driver is a "deriva" but the best one to date remains the Kiswahili for roundabout......the "kiplefti"!!

12 October 2010

Something about money and what it costs to live here. We are to live on a little more than a high school teacher's salary. I'm told we will be relatively well off, with our accommodation costs already met and my salary intended to meet food and local transport costs only.

I'm still making the mistake of converting prices into sterling. This distorts my fuller understanding of what life is like for Tanzanians. A journey on a daladala is regulated by the government, every trip costing 250tsh, about 11p in sterling. 11p is approximately 1/1000th of a day's wage in UK. It represents more than 1/20th of a good wage in Tanzania. Five big oranges cost 700 shillings, about 1/8th of a day's wage or equivalent to more than £10 in Britain. These calculations might seem geeky but they help me start to understand what poverty means for 80% of the population here.

Some things are so expensive here, the ordinary shops don't stock them. I can't find shaving gel anywhere. Airtime for phones is on sale everywhere but actually quite expensive for Tanzanians. 20p for half an hour at an internet cafe might seem cheap to us but it's nearly an hour's wage here.

Tuesday, 19 October 2010

The Amabilis centre where we are staying is run by the Mgolole Sisters. It is beautifully clean, built in a square around an open courtyard, in a Spanish style; with short corridors housing six rooms, each with two beds in each wing. Two toilets, two wash basins and two showers serve each wing. Each room has an electric fan and each bed has a mosquito net. When the electric fan in one room broke yesterday, an electrician was called quickly and the fan was mended by the end of the day.

The same can't be said for the water. In each shower and in each wash basin there is at least one tap that drips. Last week, water was running down the tiled floor threatening to enter our rooms. When the plumber was called, he stopped the drips but failed to install the taps correctly so exactly the same thing will happen again in a few weeks' time. I won't go into the need to take a large bucket of water to the toilet to ensure all waste actually leaves the building! Suffice to say it uses a lot of water. In the garden, an outside tap fed from a natural spring in the mountain above us, runs – not drips – continuously; this in a country where water is scarce and where most travel long distances carrying water precariously on their heads or the back of a bicycle. Continuing the review of kiswahili words with an uncanny similarity to English, we have "foleni" (full lane) for traffic jam, "baisikeli" for bicycle and my favourite today, especially for my son Peter, an electrician ... a "spaki" (pronounced sparky)!

17 October

Up early this morning to catch a glimpse of the wild animals in the Mikumi National Park. Our coach was here at 5.00am, the nuns had packed a superb breakfast of samosas, hard boiled eggs, bananas and bread and jam and we raced to the park gates to be there before the animals could wake up. We were not disappointed! Giraffes, elephants, wildebeest, buffalo, and warthogs abound; but on a tip-off on a mobile phone we headed for the water hole where a submerged hippo was basking in mud and on the other side under the shade of a twisted tree, lay four very sleepy and very full lions – three cubs and the lioness. Next to them was a half-eaten zebra, presumably snatched at the water's edge.

Both days this week-end Morrogorro – a town of 100,000 people – has been without electricity. Shops with small generators could just about carry on business but most places had fridges out of order. The fact that so few places have air conditioning anyway is perhaps one reason why people accept quietly this disruption, which in Europe would probably bring people on to the streets.

This evening we visited Elvis' bar or "e-pub" as Elvis's barmaids' tee shirts proudly pronounce. It's easily the best bar in town and five minutes' walk from our residence. It's run by a huge and hugely impressive man called Elvis whose dad was a fanatic for "The King" and who has tried to cash in ever since. The music is 'country' and the TV is always on. Tonight, the TV was screening east Africa's very own version of Big Brother. It was just as dire and depressing as the UK version and perhaps, even more depressingly, a collection of local Tanzanians, wearing Arsenal shirts, whooped and cheered throughout.

Hardly any wazungu (Europeans) frequent this bar and we are always looked after because we tip well and the atmosphere is very friendly. I haven't witnessed any aggressive behaviour since I arrived here two weeks ago – early days I know, but this bar in any small town in England would be stopping fights every Sunday night.

19 October

Our kiswahili lessons are drawing to a close. I am able to conjugate reasonably fluent sentences in past present and future tenses, use all seven noun classes reasonably accurately and deploy a good variety of vocabulary – all in writing. However, I'm not sure I'm any closer to being able to negotiate a sensible price for five oranges down the market than I was ten days ago. I'll find out later today as we need to practise our language skills on real live people.

On matters of local culture and etiquette, we've learned quite a lot also. We know for instance that we ought not to blow our noses whilst eating, we should not put our feet on the table, we should show respect to older people and we should not sniff the food we are served. I know. My mum and dad told me all these things when I was young too!

What they didn't tell us however, was not to wash our underwear and put it to dry in public. We, particularly the women amongst us, have been given detailed advice as to how and when and where we should wash our underwear. I wish someone had told the two African women on our corridor who insist on leaving their voluminous knickers on the towel rack right next to where I wash my face each morning. I've dried myself on them twice already.

22 October - T.I.T.

We were told at the beginning of our induction to remember an important phrase with the acronym T.I.T. – This Is Tanzania. It's used to accommodate every foible, every inefficiency and every maddening incompetence we meet. In fact it is quite unfair. At the big Vodacom shop in town, staff are unhelpful and uninterested; in the big hotel for *wazungu*, staff are unhelpful and service is very, very poor; so it is easy to see why tourists' experience of Africa is of inefficient slow moving people. But this is only a very small part of the story. Caroline's skirt was made in a few hours by a man working out of a container unit and the market is teeming with budding entrepreneurs who will move quickly to earn some extra money.

So a pattern is emerging, that the large organisations with salaried staff quickly gain an attitude of unhelpful indifference and these are the people – police, customs officers, civil servants, the staff in large hotels – that tourists meet first. The majority - 80% living on less than tsh5000 a day (£2.00) – are more friendly and more helpful than any of us deserve.
For those thirsting for more Kiswahili vocabulary, please note, Caroline's skirt is a "sketi", my shirt is a "shati" and when we've paid for both I expect some "chengi" (change).

24 October - It's the Wikiendi

Well it's the "wikiendi"! The course is over and we are getting ready to leave. This morning we did a short trek with a local guide into the Uuruguru hills, home to a small matriarchal tribe where women own the land and men do the menial work. We climbed about 500 metres to a beautiful waterfall where two of the party went for a dip in a shady plunge pool. A woman came out of a small mud-built house to shout at us not to take photographs of her vegetable patch further up the hill. I wanted to say to her that once you've seen one cassava allotment, you've seen them all; but my Swahili was not up to it.
We've walked under banana, aubergine and avocado trees, seen pineapple and yam and lemon grass - so many tomatoes and oranges, you'd wonder why they need to import food, but we also met a young mother, with her 18 day old baby boy. I asked the little girl by her side how she liked her new *kaka;* she just shrugged. Perhaps they were waiting for the health visitor to arrive. Maybe not. Anyway dad came out on to his porch and with a beaming face shouted "karibuni nyumbani" - welcome all of you to my home. The family had one room, two windows, a mud floor and two old sofas.
We passed scores of women laden with baskets on their heads returning from Morrogorro where they had been selling a few bananas. We wore the best approach shoes and walking shorts – they wore kangas with worn rubber flip flops.

We pack our bags again this week-end to prepare to travel to Mtwara, journey of about 200 miles from Dar-es-Salaam. We are girding our loins already preparing for a journey of unknown length and discomfort. Most people we speak to say, "ooh that's a long way!" The bus leaves at 06.00 and arrives in Mtwara at 5.00pm" - 10 hours (sic)! We are to be collected from our hotel at 05.00 with all eight suitcases packed and ready and then take a 40 minute taxi journey to the bus station, a huge sprawling complex full of buses cars, vendors of every kind. The Principal, Mama Eliwaja has said that she'll be there to meet us on Monday afternoon.

We're both very excited now, glad this "soft landing" is over and looking forward to setting up home and doing some work. Without that we would both miss home far too much to stay here.

25 October

Up to the great sprawling bus station for 5.30am, all our luggage squashed into a small family car, with Caroline looking like a contortionist on the back seat. At that time in the morning Dar-es Salaam is alive with, commuters, the ubiquitous daladalas' horns blaring and men and women selling food from small stalls; newspapers, bottled water- all you need for a hectic commute.

At the bus station, John - the pushiest porter - soon identifies himself and for a good fee carries all the luggage – yes, all the luggage!- singlehandedly across the huge coach park. Once aboard in the best seats (I think Benjamin had paid a premium to make sure we were comfortable) we set off in a coach which I estimate was at least 25 years old, had cracks across the windscreen which had been sealed with yellow sealant to match the company's logo. The driver had installed his own distinctive horn system, a selection of garish, sometimes vulgar, always loud sirens, which he used every few minutes to move cyclists, pedestrians, cars, in fact anything smaller or slower than him out of the way.

We were making good time, perhaps because the *dereva* made no allowances for speed humps. After two hours, not long after we had hit the open road, a loud rattling came from the engine housing and we pulled over. The old man next to me was clearly angry. I think he blamed the driver for recklessness. I was despondent, thinking that in the UK, this would mean a lengthy wait for a replacement coach. At this point Caroline suggested unhelpfully that it might be the fan belt. The driver opened the housing and with his only spanner and the ignition key rammed into the gap between spanner and bolt, he began painstakingly to remove the alternator casing. We limped to the next small town, ramshackle collection of mud houses, where he found a man with a spanner that fit and within twenty minutes, he had the fan-belt – yes, Caroline was right! – back on.

We continued, at one point covering a 60km stretch of unmade road, avoiding humps, crevices and holes, at speed, with great skill. It was impressive but incredibly uncomfortable, and after an hour or so, the sense of adventure had turned to tedium.

We arrived in Mtwara an hour late, but to find Francis, a fellow tutor, waiting for us with a Landcruiser. Our shared sense of relief was palpable. Mama Eliwaja, the Principle, was waiting for us at the college and we moved into our new home. We ate *kuku na chipsi na bia* – yes you're getting the hang of it, that's chicken and chips and beer – with our new colleagues at the cafe across the road from college. At night everyone eats outside where there is no electric lighting whatsoever. It was relaxing, but eating in complete darkness, is a testament to faith rather than discernment, as no-one can have any idea what they are actually putting in their mouths. More about our new home later. This morning, we feel tired after a sleepless, sticky night. The house has no fan, no water and single beds with ill-fitting mosquito nets. We feel it will be a challenge but in the fresh light of day, all will seem better.

26 October - No 1 Staff House, Mtwara Teachers' College

We were woken at 5.00am to the loudest call to prayer I've heard since we arrived in Tanzania. The voice is insistent yet soulful and strangely comforting, considering the time and the lack of sleep. We'd better get used to it because we're here for at least a year, so it's early to bed and early to prayer for us from now on. The call to prayer wakes up the roosters who live right outside our house. Our house has no windows, just mesh, so when the rooster crows, it's like having him bed with you. You literally, yes, literally, jump! We had a busy day planned and Francis did not disappoint. Francis had been appointed by the Principal to be our guardian and guide in our first days in Mtwara. We were to discover that generous as this gesture was, Francis' lack of knowledge and charming unworldliness would be more hindrance than help.

After a small misunderstanding about where we might buy coffee and how we would take our breakfast Francis took us to an idyllic hotel overlooking the Indian Ocean. The hotel is pricey and as a result Francis was the only African there apart from the staff. We had eggs, sausage, papaya, fruit juice and brown bread with 'Blue Band' and coffee with milk, all for £2.00.We watched women cockling at low tide and fishing dhous skimming the azure horizon in the distance. We were briefly on a clichéd film set.

From here we went on to the hardware store where we bought a fan, a water heater, extension cables and a mop and bucket. Buying these was not easy. First we had to persuade the assistant to serve us, rather than constantly allow herself to be interrupted by others. Then we had to persuade her to let us see the product before agreeing to purchase:
"You want a fan? Yes, we have one. 40,000 shillings.... What you want me to drag it out from the back so you can look at it?.... Wait a minute...What sir? You want a toilet coupling?.....What?. Yes. Fan - 40,000 shillings. No, no discount. The bucket you have to collect from across the road...."

At this point I had to turn away for fear I would laugh in her face. We had to cross the road and disturb two elderly ladies eating snacks and ask them first to let us see the electric cooker they had in store and secondly to supply the bucket we had already paid for. The cooker was broken and they didn't know the price. The bucket was somewhere else, so she got in our car...yes there were now five of us in a car, Caroline clutching a mop, whilst the elderly lady directed us to another store where we could collect the bucket. Such fun I had not had in quite a long time.

By this afternoon, boys had come round to assemble the brand new king size bed which the bursar had personally been out to purchase that morning, the fundi came round to mend the table, the light fitting and the mosquito net, Caroline and I scrubbed sinks and floors and two young girls, Rosemary and Doreen, came round to scrub our brand new pans. They would not accept the offer of even a bottle of pop for their trouble. When we thought things could not get any better, we heard a gurgling in the toilet, looked at each other in eager anticipation and shouted, "Yes! Water!"

We leapt into the shower, washed hair, filled buckets and thought ourselves very lucky people. Apparently the timetable for the availability of water is irregular. I pointed out to Francis that if a timetable is irregular, it doesn't usually qualify to be called a timetable. Francis chuckled and said, "No. You are right."
Of these wonderful events today, the most moving was the arrival of the post. The Bursar brought the letter round personally. Yes. I know we only arrived last night, but this afternoon we opened a welcome letter from Gerard with his regular prayer sheet for Caroline. It took ten days via Dar-es-Salaam. Getting post from home is easily the best way of making us feel we are in our new home.

It's 6.00pm. We are both showered and cool. Students are playing basketball outside and we are going round to Francis' house shortly where he will demonstrate the use of the charcoal cooker we have purchased this afternoon. Provided our bed has been assembled correctly and the mosquito net doesn't fall down, today will have been easily the best day since we arrived in Tanzania.

27 October

A note about protocol on the road, whether you're a pedestrian, a *baisikeki*, (bicycle) a *bajaj* (small three-wheeler taxi), a *piki-piki* (motorcycle) or a *gari* (car); you always give way to the stronger, bigger, louder or more dangerous. This list of attributes is nearly always attributed in ascending order as listed. When walking down a deserted dusty road and a small motor-cycle approaches, you should stand aside and not expect him to veer one inch from his chosen course. If you don't, he will surely hoot you.

I thought I'd got the hang of prices out here. Everything it seems is about ten times cheaper, the people are fifty times poorer than in the UK and the quality of manufactured goods is nearly always inferior. Last week in a reasonably good conference centre, chairs simply broke under the weight of our bottoms. Today, tea-bags disintegrated in the tea cup and the toilet seat cracked.

You'd be forgiven for thinking that Tanzanians stoically accepted these failings and wished that they could afford the higher quality imports. Not so. When I enquired about bicycles, I was told that the second-hand bikes are dearer than the brand new ones. Then there's clothes pegs, cheaper in the UK than they are here. Here, everyone washes everything by hand, sorts them out into mentionable and unmentionable and pegs them on the line (underwear hidden by kanga). You'd think pegs would be cheap. Not so. They are just poor quality.

Our second day is almost over. We have equipped the kitchen with plastic containers for water, rice, beans, onions, garlic and spices and every utensil we possess. The ants will starve before they find their way into the sugar again. Gilbert the gecko seems happy enough, even though he must be scared stiff of Caroline. Every time he appears from behind a door, or up a wall or under a pan, Caroline screams, Gilbert scarpers and then Caroline reassures me – even though I wasn't scared – that it's OK and Gilbert is good 'cos he eats the mosquitoes. I just don't think anyone's told the mosquitoes because they don't seem particularly scared of Gilbert.

We have a superb bed now and a superb mosquito net. We have invested in another quieter fan and hopefully we'll be able to get at least seven hours before the call to prayer and the roosters start again.

28 October - At the tailors

We live close to a relatively affluent shopping district called Bima. Bima is the crossroads of two small shopping streets, predominantly Indian owned. The more substantial buildings date back to the 1950s, when Mtwara was being developed by the British as a ground-nut export base with a deep water port. Today's mission included the hairdresser, tailor, more household items for washing clothes and water. At least two of the shop-owners smile and say "habari". I'm sure they wonder what on earth we could be doing with all these cheap plastic household goods. Our kitchen is beginning to resemble a Betaware catalogue. We were looking for tailors. We walked past three. We could tell they were tailors because they were sitting on the pavement at their sewing machines. Francis asked for patience. He wanted to take us to a good one. When we got there, he was indeed a good tailor. His pavement had the advantage of shade. We waited while he sewed a loop in a pair of bedroom curtains and hemmed a pair of my trousers. Francis started discussing prices and the tailor's face fell. I asked for translation. Francis told me that the tailor wanted 2000 shillings and he was trying to get him to accept 1000 shillings. I paid the tailor 3000 shillings (£1.25) and explained to Francis that we might need a good tailor again and that it was worth paying an inflated price. Francis sighed and said, "You are right."

Later we went on our first tour around College. I met the Head of the English Department, a quietly spoken, dark-skinned woman called Lucia. She was earnest in answering my questions and when she laughed as she did often, her mouth showed a wide array of gleaming white teeth. She explained to me in very simple terms the Tanzanian education system and how the College functioned. She explained that the academic tutor would first need to assign me an office and then I would be allocated some classes to teach. This order of proceedings seemed important.

By two o'clock the College has finished for the day, students are sitting in the shade of large trees, eating ugali – a stiff porridge made from maize flour and cooked in the cavernous kitchen at the back of the main hall - and some tutors are standing chatting. The classrooms and the library are empty. The place has the feel of a run-down high school in the UK rather than a college and I begin to feel nervous about my ability to make a contribution. Mama Ngonyani (Lucia) assuages all concerns by reminding me that I first must have an office and that she will call for me shortly before 7.30am so that I can sign the attendance register in good time. In time for what, she did not say.

Later, before sundown, we sat on the terrace of the Southern Cross hotel, drinking cold beer and nibbling cashews; we watched the *dhous* (small fishing boats) tacking their way back to port for the evening fish market and thought ourselves very lucky indeed. This might become a place of respite. We both feel that we've taken a lot on.

30 October 2010 - Mr Ratty

We need a *spaki* to fix our *shoti*. Our neighbour, the doctor, confidently tells me that this is the reason for the intermittent and irregular power cuts we are experiencing. At home, there would be chaos – the freezer would need de-frosting, the central heating clock re-setting, the shower would run cold, TVs PCs and X-Boxes would cease to function. Here it makes very little difference. Our shower is a jug of cold water poured over our heads, and we can cook our rice and beans on our charcoal stove or *jiko*. Living here for the past few days has made me reflect on one big difference between here and home – between the under-developed and the developed worlds. Here things are dear, but time is cheap. In *mzungo* land things are cheap, but time is dear. It cost me the same for half an hour's time of a skilled tailor as it did for a packet of clothes pegs. I might see if I can employ someone to make loud noises in the kitchen all day to keep Mr Ratty away. Caroline found him sniffing in our pantry last night and all is not well. I wonder what his relationship was with the huge cockroach I killed yesterday; I say cockroach, but I'm not sure. This creature was prehistoric in its dimensions, scurried across the floor, leapt a yard when I first attempted to tread on it, and was the size of a small hamster; absolutely nothing cuddly about it however.

In first day in College I could see at close quarters the meagre resources and dreadful constraints facing education in Tanzania. I sat in on an English lesson where approximately ninety students, some sitting or standing outside the classroom, notebooks balanced on their knees, listened to a talk about reading skills, given by an under-stated but confident tutor. Most students listened; all were quiet throughout, except for the couple of minutes when they were asked to discuss in pairs, their ideas for getting early readers to read aloud, or the benefits of the class reader as opposed to the library. The lesson ended as unremarkably as it had begun and I had to be signalled from the front of the room that it was in fact, time to leave.

Tomorrow we will pay a visit to one of Caroline's favourite stores, a so-called *mzungu* store. They are called *mzungu* stores because it's only white people that want or can afford to shop there. I had first imagined slick window displays, air-conditioning and expensive and unnecessary beauty products. This collection of *mzungu* stores turns out to be predominantly Indian owned shops, with the atmosphere of an American frontier store at the turn of the century. They sell everything from beans to biscuits and from Vim to Vimto. I wandered round bemused, determined to treat us to something from our world. I settled on a Knorr packet soup. Tomorrow I think it might very well be time to get something for the *wikiendi* for Mr Ratty.

Saturday, 30 October 2010

Well Ratty was hungry! He ate right through a container of rice leaving red plastic shavings all over the place. I went to see Francis to see what could be done. He said, "Yes. We have rats. You should kill them." With that helpful advice we went shopping in town, nowadays, without Francis.

We've found a new bread shop which I suspect Francis has not seen. They sell fresh bread and biscuits and buns and a Tanzanian croissant which costs 1000tsh and looks as though it weighs half a kilo. We'll have them for breakfast tomorrow. It seems like a tidy little business.

That afternoon we took the *bajaj* to Mikandani and had lunch in the Old Boma. Mikindani is an old Swahili fishing port, a former centre for Arab slave traders, and the Old Boma is the former administrative headquarters for German occupation. It's easily the best place to stay and probably the best place to eat in this region. Later we walked down to the small bay where dhous and canoes were returning with their haul of fish.

I still haven't got used to being the centre of attention. There are very few white people about and the few that are around do not seem to walk about the place unaccompanied; hence we have every kind of person, young and old, walking right up to us and saying, *"mambo"*, *"habari"* or sometimes "how doo you doo – I'm fine". If we answer it's often met with peals of laughter and back slapping. Two young boys laughed like they had never heard such a joke and cried after us, *"wazungu"* (*white foreigner*), a word which has none of the pejorative connotations its equivalent in Europe might carry. It makes me consider the comparison between the reaction to our presence here and the reaction to migrants' presence in Europe.

We've had *chai and biskuti* for tea and, as we'll be up with the rooster, if not the *imamu,* we'll be early to bed. We're off to 7.00am Mass tomorrow with Francis. We plan to force ourselves on some unsuspecting nuns or priests, with a view to them giving us some voluntary work. I don't know what the collective noun for *wazungu* seeking to do good works is, but it's probably something terrifying.

31 October 2010 - All Saints Day

All Saints Day and we attended Mass in All Saints Cathedral, a large white concrete building which is less than fifty years old and is crumbling around our heads. This is the Catholic Cathedral for the Diocese of Mtwara. It looks more like a municipal sports hall on a run-down estate. It is packed with young and old. Very obviously, Africa is where the Church's future lies, but its congregation seems oddly served. Great RSJs prop up the ceiling and the splashed paint over grey marble shows the general lack of craftsmanship that seems so depressingly evident across the country. The RSJs are held in place with irregular wedges of timber – quite unsettling, as we were underneath one.

There is certain to be a broader economic explanation for this. I suspect it has something to do with time being cheap, with skills being home learned, with craftsmanship going unrewarded and for technical education being under-funded. If we compared craftsmanship in UK with, say Italy or Germany, we'd be sadly lacking after so many years of diluted labour and the reduction of skilled apprenticeships. Whatever the reason, the country's poverty is displayed partly through this ineptitude. There are widespread displays of industry and enterprise, however. You only need to look to the men mending buses on the side of the road, or those making cement blocks by hand, or the tailors sewing and mending on the pavement, to see the enthusiasm for work; but so much of it is undone by poor materials and tools. I thought at first that it might be the absence of quality tools that made for such poor quality furniture, and then I thought of Chippendale of Otley in the eighteenth century. What this country lacks is high quality training. The skills shortage is evident at every level.

Today, clocks go back to Greenwich Mean Time in UK. In Tanzania we are on Swahili time. The day starts with sunrise and time is measured in hours from sunrise. So 7.00am in *wazungu* time is 1.00 in Swahili time, midday in *wazungu* time is 6.00 and 6.00pm *wazungu* time is 12.00. There is no 24 hour clock and time is therefore described as being of the morning, afternoon or night. It's sunrise every day of the year at 6.00am and sunset at 6.00pm, so you can see the logic.

Having spent a delicious hour on the beach at Msemo, we bumped into the lovely old Polish lady who runs a container unit for wazungus, selling everything from shower gel to tomato soup. We bought a bag of mince-meat from her as she was about to freeze it and having discovered the tiniest market about two hundred yards from our house, where we can buy fresh vegetables, fish and eggs, we came home to eat rice and mince for lunch.

2 November 2010 - Ratty lives on!

Well the anti-rat glue might work in the cartoons, but I reckon Ratty took one look at our pathetic trap and sniggered, perhaps laughed. He picked daintily over the glue and nibbled all the grains of rice. He sniffed at the banana skin and then found a fresh banana in the living room. He'll be back, no doubt.

Teaching English at Shangani might be more challenging than I first thought, not because there are sixty pupils crammed into one classroom, not because they don't have enough desks, nor because not everyone has an exercise book, nor because the chalk is dusty and the board is pitted. The main challenge is that the pupils' exercise books show neat tables of sentences with pronouns underlined, a table for past future and present tenses, a glossary of literary terms which would grace 'A' level candidates' work – and yet they cannot choose an adjective to describe themselves. Many of them know what adjectives nouns and verbs are – that is they can repeat a definition they have previously copied - but they cannot identify one for themselves. Knowing where to 'pitch' the lessons, I will find difficult.

As I arrive in school, a boy runs to carry my bag. Mtumbi advises that this is their way of showing respect and I should oblige. Each morning school starts at 7.00am with Cleanliness. Pupils patrol the school brushing and watering and tidying. Inspection begins at seven-thirty. This is led by students and I am introduced to the school. Classes begin at eight o'clock. The two classes I taught today were docile to the point of unresponsiveness. They are polite, but the combination of my accent and their unwillingness to do anything other than precisely what they are asked, makes for a dull lesson.

The heat is unbearable. It rains for about twenty minutes and then the heat returns with a vengeance. At break, I ask if there is water, "No," comes the response from my colleague. "This is Tanzanian education."

For lunch we sat at a rough wooden bench and table in the small thatched shelter or *banda,* a few yards from our house. Here we were served *chipsi mayai* - a chip omelette cooked on a charcoal stove, washed down with a bottle of soda. The shop had no soda so the cook rode off on his bike to a shop off campus, a gesture of kindness on his part - no reward expected.

After lunch we had a power cut. No-one expressed any surprise, but I was told that's the fundi – the *spaki* – would be along. I'm ashamed to say I assumed that this would be like the UK and I would wait in all afternoon for the guy to turn up at tea-time and say he needed to order parts. Not at all. The fundi possessed the ubiquitous screwdriver and a hammer! He fiddled with the fuse box, looked at it, prised it apart, bent it, fiddled with it some more and put it back. When the lights came on, he was more surprised than I was. He didn't expect a tip, but he brought his boss, Francis, along later just to bask in the congratulations of actually having mended it.

Wednesday, 3 November 2010

"If Mary had been here....," retorted Caroline, as I laughed at her because a small herd of cows raced towards us. Our credibility suffered quite a blow as Caroline screamed and squeezed my arm tightly. What was strange about the scene was that we were shopping in Mtwara's main street and no-one else blinked, least of all the young boy shooing the cows across the busy road.

I was off for a haircut *a kunyoa.* Daniel, the hairdresser, was very attentive. He took twice as long on my hair as other customers. Maybe it was because he wasn't as confident with mzungu hair or maybe he just felt better about charging me triple the local price. (£1.25 as opposed to 40p). I smiled and told him next time I'll pay him the right price.

We had a cold beer in the Green Garden pub where there is no garden in sight, just a dusty yard, plastic tables and Eminem blaring out. From there we went home for a shower (five jugs of cold water), rice and beans for tea (local chillie sauce as well) and an evening with Henning Mankell (novel). It was the end of a tiring and trying day for both of us. The heat is relentless and the absence of the comforts we're used to at times makes life hard. We were reminded yesterday, however, that living with a flush toilet probably places us in the top 5% of Tanzanians. Being able to buy cold beer when we want, being able to take a *bajaj* up the coast when we want and all manner of other comforts that we afford ourselves that few here could afford, cossets us from the true harshness of life here.

The cows that alarmed Caroline earlier were, I think, joining the others that have been moved to graze near our house. They have mooed loudly all afternoon. Roosters, rats, dogs, cows, geckos, even a stray cat comprise our nearest and noisiest neighbours. The gecko isn't exactly noisy, it just poos a lot.

4 November 2010 - Water, water everywhere...

At home we have three grades of water: dirty water straight from the tap. This comes out of the tap brown and scummy; it is stored in large plastic vats in the kitchen and transferred to smaller buckets for use in the toilet, shower and wash basin; clean mineral water bought from the shops in plastic bottles and costing 350tsh a litre; only used for drinking and rinsing; filtered water, which is dirty water filtered through our chalk filtration system. This is cleanish, but needs boiling for 3 minutes before consumption.

Plastic water bottles are cut down for use as toothbrush holders, pots for pan scrubbers, tubs for organic waste. It's best to keep your wits about you, which I should have done last night, when I swigged from the one bottle in the kitchen with a plastic top – not water, sadly, but Milton cleaning fluid. Caroline had labelled it with permanent marker but I failed to notice and this, and a surfeit of beans for tea, played havoc with me all night.

This morning we were entertained by fifteen three-year-olds dancing and singing their welcome. They had been rehearsing for the kindergarten graduation ceremony later this month. We were visiting the Montessori kindergarten and training school. Fifteen years ago the Sisters of the Holy Redeemer established the nursery and since then the network of training colleges and kindergartens has been growing across Tanzania. Sister Tadea responded warmly to the suggestion that Caroline might want to help by organising at about three minutes notice, a tour, a reception, a small breakfast and transport. And this is supposed to be a country that can't organise anything!

While Caroline plans to start volunteering in the kindergarten I continue to volunteer a few hours each week in the neighbouring secondary school. There is much to admire about the way in which schools manage with so little. Discipline is strong but the method of imposing punishment, challenging. Pupils stand without instruction when I enter the room, the blackboard is wiped clean before I ask, and when the lesson is over, I simply tell them that the lesson is over and I leave. The class in unison stands and says, "Good-bye sir." This idyll sits uncomfortably, then, with the other scene played out yesterday in the staffroom. One young girl was made to kneel as she was caned across her hands, whilst another boy was made to hold his body weight prone on one arm whilst his buttocks were caned; this latter caning delivered by a woman teacher and I suspect intended to maximise the humiliation for the teen-age boy. Challenging, to say the least!

After a risky, but ultimately, reasonably successful drama lesson with Form III, I began to feel at home here. First, pupils from Shangani secondary school, then trainee teachers from the college greeted me with, "Good afternoon, sir", as I wound my way along the path marked by three huge baobob trees, to my house.

5 November 2010 - **Fish heads and biscuits**

Today I have two short anecdotes from today's foray into town, which, in some ways, encapsulate the contrasting experiences of living here in Mtwara. I've been wondering for a few days, why our moods seem so helter-skelterish – sometimes high, sometimes low, not always for any discernible reason. Perhaps it is the unpredictability of day-to-day life which brings its own form of powerlessness; or perhaps it's the pressure of constantly being a stranger in a strange land. That strangeness is sometimes exciting, enervating; at other times, it's stressful and depressing.

We went for lunch today to our favourite day-time restaurant. It's situated just off the main street and comprises about 15 plastic tables. You can tell that it is relatively high class because each table is located immediately below a fan and the hand-washing facilities – which incidentally are *de rigeur* in TZ – are high quality, with warm water from a tap in a bucket and some liquid soap. The menu is fish or chicken with rice or ugali. We nearly always choose fish and rice. Today the fish was a complete fish-head. I can almost see Mary's reaction now, but believe me, there's loads of fish on it and once you've got the hang of the bones and taken care not to eat the eye, it really is very tasty. The best advertisement for the place is that it's full of people, all sorts of people. I complemented the owner on his food last time and today he came over especially to welcome us. It is a fulfilling experience in more ways than one and, at 6000tsh (£2.40) for the two of us, including a bottle of water, extremely good value.

The good value lunch makes up, perhaps, for the contrasting experience in the bakery. I had said the other day what a good little business it is. Today, Caroline bought a pack of three crumbly biscuits which should cost 800tsh. I paid with a 1000 tsh note and the woman smiled at me, almost grinned, and said that she didn't have change. Instead of standing my ground or demanding my money back, I sheepishly accepted this daylight robbery and tried to make a joke about her owing me 200 tsh. "It's about 8p. What are you going on about Adrian?" I can hear you say; but that doesn't go anywhere near describing the debilitating effect that being looked on purely as mzungu, a man with loads of money and someone ripe for being ripped off, day after day, has on your state of mind. Imagine in the UK, a wealthy man buys a pound of apples from the market with a £5.00 note and the trader decides not to give him change because the man is rich. I've considered that if this is the price rich people from the developed world have to pay, then they've got off far too lightly. I don't need to be reminded of the politics of world development. I'm talking about the personal affront that you feel when one human being looks you in the eye and has no respect for anything other than the money in your pocket. I'm determined to get my 200 tsh back from her. I'll let you know how I get on.

6 November 2010 - Another Saturday morning

What a delicious sound to wake up to! The steady flow of water into the toilet cistern! We leapt out of bed and rushed for the buckets. Our huge vats were nearly empty and we had already decided that if we got no water today, desperate remedies would be called for. No need. Our cups overfloweth, almost literally.

Having said all that, we wouldn't have been exactly lying in. Whilst the imamu seems to have had a day off, no-one told the roosters and then lad next door seems to love nothing more than run errands for his mum on his motorbike, revving it up outside my bedroom as he passes. One of our tasks today is to dispose of rubbish. Yes, we set ourselves fairly limited goals. We seem to be required to burn it outside our house, but am concerned that no-one else seems to have acquired the number of plastic water bottles that we have.

Last night, we spent an enjoyable evening at the Upendo grocery. It's a general store with a small verandah with plastic tables and chairs. Next door is Kia's chipsi stall where you can buy chipsi mayai (chip omelette) for 1500 tsh. We drank bia baridi with Philbert, a retired schools inspector and two young doctors, Tom and Deo, til quite late.

Philbert is working as an adviser in the King David School, a Seventh Day Adventist school, working on their school development plan but also advising them on other religious denominations, something they got into hot water over recently. The private schools, nearly all religious, have more resources, better motivated teachers and, as a consequence, better attainment levels than government schools. Tanzania's efforts to meet their Millennium Development Goal (MDG) for access to education have been so successful that there is now a dire shortage of teachers. In these conditions, the gap between schools with money to pay teachers and those without the same resources, is stark. Philbert, unsurprisingly, identified the shortage of teachers and poor school buildings as the priorities. We talked about my placement to improve the quality of teaching, but as he quite lyrically put it,
"Before you wear socks, you must first have shoes."
I asked Philbert what he would do. Nyerere had recognised education as the force for change in society and nationalised many private schools at Independence. This allowed the formerly dispossessed, the Muslims, the non-alligned, to receive the same education as the Christians. For Philbert, Nyerere was right, and if he had his way, the private schools would be nationalised again. He agreed with me, however, that it is not likely to happen any time soon.

For those of you interested in our menagerie, you might like to know that a small herd of large goats, the size of cows, has taken up residence just beyond the hens. They have huge horns and, again, Caroline embarrassed us both by squealing as we hurried past. After a short lull in hostilities, battle with Ratty is due to recommence after he got stuck into Caroline's knickers last night. (She wasn't wearing them at the time!). We have a new lethal weapon, though - a deadly white powder - which will be deployed at nightfall.

Sunday, 7 November 2010 - **Fish and fishing**

I think we started to feel at home here today. After a dreadful night's sleep we woke late to go to 9.00am Mass at Shangani Church, a much more attractive church than the Cathedral and very obviously a parish church serving the relatively well-off district of Shangani. The choir was in fine voice; the singing is powerful, the harmonies rich and the rhythms compulsive. The ululations which emanate spontaneously, made the hairs stand up on the back of my neck.

One interesting feature of Mass is the emphasis placed on the collection. Before the offertory, four children processed to the altar bearing four wooden chests, each marked with the name of a saint. Members of the congregation step forward and make their donation in the saint's box of their choice. The boxes are closed and the children are followed by four more children bringing four more boxes for four more saints and the collection is repeated; and finally, four more children and four more boxes for four more saints. Twelve children, twelve boxes, twelve saints. We were spoiled for choice. Caroline went for St Benedict and then could have kicked herself. If she'd waited, she could have had Padre Pio.

After Mass we went down to the fish market and watched small wooden canoes empty their catch. One man had caught the most enormous sting-ray, whilst another was gutting and cutting a huge tuna with a knife a mallet resting on a piece of old lino. This is subsistence fishing. It can seem quaint and the fish market is included in Lonely Planet itineraries, but it looked a hard life to me. Wives and children were waiting in the stinking shade of wooden lean-tos for dhous to return at sundown. There was a stench of rotten fish everywhere and the beach was littered with debris and fish carcasses.

The legacy of the economic regeneration planned by the British fifty years ago, is to be seen a few hundred yards down the shore from this daily fish market. It's a great white elephant of a port, intended to support a ground-nut export scheme. The British, having coerced local farmers to switch to ground-nut production from subsistence farming, only then discovered, that neither the soil nor the climate could support growth of ground nut plants, and the whole project folded, leaving Mtwara a dilapidated backwater.

After lunch, we ended up on the beach at Msemo and I tried snorkelling for the first time. The sea was murky, being stirred up at high tide but even today, in two feet of water, the sea was teeming with fish. Two young boys approached us. I was, I am ashamed to say, apprehensive at first, having being warned so strenuously to be on one's guard. These two boys, Kevin and Muksini, turned out to be two Form I pupils of mine who had recognised me and chose to sit and chat about themselves and their families for half an hour or so. They were clever, very polite and Kevin even made some helpful suggestions as to what I should teach them tomorrow morning.

Monday, 8 November 2010

Shangani Secondary school has started examinations for Form II. Form IV has already left, following their examinations ('O' levels), leaving just Forms I and III. At least one external invigilator has been brought in and so you would have thought that the remaining lessons would be covered from existing staff. Not so. I'm not sure why, but the staffroom has nearly always got two or three members of staff sitting chatting. There are only ten teachers altogether and two of us are volunteers. What, you might ask, are these teachers doing? And why are classes still without teachers? I'm not sure, but I think Philbert might be able to shed some light on the matter.

On the subject of righting wrongs, I went back to the baker's today. You might remember how aggrieved I felt at the off-hand way in which she had failed to offer me the correct change. After we had bought bread and sausage rolls today, I reminded her that she owed me 200tsh. She smiled. I paid. I now needed 100 tsh (4p). She asked her friend this time, in a tone which sounded like,
"Give the tight-fisted mzungu his 100tsh, will you?"
But I could be wrong. Still, we probably both feel better now that the air has been cleared. I certainly do. Not sure about her. On battles fought and won, it's early days, but we haven't seen or heard Ratty for two nights now. It could be Caroline's cleaning and bleaching regime. It's certainly not the poison. He doesn't touch it. It could be simply that he's given up on us ever having any food in the house. We have a tub of uncooked beans, half a tub of Blue Band and a jar of jam. I reckon even Ratty thinks he could do better elsewhere. Actually, the geckos – Gilbert and his brothers – are starting to get to Caroline. She has polystyrene trays placed strategically around the house ready to collect gecko poo. They always seem to confound her, and tonight she has re-doubled her efforts as she found gecko poo in her hairbrush.

The heat seems to drain away appetite, along with the pints of fluid which seep from every pore of my body. I still wear a vest to try and disguise the moisture, but Lucia takes pity on me, I know; for she smiles as I sit in the staffroom, dripping, after having walked seventy-yards. "Phew. It's warm," she says, but I'm pretty sure she doesn't mean it. She just wants to make me feel better. And I do; just not cooler.

If we are to feel truly settled here, we must start to learn more kiswahili. Since leaving Morrogorro, we have hardly spoken any in any prolonged way and we are already forgetting the basics. A Form III pupil approached me at break-time this morning. Actually, he walked into the staffroom, approached my desk and said, "Teacher. Excuse me. I want to learn English."

I was taken aback, but walked to the shade of a tree with him. We ate a samosa together and I spent twenty minutes in conversation with him. He was appreciative, but, I thought, "What enterprise! That's what I should do." Caroline confirmed this. As she came home this lunch-time, a group of three-year olds from the nursery ran up to her and surrounded her with questions. She, like me, has said that we won't be able to share anything, least of all our skills, if we can't share some of their language.

Tuesday, 9 November 2010

Caroline has started helping at the Montessori nursery attached to the local Catholic Church. Singing, dancing, eating porridge and washing up the plastic beakers is the order of the day; but all routine is secondary to the number one priority at the moment, of rehearsing for the older children's 'graduation ceremony', to be held later this month. This involves a series of intricate singing and dancing routines, of which we had a sneak preview when we went to visit last week.

There is a Montessori training centre further up the road where students can enrol at seventeen years to train as Montessori teachers. They are apprenticed in the theory and practice of the Montessori methodology of learning through sensory perception. It costs Tsh1m (about £400) per annum and for that, each student receives full board and lodgings as well as training costs. To put that into context, a teacher here earns about Tsh4m, so it's not chicken feed. But students get what seems to be high quality training in relatively small classes.

The beach close to our home in Shangani is beautiful. It has clean white sand and the sea is at times blue, green or turquoise, depending on the tide, the sun and the time of day. The beach is littered with shells, small crabs, sea urchins and tiny jelly fish, along with sea-weed and what we think are broken sections of coral. The only blot on the beachscape is the ubiquitous plastic bottle. In a region, a country, where virtually none of the water is freely drinkable, bottled water is the simplest, if not the cheapest way, of drinking water. The drawback is that the plastic bottles are everywhere.

On the beach we had noticed that young boys can often be seen collecting the numerous plastic bottles that form part of the flotsam. We couldn't work out why they would do this until we noticed some of them binding them together to form a makeshift float. About ten of them tied together form a girdle or buoyancy skirt that will help keep you afloat. They need this because as we watched groups of boys playing in the sea more closely last night, we realised that very few of them can actually swim. You need to be taught to swim – it's not like dancing or singing. It explains the fascination that some boys had shown when I was swimming the other day. I thought they were curious to see an old, fat, white man in the sea. I think now that they might have been impressed by my swimming.

Swimming, or rather playing in the sea, seems to be something for young people. Tanzania is full of young people. It has a population of 40 million with an average mortality age of 52. That makes me and Caroline revered elders. We are old and still walk like Europeans; that is, briskly. Francis, the legend, reported to me yesterday that he and colleagues had been impressed with this.
"You need not worry about the robbery which occurred just behind our house. When the robber sees how energetically you walk, he will run away."
I don't think I'll test that theory out.

Wednesday, 10 November 2010 - Cacophony

For those of you who might think that Caroline and I are living in some rustic African idyll, let me disappoint you. I want to describe for you the early morning hours through the sounds around us. Before I start, understand this; the house has no windows. It has large openings where in a cooler climate there would be glass, but here there is only mesh to stop insects. The houses are about ten meters apart and it has the feel of a cheery campsite, where every sound in one house can be heard in its neighbours- talking, snoring, farting and sneezing. Every sound can be heard.

At 4.30, the first rooster starts to crow, at 5.00 someone starts banging the inside of a pan loudly to call animals for feeding. At 5.30 the first call to prayer from the mosque across the field can be heard. At 5.45, a group of boys starts practising basketball on the pitch, yards from our house, the steady beating bounce of a heavy ball is not rhythmical enough to be soporific, just annoying. By 6.00am, the whole area is alive with children crying, women brushing their yards, and the general hubbub of people rising and preparing for another day. The man next door turns his radio on with a booster bass at 6.20am. At 7.30, the mosque across the field is testing its PA. I wondered why I had only heard a muted call to prayer. I suspect the PA has been broken and this morning, he can be heard shouting, "Testing. Hallo. Hallo Mama. Hallo", at the top of his voice. Imagine what he's going to be like at 5.00am tomorrow morning. There's actually so much noise, the hens, cows and goats don't get a look-in.

On a much, much more pleasurable note, the Vice-Principal greeted me this morning with urgent news.
"A parcel has arrived." Actually, it was three small parcels, each containing gifts from home. They made us consider what we miss most. The Italian coffee is still one of my deepest pleasures. The plastic clothes airer contraption solves Caroline's underwear problem at a stroke. But the chocolate......thoughtful ......lovely..........briefly nostalgic ......but this country is too warm and WE HAVE NO FRIDGE. I've just scraped the last of the Milky Bar from its wrapper with my tongue, but a good deal of the pleasure was wasted.

Caroline is planning new ideas for meals. I particularly liked this delicacy from the VSO cookbook.
Kumbikumbi (flying ants): Ingredients: flying ants, salt, oil

*These are in fact the dispersal stage of termites and can be collected in great
numbers at the beginning of the Rains. Once collected, fry the ants dry, remove
from the pan and winnow to remove wings. Pick over carefully to remove any
stones and remaining wings. Heat the pan with or without oil, add the ants and a
little salt. Fry until ready. Serve as a relish or tasty snack.*

Thursday, 11 November 2010 - Valentine

Adrian has been in college today. He's made a few new friends and this afternoon
was left invigilating 100 students in an English exam. I went off to nursery as
usual, and, as usual, the children were practising for the graduation ceremony.

Half way through the morning, a man brought in a tortoise for the children to see. I
thought at first it was a bit gruesome, as I thought he'd brought a headless tortoise,
and then I realised that its head was in its shell. I felt stupid. Fortunately, I hadn't
admitted to this in swahili and Angela's English isn't that good yet. Valentine,
who is three years old, was entertaining us all as usual, gyrating his hips and trying
very hard to keep in time. I don't know what the words to the song mean, but I
wonder if they're rude because if Deonicia could blush, I'd swear she was
blushing today. Valentine's gyrating hips led me to ask Angela if she was a fan of
Elvis. She didn't know what I was talking about. I tried to explain, mentioned
Jailhouse Rock, but still her face was smiling, but blank. I'll sing one of his better
known songs to her tomorrow.

We needed an umbrella today. It rained nearly all day. I regretted leaving
Elizabeth Holdsworth's umbrella behind as it's far too warm for cagoules, but the
rain is heavy and it drenches you in seconds. I know we've said previously that
this is quite a comfortable district, but that doesn't mean that all the children at this
nursery are from comfortable homes. Sister Tadea had explained that some parents
pay their fees 'in kind' by doing odd jobs around the church and the school. I've
decided it is a very worthwhile project and when I hear Sr Tadea talk of parental
commitment to building a Montessori primary school with their own cement and
their own hands, I feel quite humble.

The Sisters also run a dispensary – a common African term for a social welfare
service – feeding children, elderly and the sick, arranging for nurses to visit the
homes of the sick and housebound, and dispensing medicines to those in greatest
need. They spend about Tsh500,000 a week (about £220) on food, wages and
equipment, but could spend much, much more than that if they had it.

It rained all afternoon and most of the evening. We went for fish curry in town and
sat in the darkness of a power cut wondering if food would arrive. It did,
surprisingly quickly. We walked home down unlit, busy streets, avoiding pot holes
filled with muddy water where we could, and playing Russian roulette with the
motorcyclists who tooted assuming that we would leap into the gutter rather than
cause them to veer from their chosen course. We stood our ground and are here to
tell the tale.

Friday, 12 November 2010

Health matters

We mentioned yesterday the dispensary run by the Sisters here. They treat private patients as well as those unable to pay. Many people choose these private clinics rather than the state hospitals because the service is so much better. Medicine for under 5s is free, but for everyone else they pay.

Francis told us yesterday that he has been diagnosed with malaria. He tells us, like he had been told he has a minor throat infection. He is suffering all the symptoms –fever, aching joints, tiredness – and has the anti-malarial medicine to take over the next few days, something he paid for privately, rather than through the hospital. Tonight we found him cycling off to the shop for water. Yes, water. He has no clean water in his house and he thinks that the medication he has been prescribed is making him sleepy; therefore he plans to drink water to dilute the medicine to make him less sleepy. Our entreaties to him to rest, fell on deaf ears.

We ate in the local bar – *chipsi na mayai na kuku na nyama* (chip omelette with four pieces of beef) – with Deo, a local clinical officer, the equivalent to a junior doctor. In his spare time, he is a senior manager with a small NGO organising health education projects around this region. The funding they receive is to promote health awareness around HIV/AIDS but the big killer round here is not AIDS, but malaria. We reflected on how malaria does not hit the headlines like HIV does, unless Cheryl Cole or Didier Drogba gets it; because of course, apart from those rare cases, malaria is pretty much an African problem. It doesn't cross borders the way HIV does. Draw your own conclusions.

Back to Tanzania and tolerance; we also reflected on how it is impossible to tell a Christian from a Muslim here. Perhaps if you know their name it might give you a clue, but not always. Deo is a Catholic, sings in the choir at Shangani Church. He is engaged to a Muslim. I suggested they invite John "He's not a Muslim; he's a good American" McCain to their wedding. Francis is a Catholic and a Makonde (his tribe); the Vice–Principal is a Muslim and a Makonde. The Vice-Principal was keen to tell me proudly, that Francis is not only a committed Christian but also a Makonde. I need to know more, but it seems at first sight that your tribe is far more important than your religion. In many conflict areas around the world, it's because your tribe is the same thing as your religion that there is conflict. Not so here.

Sunday, 14 November 2010

Saturday and Sunday

A surprisingly quiet night; I know, because in spite of the silence, I still lay awake through most of it, until 4.50 when as loud as you please some bouncy gospel music started blaring out from across the field. I really can't work it out. It was certainly one in the eye for the call to prayer, though. He started up about 10 minutes later and I could barely hear him. I really like the soulful and slightly haunting tones of the call to prayer and if I could have found the source of that bouncy, bass, gospel schmaltz, I'd have cut his wires.

Kelvin, a pupil from Shangani school, came round this afternoon. He is quiet, conscientious and clearly enterprising. I set him up with an email account and then on Facebook and then he came with us to the beach. Naively I thought he wanted our company and to practise his English. In fact he wanted me to take a series of photos of him, looking cool and macho, to load up on to his Facebook profile. The long Christmas holiday is fast looming and Kelvin for one is looking forward to travelling to Arusha, where he will spend the long holiday with his mother and grandparents.

Probably the highlight of Saturday afternoon for me was snorkelling with Philippe, who I met on the beach with his family. He took me out at low tide to a deep channel where we saw the real beauty of the coral and the amazing array of coloured fish, sea urchins, jelly fish, even a huge turbot. I felt like Jacques Cousteau.

At Mass this morning the twelve collection boxes were explained – one box for each of twelve districts within the Parish. We are supposed to give to St John the Baptist. Seven o'clock Mass was packed. It took me back to childhood with ushers finding spare seats for latecomers and directing the congregation at Communion. Almost as long as Mass was the announcement at the end of Mass, of the broadcast scheduled for next week by Radio Maria, the national Catholic radio station. Apparently the show will be broadcast live from Francis' house next Sunday evening and we along with other Catholics in College should be there. He's going to have to move the enormous fridge and TV from his living room if there's to be room for us. He's also better tell the Bursar to do something about his roosters and the other tutors about their goats; otherwise the broadcast is going to sound like Farming Today, rather than Songs of Praise.

Monday, 15 November 2010 - Caroline's day

I went through the register at nursery this morning to see if I could remember any of the children's names. There was Judith, Irene, Valentine, Omari, ...I'm getting to know each of them, but I came across one I didn't know, God's Love. I'll make a point of finding that little one tomorrow.

We have lunch in the staff room at college now. Rice, meat stew, cabbage or spinach and a banana or mango - all in the same bowl. It's welcome though and nice to eat with others. Today we were handed a letter from Les, our brother-in-law. Receiving post from home is more of a pleasure than you would think. He had taken such trouble to write such a long letter and, for us, news from home seems more important than ever.

Last thing, we went for our evening constitutional along the beach; low tide tonight and it was a riot of small pools full of crabs, tiny fish, shells of every colour and size, and then, swooping in for supper, two most graceful stork-like birds. They weren't storks, they were too small, I think; but they were beautiful.

Tuesday, 16 November 2010

Strange day today. As the exams come to a close at college we tutors are marking the papers and trying to get everything finished as soon as possible. I have been given the English papers to mark so I am left alone with two lots of about two hundred papers to mark, whilst the others take a whole paper between them, marking one or two questions each and arguing all the time between themselves, whilst listening to soul music from the computer. It's impossible to concentrate.

At morning tea break the Deputy Principal- you will recall that he's Muslim – came in to remind us of the public holiday for Eid tomorrow, but also to tell us that the local MP, in thanks for her re-election, has donated a cow to the college and we should collect our share after lunch. Yes, a cow! I don't know what electoral law has to say about that, but Caroline is cooking the best quality beef and onion stew we've had in a long time, as I type this.

Just cut up a huge piece of beef given to us by a local MP. Remember the sleepless night as the ballot boxes came in, well if we eat all this beef, we'll be up all night with indigestion. The lack of water and a fridge mean that I'll have to be inventive in how to prepare and store the meat.

I asked to be introduced to God's Love today. I think he and the teachers were surprised when I shook his hand. Sadly, I am not yet able to ask him why he was christened with such a lovely name. I will have to practise my Kiswahili. The dancing is a very complicated form of line dancing – African style. I know from past experience not to join in the dancing until this crowd has got to know me.I walk through an amazing piece of land on the way to nursery. I counted at least eight baobob trees. I'm sure Les could make up an amazing story – animated of course – of the scene and all the creatures – Ratty, Gilbert the Gecko, as well as all the other animals. I'm told there are snakes, but I haven't seen any yet. Ironically, for a house without water, we are waiting for the *fundi bomba* (plumber).

The kitchen tap came away in my hands and the waste pipe has corroded away to nothing, probably from disuse. Francis told me apologetically, this afternoon, that the fundi has a lot on and will be round tomorrow. I was quite pleased to be able to make him feel better about the situation, when I explained that in UK, to have a plumber turn up the same week, would be quite an achievement.

Postscript
Our beef stew was lovely - made with onions garlic tomatoes and beef; each grown, reared, picked, peeled, butchered and stewed within about a hundred meters of this house.

Wednesday, 17 November 2010

Eid al Adha – The Feast of Sacrifice

Mtwara is a sleepy old town. It's spread out over a square mile or two. We live in the relatively comfortable district of Shangani, we shop in the small district of Bima, which boasts banks *(benki)* and the Post Office *(poste)*. We occasionally go to the poorer and more bustling area near the market *(sokoni)*. We haven't decided yet whether to buy two bicycles *(baisikeli)* yet. They would make our trips to the beach much quicker and there are parts of Mtwara that we have not explored yet because they are just a bit too far to walk. We'll have to see if our *bajeti* - See! You're getting the hang of it- can stand the cost.

Close to the fish market, looking out over the bay, are the old slave sheds, a decrepit reminder of inhuman practices. They formed the market place for a trade in African slaves with Arab states further north. This Swahili coastline has a number of such reminders, the best preserved being here in Mtwara and Mikandani. Our new friend, fellow tutor Aviti, has offered to take us on a short guided tour of the slave markets.

The Feast of Eid al Adha, commemorating the sacrifice made by Abraham when he offered his son to God, is observed here as a public holiday. The beef we were given yesterday is part of the Muslim tradition of charitable giving, sharing the slaughtered animal with family, friends and the needy. It causes me to reflect on the role of religion in this culture. I admit I had to do research to understand the roles of Ishmael and Isaac and have concluded that Abraham, being the Father of Islam, Judaism and Christianity, it doesn't really matter. Certainly not here, anyway. Here, if you were to say, "Sorry, I'm an aetheist." You would be thought of as quite strange.

I don't believe you could find a greater ambassador for this country than the humble, well spoken, caring and hospitable man we met on the beach. He is perhaps sixty-five, quite fit, and wears a full, long white beard. He is staying in Mtwara with his son and grandchildren. His grandchildren love playing with him on the beach. His daughter, newly qualified from university, is to be married in their home town of Moshi, far in the north, on Christmas Day. He wants to return to make the arrangements, but mainly because he misses his wife. As he said, when you get to our (!) age, it is good to be with your wife. I agreed. He likes to meet people and to offer acts of generosity, as it might be God's will that he needs my help at some point in the future. We should all prepare for these eventualities. It is this capacity to look passively on life's vicissitudes and to trust in God which makes this such a religious country.

Friday, 19 November 2010

Simple things.....

It's the last day of term. We have marking to do and the students are eager to get away. The students are all aged eighteen to twenty-five, have to where uniform all day during teaching hours and are not allowed off campus without explicit permission. Should these or any other rules be flaunted, punishments are imposed. This morning a group of eight students – men and women – were to be seen digging a large pit just outside our house. You might recall that I had queried the issue of waste management; well, true to his word, Francis had dealt with it. These students' punishment was to dig a fresh pit for our waste. These punishments are observed by tutors and students seriously.

Most students were giddy with the prospect of travelling home to see families, but forms had to be signed and punishments had to be observed. The Principal addressed the student body this afternoon at a meeting of the whole College held in the great Benjamin Mkapa Hall. The matter of discipline was high on the Principal's agenda and two women were made to stand up in front of everyone, to shame them. They had committed the crime of being off campus out of uniform and this is taken very seriously by this Principal. When I had previously challenged the notion that uniforms for young men and women whom we were encouraging to be strong independent thinkers was inappropriate, she disagreed robustly, saying that in previous times when uniforms had not been obligatory, standards of discipline were low.

Strange as this was, our presence in the Hall was greeted enthusiastically. Caroline greeted a hall full of 600 students with "Habari za mchama" (good afternoon.) They were all very appreciative and cheered. It was quite humbling.

Later in the afternoon, as I went for a swim, another humbling thing happened. As soon as I went into the sea and started my first few strokes, a young man, perhaps twenty years of age, a student at the nearby seminary, I later learned, came over and we greeted each other:

"Shikamoo," said he
"Marahaba", said I.
"You can swim," said he. "Will you teach me?"
That was it. Just...you can swim. I want to swim... will you teach me.?
In about ten minutes, I had shown him the basics and he was, through sheer determination, rather than any technique I had imparted, doing a passable breast stroke.

Later, we sat drinking our *bia baridi* on what I suspect is the most beautiful terrace in east Africa, under a full moon and considered ourselves very lucky indeed. As if the day could not get any better, we came home to hear that most delicious sound - water overflowing from a bucket.

We had, today, run out of water completely. Our large plastic vats were empty. I had mentioned it to Francis. He had replied, as I suspect you can guess by now, "Yes. I have nearly run out. My buckets are empty. But the timetable is not regular. I think we will have water tomorrow." Fortunately, for once, he was wrong. We spent our Friday evening ferrying buckets round the house, filling our vats and feeling very lucky indeed. We showered, sat down to a beautiful potato and tomato stew, and I am finishing the evening, thanks to a kindness from home, sipping a fine single malt.

Saturday, 20 November 2010

Ratty's back!

Adrian: I think Ratty's back. I haven't told Caroline. She doesn't read this so she needn't know. We already know that something had taken a liking to the plastic bag containing my plastic sea shoes – a large six-inch diameter hole appeared in it one morning. Now I find a whole slice of bread at the other end of the house, close to where the large hole in the ceiling had been covered, following the previous invasion. I don't want to see it. I don't particularly want to catch it. I think IT is probably THEM anyway; so when I get up in the night I whistle, as loudly as I can. I don't know what the neighbours think and it doesn't wake the rooster (bless him!) and – touch wood – I haven't met a rat yet. So, Les, if you're reading; the humane, sonar, anti-rat device works. Just whistle!

Caroline: I wasn't going to tell Adrian, but the last cake left out on the table last night was, this morning, behind the chairs on the floor! I also had my suspicions about it/them still being around but I thought as long as I didn't see it, I'd stay sane. I do miss my pets, Jack, Holly and Lucy on mornings like this, but there have been so many things to think about, that that hasn't been often. Our neighbours obviously become frustrated with the wildlife too: Today, a young woman came to her front door, raised her arms, I assumed to wave at us; but, no, she was throwing a hen out of her house!

Sunday, 21 November 2010

Enterprise

When we've finished moaning about rats, lack of water, the heat, all manner of discomforts we suffer, let me share with you some perspective by illustrating what I think many, many Tanzanians live on. An average wage – a difficult thing to assess here as the difference between rich and poor is so huge – is about 10,000 shillings a day. It is possible to live, but you will rarely eat other than at home, rarely drink beer, hardly ever take a taxi, drink tap water not mineral water, and travel out of town only if you have to.

If 10,000 shillings a day is a good wage and £100 a day is a good wage in UK, then you should be able to make the comparison and see what I mean when I say that THINGS are dear here. It means that 1000 shillings is about £10.00. It means a bottle of soda is the equivalent of £5.00. But time is cheap. I could have a housemaid for as little as 1000 shillings a day.

Enterprise is plentiful however. Tonight on a dark and dusty unmade track speeding over the bumps and humps in our bajaji, we came to an abrupt halt, the bajaji lifeless. Dogs were howling, we weren't sure exactly where we were and I thought, "Crikey. This could be a bit scary."
Not a bit of it. Our *dereva* jumped out, opened up the engine and removed the pipes from the fuel pump. Petrol was spewing out over hot pipes at this point, but he sucked and blew all the muck out of the fuel pipes with the help of the light from his mobile phone, put the whole thing back together and had us back on the road in about three minutes. Impressive or what!

Monday, 22 November 2010

The Masai, religion and the President

Caroline: We had loads to write about yesterday so we've saved some of it up for today. I didn't tell you about Mass, the swaying and shimmying of the little girls for Christ the King. They shassied their way to the altar and did a sort of hula hula dance next to the priest. It had all been beautifully choreographed by the nuns. And then there's the fact that Adrian meets people and doesn't ever remember a face, so people come up to him, ask him how he is and he says, "Hullo. My name is Adrian." and they say. "Yes. I know. I am the Deputy Headteacher at the school where you've been teaching. Or, "Yes. We met yesterday." It happens all the time and is quite embarrassing.

I also wanted to write about the Masai. We watch them every evening, playing football on the beach at 5.00pm. They start at 5.00pm and finish at 6.00pm, almost to the minute. They can't play football, but shout at each other, their language is guttural and not all like Swahili. They are employed as guards for the hotel. We asked why and were told that, as they are notorious for killing lions, they could easily see off a thief.

Last week, a group of boys had approached us and were being a bit cheeky, a bit rude, asking for things and touching our bags. One of the Masai saw them from the distance, walked over slowly, muttered about four words and the boys ran for their lives. They didn't even look round. We don't know what he said, but we think it was something about little boys' bits for his dinner.

We have *baisikeli* now. I just hope we don't get a *pancha*. It will make getting around town a lot easier and our visits to the beach even shorter

Adrian: I asked Francis the other day why religion featured so prominently in Tanzanian life. He said, "There are three reasons."
There is nothing equivocal about Francis.
"Ignorance, poverty and fatalism."
"Fatalism?" I asked. "What do you mean?"
"Let me give you an example. When our President, President Kikwete visited America, he stood in the White House with President Bush and looked out one evening on the Washington skyline, a bright sea of lights, except for one dark patch on the horizon, where there were no lights. President Kikwete turned to President Bush and said,
"So, Mr Bush, even in America, this land of plenty, you too have power cuts."
Mr Bush looked at President Kikwete with surprise and then smiled,
"No, Mr President. We have no power cuts. That's the Tanzanian Embassy."

Francis snorted and chorkled like a drain, at his own joke.

Tuesday, 23 November 2010

Rehearsals, bicycles and the Pope

Caroline went off this morning on her new *baisikeli*. Final rehearsals for graduation are becoming tense; nuns throwing shoes, children crying; but still they find time to serve Caroline with a bowl of rice specially saved for her. She is the elder after all.

We cycled to the University – actually St Augustine's Catholic University, to give it its full title - for lunch. Lunch is served in a huge wood and concrete gazebo. It comprises the standard Tanzanian fixed menu which we seem to find everywhere – rice, a small amount of fish or meat in sauce, beans, cabbage, fruit – all served in separate compartments on a prison-like food tray. At the University, this ample, freshly cooked and very tasty meal costs 1000 shillings (that's 40p to us!).

As we ate our lunch I reflected on the massive impact the Catholic Church has had on this country. In the week that the Pope has issued some welcome remarks on the condom I paused to think of what my dad told me about such things.

What goes on under the bed-sheets is a private matter – between you and God; not so, the state of Africa and the world's poor; that is a very public matter. Those liberals in Europe who would condemn the Catholic Church might want to reflect on this. I can only comment on what I've seen around Tanzania, but from kindergarten to university; from hospitals, hospices to homeless shelters, if the Catholic Church should remove itself from this country, the country would implode. The lives of so many millions of people are inextricably tied to and dependent on the Church.

Back home, this evening, our lives have become quite quickly much simpler than they were in Leeds. A bike ride, a swim, a beer and home for supper. Aubergines, beans, onions and rice – all grown locally; these vegetables are plentiful, yet expensive for so many who have so little. Being rich in a poor country brings dilemmas hitherto unforeseen. Tomorrow morning, I will have Italian coffee for breakfast, which now seems inappropriate, Mum has sent us loads of chocolate. It's mostly Fair-Trade, but Ratty isn't fussy. I've hidden it well. We'll see if Ratty finds it.

Wednesday, 24 November 2010

Malaria

Timothy, another fellow tutor, has also contracted malaria. He is quite poorly, but, like Francis, stoical. Unlike many Tanzanians, Timothy and Francis have access to the medical services where they can buy the medication to fight the parasites in the blood, which are causing the illness. Babies and older people, particularly, die every day because they are weak and they have not got early access to the medication.

A government programme to distribute nets is widely seen as largely ineffective because everyone knows that without other preventative measures, the nets are almost cosmetic. Babies are particularly vulnerable, especially as the bites that occur later in the night, when it is more difficult to protect little ones, are more likely to carry the parasite than those earlier in the evening. This is because the parasite matures in the mosquito through the night and is most potent in the middle of the night. A six month old baby, a neighbour of Philbert, just down the road, died at the week-end.

We are pretty upset when mosquitos are about because Caroline reacts quite badly to the bites. Her ankle has been swollen all week, following a bite at the week-end. But that's it. She gets a swollen ankle and sometimes some nasty sores. We have the nets, the repellents, and most critically, the prophylactic tablets, that mean we are almost guaranteed not to get the illness. It's a killer disease – thankfully not for Timothy or Francis, as they are both young fit men and they can buy the medication – but for many, it's fatal.

Before we left UK, we met one or two people who were concerned about the side effects of the medication and decided not to take the prophylactic. These side effects include nausea, bad dreams and rashes. Those with a known history of adverse reactions to the cheapest, Larium, can be prescribed the exorbitantly expensive, Malorone. This costs approximately €50 a week! I now feel almost angry with those who would refuse the treatment. It seems carelessly disrespectful of those millions less fortunate than us. I feel guilty when I explain to colleagues that I am almost certain never to get malaria. They are too polite to say what I would surely be thinking, if I were them!

Back to more pedestrian, or rather, perambulatory, matters. We took one of the baisikelis back to the shop today to have a back brake fixed. He was charming and greeted 'mama' (Caroline) with a chair, while he went off to find the fundi. Mama hasn't yet come to terms with the rules of the road here. She's showing great fortitude, but insists on alighting at the approach of any motorised vehicle, which is quite often. The shopkeeper, a short fat man, with a big smile until it comes to talking about discounts, was surprised when I wanted him to mend the bicycle. Next to his shop is small dark-skinned tailor, who sewed while he smiled but never spoke.

The beauty of taking the bike though is that we start to feel at home. People shout 'mambo', we reply "poa"; people shout "jambo", we reply "sijambo"; people call "shikamoo" and we reply "marahaba". Sometimes, embarrassingly, one of us gets these mixed up. Caroline sometimes calls "Hodi!" when she wants to say 'hello' to small children. It means "Can I come in?"; but probably more embarrassingly, when boys shout, "jambo", I have once or twice become utterly confused and shouted "Sambo". Fortunately I think few are aware of the offensive connotations and just offer me a bemused smile in response.

Thursday, 25 November 2010

Heat

Apart from one day, it has not rained since we got here. That's seven weeks of unbroken, blistering, sweaty heat. Each night I go to bed thinking of ways of avoiding getting too warm. Should I lie on my back or on my side? Should we have the net open? The fan on or off? Should I shower - (chance would be a fine thing) - before bed or will this cause my body temperature to rise? The business of staying cool consumes my thoughts as I'm preparing for sleep.

The students have gone home for the long holiday now and this seems to have led to a reduction in the noise level at night too. We'll have weddings at the week-end, but on the whole, the place is very quiet. The marking of end of term examinations is almost complete and then we'll have nothing to do for eight, long, hot weeks. We plan to get involved in one or two local projects; otherwise being here, doing nothing will cause us to miss home and family too much. None of us can work out why VSO brought so many teachers out immediately before an eight week holiday.

Caroline: The big day, the day that all this tireless rehearsal has been for, is upon us. Tomorrow, we go as honoured guests, for the graduation of about seventy-two five-year-olds from their Montessori kindergarten and progression to primary school. The dancing, singing, shouting, shimmying, drumming, tantrums, shoe flinging and even crying will all have been worth it. Honoured guests will also be treated to a handsome meal as I spent the morning helping staff crush garlic, scrape ginger, cube beef and peel vegetables for tomorrow's feast.

The respite from the heat comes at the end of the day with our daily dip in the ocean at four o'clock. It is fast becoming a group swimming lesson with Kelvin, Muksini, Joshua and another boy there today, all wanting swimming lessons. I've promised them all another session tomorrow and I'm expecting them to practise their strokes before I get there. The goggles and snorkels have already proved extremely good value. Even better value is William's fridge, which we used to freeze some bars chocolate, courtesy of my mum, which we shared tonight for supper. Perfect!

Saturday, 27 November 2010

The Big Day

Well, the graduation ceremony was every bit as grand, noisy and thrilling as we had hoped after seven weeks of intense rehearsals. Mums and dads (about ninety per cent were women!) came in their finery to whoop, cheer and ululate as the children shimmied and sashayed their way on and off the performance square. It was hot, at times, uncomfortable, but women and children were all very patient. Mercifully, there were no speeches; just a presentation to each child at the end, of a pencil sharpener and three boiled sweets wrapped up in a piece of paper towel. Then they all tucked into a tray of pilau. Each tray served about six children, each of whom sat chatting comfortably, eating sociably.

The kindergarten clearly serves the slightly better-off district of Mtwara. The fact that parents choose this school for three-year olds, indicates an awareness of the power of education in a country where skills are the primary route to sustainable prosperity and shows that these parents not only have those middle-class aspirations, but have the disposable income to pay the modest fees. There are parents who cannot pay the fees and these parents are invited to work for the school – cooking, cleaning, gardening- whatever jobs need doing – but children are not excluded on financial grounds. These children are getting a head start in life. They would in Europe; so much more so in Africa. Should we resent or celebrate this?

I feel torn, when I think about Philibert's comments a few weeks ago, about private education. Nyerere saw the need to force an equitable distribution of access to quality education. It certainly seems true that the distinction between faith school and state school is stark. I'm not sure that bringing small gems of excellence like the Montessori school into state ownership is the answer. Broadening access to that excellence is the key.

Cycling home from Msemo last night, the bikes have proved their worth. The journey takes about fifteen minutes across open brush land, along dusty tracks. There are no roads as such, but everyone knows the way and as the only wazungu travelling like this, people always stare. Our favourites are the two small children who wait for us to pass each day. They live in what we would call a concrete garage. Their mum can be seen working, sometimes cooking on her jiko outside, sometimes digging the patch of soil outside their home. The two children aged about three and five, wave and call, "Hi" each time we pass. Caroline always calls 'Mambo', if not 'Hodi'. Today I was a minute or so ahead of Caroline and as I passed, they didn't call 'Hi'. They shouted, 'Lady?' I realised that it's Caroline, not me, who they like to call.

Sunday, 28 November 2010

Advent

Father Mwenge looked grumpily at his altar servers; the altar candles remained unlit and he didn't look happy. Father Mwenge has the sort of face you could wear as a mask. The altar boys scurried like ants. It is the first Sunday of Advent and although the wreath was there, Mass was still a rather perfunctory affair, with even the choir less than impressive this morning.

From Mass we cycled up to town to find some breakfast. Having dealt with Ratty, I'm now having to come to terms with ants. Every morning, we find they have managed to find their way into some place we were convinced was impenetrable. I had bread in a plastic bag, wrapped in a cellophane bag, in a cool box. I opened the bags and every slice was alive with ants. So off we go, looking for breakfast.

Today we had a samosa, a dough-nut and sweet chapatti with sweet milky chai – not everyone's cup of tea, but I was starving, so wasn't about to complain. We bought fresh spinach, *mchicha,* for 4p and wilted it over a fierce stew made with onions, tomatoes, potatoes, chillies and an ounce of ginger. The smells are delicious and I'm now convinced of the benefits of organic vegetables. The meal is completed with fresh mangos, just coming into season. They are the perfect anti-dote to a stew in which there were about two chillies too many.

We went for tea yesterday with Roger and Francisca, a Swiss couple working at the Benedictine Girls' school. They have two young children; the youngest, Mattheo, almost exactly the same age as our grandson, Harry. Francisco told us of the challenges they faced over the last three years raising two young children here. The closest hospital where you would risk going with anything serious, never mind a baby, is Ndanda, about four hours away on a bumpy road; other than that, it's Dar-es-Salaam or Nairobi.

Roger and Francisca live next door to the bishop, in a house with a huge garden, an even bigger fridge and air conditioning. They own a car, three bicycles and a huge mango tree; and the school where he teaches has only thirty-five in a class. Yes, I'm jealous.

We were late coming home from Msemo tonight and Caroline showed just how confident she has become on the baisikeli, weaving her way between sand dunes, shrubs and youths calling "Mambo". We needed to get home before dark as night falls like a blanket here.

We made it, in time for tea with some melted chocolate, and another hot sweaty night ahead.

Monday, 29 November 2010

Absenteeism

I signed in dutifully this morning at 7.30am but on reporting to the academic tutor, was told, "No, no work today."
You see marking has finished and now there is the long holiday upon us.

Officially we get only four weeks holiday a year, but that does not mean that tutors work for the remaining forty-eight weeks; far from it. I asked one of my colleagues why there are so many tutors away. It was explained that after two years, every teacher and tutor is entitled to apply for study leave, with pay. Unless he or she has shown some level of incompetence, study leave will almost certainly be granted. When these tutors and teachers have completed their study leave, with pay, many look for better paid work.

My job here is to support the improvement of classroom teaching, but, in fact, I will be used to fill the gaps left by tutors on study leave. I will also teach part of my week at the nearby secondary school, which has no dedicated English teacher, because she is on study leave. I am reminded – again – of what Philibert the other week, so aptly said,
"Before you wear socks, you must first have shoes."

On a more positive note, Caroline spent an hour with Sr Cecilia this morning, who explained the need to have one member of staff fully trained and accredited as a Montessori assessor, in order that their dream to open a Montessori primary school be realised. Staff at the nursery, today, were not idle. They were preparing resources and materials ready for the start of next term.

The University is becoming something of a favourite place to eat for us. It's so cheap, wholesome, and the atmosphere is lively, with young people chatting. We met Father Mwenge, completely by chance, again, this lunch-time. He was there in his capacity as student today. I noticed that his face, whilst rubbery, never actually stretches into a smile. I'll have to introduce him to Francis.

Tuesday, 30 November 2010

Bureaucracy, the Bursar and a beaten brow

I had an interesting meeting with the Deputy Principal this morning. I asked for leave to go to Dar and then take a holiday. He looked perplexed, which perplexed me, because no-one is actually doing any work here anyway at the moment. When I explained that I was to attend a conference and make some visits, his brow un-creased and he said, "No problem." It was the word 'holiday' which seemed to furrow his brow.

Next, I asked when I would be paid. At this, he smiled and said, "No problem." I pressed him and asked, "Well, when?"
He said he would ask the Principal.
"When will the Principal be back?" I asked
"Probably next week."
OK, I thought. Let's press on.
Next, I asked if the College would buy a fridge for the house, if I agreed to pay a monthly rent. His brow furrowed at this again and said he would discuss it with the Bursar. "Oh good," I thought.
"When will the Bursar be back?" I asked
"Not later than the middle of January", he said.
I love it, that by saying "not later than..", he manages to make me feel that this is quite soon.
Quite a successful meeting, I thought

Today I was concerned that our passports had gone missing in the post on their way to Dar to have Visas extended. One advantage of an over-staffed, heavily bureaucratic organisation is that it relies entirely on procedures; and when those procedures work, it's a joy to behold. So it was, as our registered package was traced to Dar. The passports are important not least because I have not been paid yet.

I have been told that I could be paid 'properly' by cheque; but I have also been told that I will be paid in cash. The trouble is that neither option is actually possible at the moment. Option 1 – being paid by cheque, would require the Ministry to make the payment and for me to have a bank account. For me to open a bank account, I need a work permit. To get a work permit, I obviously need a passport. None of that is going to happen before mid-January. Option 2 – being paid in cash requires the Bursar to be present; that's the same Bursar who took me to watch Arsenal the other week, has gone to Dar to be married and will not be back here before the middle of January

Wednesday, 1 December 2010

Thomas Aquinas

As there is so little to do at college, I spent the early part of the morning visiting another secondary school, the Catholic, fee-paying, selective school of St Thomas Aquinas. Actually, it's a modest, modern school on the outskirts of Mtwara, close to some of the really poor semi-rural areas. It was opened three years ago with a capital injection by the German Benedictine Order of nuns that have become part of the fabric of life in this area.

I cycled there down dusty roads and unmade tracks, passing mud houses where women were heating water on charcoal jikos, babies were being washed, men were cycling, walking, sitting, talking – all manner of busy activity at 7.00am. It was a side of Mtwara I had not visited before. Cycling within feet of families with a mud floor for their living space, a charcoal fire for their kitchen and a pit for their waste, came as something of a rude awakening to me.

Sister Maureen greeted me enthusiastically. She's from the Philippines and seems unaccustomed to losing arguments. She smiles with energy, knowing she's right. But she's been brought in to turn the school into an educational and economic success. And there's nothing about her demeanour which makes me doubt she'll succeed.

Tanzania requires all such private schools to accept all faiths. I asked her how Muslims were accommodated in the school.
"They are happy to come", she told me, "and we are happy to welcome them, provided they accept our rules, and that means no Friday prayers."
I didn't question her either at this point.

The most challenging aspect of my visit, perhaps the saddest, was that although in almost every way, the school is the same as Shangani Secondary school, they are so different. The staffroom was exactly the same in its layout as Shangani, but here, I saw desks neatly set out and at 7.40, staff silently working. Each classroom, bare of all but a blackboard, desks and chairs, just like Shangani; here, each room with desks and chairs set out in neat rows, the floor clean, the door, not broken and warped, but varnished and closed snugly. Someone had taken the care to hang the door properly, varnish it to a finish, and label it with a plate and screwdriver, rather than a piece of chalk. Thomas Aquinas is a fee-paying school, but many of the differences I saw cost nothing, other than a little time and presumably a fair amount of care.

Finally back to College, where the Deputy Principal and I are getting on famously. He waves encouragingly on Sunday mornings as we go to Mass; he invited us to eat with him at Eid, and today he asked me about football. I had to explain to him that whilst we had a lot in common, I would have to draw the line when it comes to Manchester United! Now he knows that I favour Yorkshire clubs, he taunts me. He asked me,

"If you like football, Mr Adrian, who do you watch if not the Big Four?"
I explained that I would rather watch his students, chasing around trying to kick a deflated ball around on a stony, dusty square, outside my house on a Saturday afternoon than watch Manchester United. He didn't understand, but we left it there.

Thursday, 2 December 2010

HE HAS NOT LEFT THE BUILDING!

Ratty is back! But this time we mean business! I spoke to my neighbour, William, this morning and to my surprise and disappointment, he is equally depressed at waking each morning to find remnants of food packages, droppings and other tell-tale signs of rodent activity. I had thought that African stoicism steeled my colleagues to what we find so upsetting. Not so. William would dearly love to find a solution – a final solution – too.

Last night, I left rat poison hidden with some rice in an egg shell, the protein-rich egg white hopefully irresistible and spelling certain death. At the darkest hour, I woke in a sweat to hear the tin in which I'd left the trap, being dragged across the kitchen floor. I didn't go and look. I could imagine the scene only too well. At daylight, I was proved right. One of the egg shells had gone, the tin had been dragged to the other side of the kitchen, most of the poison had gone, but there was no dead rat....thankfully. I didn't actually want to find a dead rat in my kitchen.

Listening to William this morning, I wondered why he had done nothing about it. And of course it is partly to do with money, but it's also to do with a feeling of resignation. Life can be grim here. And rats are just part of it, not the worst part of it.

Caroline: I am becoming more and more confident on my bicycle. Adrian hasn't exactly helped. He's impatient of me when I stop for other vehicles and intolerant of me for going so slowly. He cycles too close to me, wanting to talk, intimidating me, and I've threatened to get off and walk more than once. Although I can see that it is relatively quiet on the roads and very flat, I cannot get Adrian to understand that I've never ridden a bicycle before and my mum and dad, who both rode bicycles, would be proud of me. Tonight, the small children who call "Lady" as I pass, on my way to the beach, got a fright as I screamed because I'd got stuck in the sand and almost fell off. It's taken me until I'm fifty-one, and living in Africa, but I'm doing the shopping on my bicycle and calling "Good morning" and "How are you" in Kiswahili as I go.

Friday, 3 December 2010

A shati, a skati and a suti

Today we enjoyed the supreme service of African enterprise mixed with hospitality. When we bought the bicycles from a shop near the market, we also bought a length of waxed cloth, a very African design, and asked the shopkeeper if he knew a tailor - *fundi cherehani* . He pointed to a man sitting right next to his shop with a sewing machine, a tape measure round his neck and a book to write notes in. This fundi doesn't speak a word of English, but people are so friendly and bemused that wazungu would have clothes made in this way, that young people, especially, simply step forward and help. So it was that we were measured for a shirt and a skirt respectively, with about a dozen onlookers smiling approvingly, agreed a price and a date for collection. Today was that day. We were not disappointed. We sipped Stoney Tangowezi (ginger beer) and sat in the shade, as he finished a kanga for Caroline.

I saw a fine piece of cloth hanging on some clothes line behind his head and negotiated a price for a suit. Caroline actually negotiated the price up, which made him laugh. I might be a bit shorter, about two stone heavier and white; but I swear, with the suit that this fundi is making for me, I'll be the spitting image of Julius Nyerere.

After he'd noted down all the measurements and made a small drawing of the suit in a margin, using his biro – who needs CAD? – I asked if he knew where I could get a key cut. He took me round the back of the bus station, to a man with a small box of keys, screws, bits of metal, a hack saw and an old tyre. He was working on the pavement, using the tyre as his form; and in half an hour he had cut my key. It works perfectly.

Life here is beginning to become quite fun. We buy freshly made samosas and doughnuts for breakfast, each morning. We eat freshly made rice and meat each lunch-time and drink cold beer, looking out over the ocean each evening. We cycle everywhere and people call "Mambo" or "Wazungo! Habari za subuhi". We feel like celebrities now, so wait 'til they see me in the suit and see what they think then.

4 December

The Taxman, the water board and the daladala

Today we visited the former maritime and slave trade centre of Mikindani. As we left the restaurant, a large party from the regional water authority were arriving for a smart reception, for which the staff had been preparing all afternoon. I was dying to ask the man in a suit, similar to the one I am having made, why we get water so infrequently and whether the details of the irregular timetable could be shared with others, particularly me. I didn't want to intrude, so instead hurried down to the beach to take a daladala back to Mtwara.

The daladala is the most common form of public transport in Tanzania. Unlike Kenya, Tanzania still regulates fares on these minibuses and they remain extremely good value. They are very profitable for the private operators because they cram as many people as possible into the bus. This afternoon, we had about twenty-five people on board a mini-bus designed to carry twelve. This included three women with babies wrapped to their bodies in kangas. The smells, sights and sounds of so many different people in such a small space made for a fascinating journey. I hope the young boy squashed into my midriff felt the same.

The journey, or rather the economics of the daladala business among other things, became the major topic of conversation with Philbert. We had joined him for a quiet beer during the Everton match this evening and our discussion ranged from taxation, a belief in the strength of local communities and why school performance might be improved if responsibilities are devolved to the lowest competent level. We were joined this evening by Mr Faustin, the Director of Public Works for Mtwara Municipality. Mr Faustin's responsibilities include water, highways, housing, sewage and street lighting. There is no street lighting in Mtwara, so we concentrated on water.

It is government policy for every household to have a water supply within 400m. Faustin explained that whilst this is a policy objective, they are well short of meeting that target, resources being so scarce. Caroline had noticed that the taps for standpipes often have small wooden boxes with padlocks. I asked Faustin why. To my surprise he was not aware of this and so we asked Philbert. Philbert explained that it is quite common, that in fact he has one, and that it is to protect your supply from being used by others. All water, whether it is fed from a standpipe in the street or in one's house, is metered. I asked Philbert how much he paid and whether water was readily available,
"Oh yes. I pay monthly and the amount covers all my needs."
"So you don't have water rationing?"
"Oh yes, the water is rationed, but that it is not due to Mr Faustin's department. That is the responsibility of the water authority."
My mind returned to lunch and the large party of men sitting down to a heavy meal and I regretted not asking the man in the suit about his irregular timetable.

Sunday, 5 December 2010

Radio Maria, a scary mzungo and a mended pancha

We were up for 7.00am Mass today. The Church was packed and the choir was particularly adventurous. We learned later that the service was being broadcast across Tanzania on Radio Maria. Francis will be gutted he missed it.

We had been at least twice, before we realised that there is a fairly strict gender division in Church – men on the right, women to the left. Children in church sit with either parent but, as they are nearly always silent and there is no 'kiddies' room for restless children to play, they literally can be seen but not heard. Not heard, that is, except for the little one who turned, caught a glimpse of me and then screamed so loudly, she gave everyone around her a fright. Her mother thought she'd been stung; then she saw me, turned the child away from me and smiled.

It is my fascination with the sounds of Swahili, the harmonies of the choir and the colours in the congregation that keep me enthralled. I don't understand a word and have asked two priests now if they can find me a missal in Kiswahili, but it has not materialised. No-one in the congregation uses a missal, a mass sheet or a hymn book and the entire congregation participates as one, throughout.

We've done a fair bit of cycling today; up to the market, twice, down to the beach and finally, I got a '*pancha*'. I've tried telling them to pronounce the word correctly, but they won't have it. Just as we thought we'd have to trudge all the way home, two guards sitting in the garden of a rather plush house called us. They had a little *fundi s* business going – repairing shoes, repairing bicycles, and if I'd wanted a rat catching, they could probably oblige. They passed two chairs over the fence and we sat and chatted in broken Swahili and English whilst they fixed my *pancha*. After lunch, which cost us 20,000 shillings, the smallest note I had was 10,000 (equivalent to about £4.00). That's about what these guys will earn in a week, so I had to cycle off and get change to pay them their 500 shillings (about 20p) for fixing my bike.

After a hot and salty day in the sea air, the cold water sitting in my bucket which I used for my shower, was the sweetest end to the day.

Monday, 6 December 2010

The first rain

It was Caroline's turn to go for breakfast, so at 7.00am she cycled up to our favourite samosa store. I'd noticed that the clouds were thickening and the air felt close. Within minutes of leaving she managed to catch the full force of torrential rain falling in sheets, whilst on her bike. If this wasn't enough, the rain turned into a violent electric storm with some of the loudest thunder cracks I have ever heard. And then she got a puncture!

I'm trying not to laugh as I type this, but you have got to picture the scene - a half-drowned *mzungu mama* pushing her bicycle to take refuge with a *chipsi mayai* stall. It was raining so hard, the *fundi baisikeli* had stopped working. She eventually returned nearly two hours later, drenched to the skin, to find the roof of the house has a leak and the hallway had become a shallow lake. I was expecting to see rats scurrying down the path, fleeing the inundation.

We have had a glimpse of what it might be like when the 'big rains' come. In minutes, almost every road is turned into a river of red mud, making walking, never mind cycling, very difficult. As Mr Faustin pointed out to us the other night, hardly any roads in Mtwara are metalled. And if it's rainy next week, when we travel to Dar-es-Salaam, people tell us it might take a couple of days, rather than seven hours. No-one has any idea, even after a General Election, when all sorts of promises are made, as to when this road, the only road from the rest of Tanzania, to the major city in the south of the country, and a regional capital, will be finished. I've not heard anger, just resignation.

In Mtwara this morning, the bajaji were in short supply. They're no protection against the rain but they're better than nothing. So it was nice to see people, soaked and dripping, being welcomed into a bajaji already taken; neighbours squashed together, sharing their good fortune.

Today women could be seen catching almost every drop in buckets and bowls, to use for washing, cooking and probably drinking. This water is not only clean and plentiful today, but it is also completely free!

Tuesday, 7 December 2010

The morning after the night before

It's the morning after the night before. The rain was heavy in the night. I know because the evidence is all around us this morning. The roads are smeared with great swathes of thick ruddy mud, branches litter the sides of the road and small lakes have appeared round the small mud and block houses where women will light their stoves to cook *ugali*. Town at 7.00am has the feel of somewhere reeling after an all-night party that went badly wrong; young men sweeping debris from their shops, an old lady spreading grit and stones to fill a huge puddle from round her wooden stall and, as I cycle up to town for breakfast, I pass men in pressed trousers, women in colourful dresses, picking their way round puddles to avoid being muddied.

Last night had a portentous feel to it. The first huge flying termites arrived with the small rains. They are called *kumbikumbi* and are so cumbersome, they seem stupid; killing themselves as they are caught in our fan, making a small whine as their wings are separated from their bodies. I am told that they are caught in large nets and slowly fried to be eaten as a tasty snack or delicacy. Caroline was not in the mood for tasty snacks as she pulled them out of her hair then, later, watched them circling our bed and bashing themselves into our mosquito net. It was as though the rains changed the balance of things slightly. In our room last night, the geckos appeared, as though for shelter. They patrol the wall near the window and Caroline believes they eat the mosquitos. They could eat hundreds and we'd never know. There are always plenty to go round.

This morning we woke and listened. Nothing. No roosters. No basketball. The call for prayer was even more haunting. As I set off to town, a centipede, the size of a bicycle pump was making its steady way across our yard. It's a Tanzanian blue-legged centipede and is poisonous,

"Yes. It can bite from both ends. If it bites, you will surely suffer," said my colleague supportively. In the sandy garden in the front, were burrowing scores of red beetles, also capable of a nasty bite and on the wall of the living room was a cockroach of biblical proportions. The cockroach doesn't bite. It just spreads disease.

By mid-morning, it's as hot as ever and a sense of normality returns to our community; our community, which includes a diversity of insects, large and small, as well as mammals, large and small, some welcome, others, definitely not.

Ratty came again last night but didn't stay. I think we've pinned him down in the pantry, where he nibbled on some tomato and egg shell. I thought I'd heard him struggling in the glue, and for a moment in the dark, I started to prepare myself for finding him trapped, spread-eagled, a gruesome scene from some Disney horror. But, alas, no; he left, presumably to take cover from the *kumbikumbi* and the rains.

Wednesday, 8 December 2010

Development, bureaucracy and cash (or the lack of it)

The Deputy Principal raised the matter of my allowance this morning, before I had chance to mention it, which I thought was very decent of him, as he still has no way of paying me. I'm not sure, but I think the Principal has gone away and left the Deputy in charge. Without the Bursar, however, he has no means of paying me, as he has neither the necessary authority nor the cash.

This less than appealing face of Tanzanian bureaucracy reared its head again when later, I asked Francis about repairs that should be done to the protective mesh across all the windows. This is necessary, if we are to keep mosquitos out of our homes. It is also forms part of Tanzania's war on malaria, trumpeted during the recent election campaign, which in the words of President Kikwete, will make "......every visit by a mosquito for a blood meal, a thing of the past."

That particular vision will remain visionary for some time to come, here in Mtwara Teachers College, as apparently, the College only has money to repair my house. The Deputy Principal's, Mama Ngonyani's and Francis' houses are all in need of these repairs but there is, apparently, no money. As you can imagine, I'm not entirely happy. We'll see what happens.

The question of what the college can afford is placed in sharp perspective when the only I.T. support I've offered to date, is to assist with the uploading of CVs for tutors applying for study leave. All the tutors, except Francis, under the age of forty, who I've spoken to, are either about to, or hoping to, undertake extended study as a means of furthering their careers. By 'furthering their career' they mean 'get out of teaching'. The pay is low, there is guaranteed access to study leave with full pay, and with further qualifications, tutors can expect to be able to apply for jobs outside education. Tanzania's route to development is through education, and that means more teachers. I have begun to question my role in this strategy, if indeed, there is a strategy.

On the matter of money, one feature of daily life in Tanzania, is the quest for change. Whilst every transaction is made in cash, the largest denomination for a bank note is 10,000 shillings. We paid for our bicycles with a large brown envelope full of cash. On the other hand, most small traders have difficulty giving *chengi* for more than 2000 shillings. With some, we are already trusted, and we need to remember, therefore, that our dinner lady at the University owes us 100 shillings and that we owe the samosa man 1800 shillings. Sometimes, you have to remember that there are two worlds here, and that, whilst two beers cost 4000 shillings, the *baisikeli fundi* rarely have anything other than 100 shilling coins.

Thursday, 9 December 2010

Independence Day

We woke up this morning to nothing except the steady irregular beat of the basketball. Two enterprising students make their way each morning, immediately after sunrise to practise their basket shooting and dribbling. I want to go and congratulate them for their commitment and enterprise; but I don't, I just shout expletives at them under my pillow.

The reason things were so relatively quiet this morning, is that today is a Public Holiday, celebrating independence from the British in 1961. No-one had warned me and there few signs that anyone was celebrating. It's a public holiday for public servants, salaried and superannuated. For the rest of Mtwara, it was business as usual. Business as usual means coming to grips with mud and poverty. It is appropriate today to reflect on why we're here, why Tanzania is one of the poorest countries in the world, and whether any of us believes that the Band Aid culture, of the rich giving a tiny percentage of their surplus to the world's poor, will ever be a thing of the past.

Tanzania is a large country with incredibly fertile soil, much of it volcanic and rich in minerals. It has a long coastline, with a port offering good access to overseas markets. A railway joining that port to the hinterland was built over a hundred years ago. Since independence in 1961, it has been peaceful – Nyerere's great success was to build one nation from many tribes. He is universally thought of here as the father of the nation, the teacher, the great 'uniter'. Many of these factors are singled out by Professor Paul Collier in his seminal book, "The Bottom Billion", as being pre-requisites for sustainable economic and social development. Why Tanzania has fared relatively worse than Kenya, but has fared much better than DRC or Cote d'Ivoire is explained in a coherent, accessible way in this book, written by probably the world's strongest authority on African economies.

As we cycled home this evening from the beach, I was still wondering what the three white businessmen – one Polish, two American – thought of this quandary. They had spent the evening discussing how bad things are in this country, how corruption and bureaucracy stifle enterprise. At that moment we passed a large piece of land which has been fenced off and we have been wondering whether it is to be cultivated or used to build homes. In fact, it is being used a storage facility for crates of Coca Cola. Two, now three, large containers have dumped hundreds of red Coca Cola crates and a motley collection of young people are moving, stacking and generally looking after them. This is not scientific, I know, but I see everywhere the possibility for progress and rarely the reality, and I don't know why.

Fortunately, Caroline and I need to focus on smaller things. Caroline has become an avid washer and ironer of clothes. We've been told that clothes can become impregnated with small burrowing ants whilst drying on the line and they must be ironed. Not sure if it's true, but I like having my underwear pressed.

Friday, 10 December 2010

You dirty rat!

Politics here, as anywhere, is about self-interest and the art of the possible. The CCM was elected with 64% of the vote, a figure disputed by many of the President's opponents. CUF, a Party for the urban intellectual, is still marginalised when it comes to the elections, because of the huge numbers of impoverished farmers who remain loyal to the Party of the father of their country. This analysis is derided by, for example, Father Mwenge, who openly describes the corruption and information management of the ruling Party.

At the Saint Augustine's University of Tanzania, where we have lunch each day, demonstrations such as those witnessed in London and other cities this week, seem unlikely. These students are well dressed, sitting chatting, reading, taking notes or watching TV. They appear calm and, dare I say, adult.

Of course in Tanzania too, education is valued greatly, not least because without it, it is almost impossible to lift yourself out of poverty. Although the country is making great strides to get more children into school, hence the need for more, better qualified, teachers, these students still represent an intellectual and economic elite, and their demeanour shows it. They don't look as if though they are about to riot.

At the risk of boring you, I thought I'd give you an update on Ratty. We've starved him of food, other than tomatoes laced with poison, and he's obviously looking for grub. Last night in frustration, he went looking in the bathroom (well, there's no bath, just a concrete stall for a shower!). We assume he'd wanted to give himself a good scrub because he left his tooth and foot prints in the soap. Then rather eagerly, he'd taken a huge block of laundry soap two metres down the hallway and left it by the linen basket. He then tried to drag some of the underwear out and presumably give the laundry a scrub. Caroline didn't know whether to laugh or, literally, cry.

I went for a haircut today, with the surliest hairdresser I've ever come across. It might be that my Kiswahili is still rubbish, or that he felt nervous about cutting a mzungu's hair, but try as I might, I couldn't get a smile or a peep from him. He has, however, given me a mean haircut, some might say a bit on the short side, but the razored and wedged sideburns make me look, in my opinion, more like a popstar. It made Caroline laugh out loud. I just hope it doesn't spoil the Nyerere look for when I collect my suit next week.

Saturday, 11 December 2010

"I'm dreaming of a white Christmas"

We woke to the rich, resonant sounds of Bing Crosby this morning, interrupted by the ubiquitous roosters. We laughed, because, of course, we are dreaming of a white Christmas and at times, missing home quite badly; but, also because, it is the first bizarre reference to Christmas that we've seen or heard here. Refreshingly, in this most religious country, Christmas is referred to only in a religious context. There are no baubles, no Santa suits, no hurriedly scribbled Christmas cards, no queues at tills to buy unwanted gifts. None of that. And it's quite refreshing and uplifting. It reminds us that Christmas was a pagan winter festival, replaced by Christians to celebrate the birth of Jesus. The winter festival, the fending off of spirits of the cold, rituals to welcome the spring, the retaining of evergreen as symbols of fecundity – none of this is part of Christmas here and it suggests that those pagan rituals are still quite important to most British people.

Shopping for clothes in the market should have been fun, but it wasn't. It's normal to buy second-hand clothes and check them thoroughly for stains and tears before parting with your money. I bought shirts, Caroline bought a dress, but the tailor is looking more and more like good value.

One problem we still face, is that, unlike in the smaller shops where our faces are known, when we walk round the market, a whisper trickles ahead of us, through the crowd, "wazungo....", so that at every stall there is usually some young buck trying to prove to his mates that he can screw more than anyone else out of the gullible wazungu. We try and seek out the *mzee,* the older traders. They are less easily impressed, less eager to trick you or over-charge you.

The shirts like the mango juice we bought, which to our shame, we discovered too late, had been imported from Egypt, are not made in Tanzania. The processing of resources is what adds value and yet so much of what Tanzania produces is not processed here, but exported for others to process. Nothing has significantly changed since Germany used Tanganyika as its back garden for growing the highly valuable 'sisal' plant, for use in the textile industry. When I commented on the effect of the rains in town earlier in the week, I should have also noted, that every Tanzanian who has commented, has referred to the rains with thanks. People are very aware of what they mean for crops, for livelihoods, for people's lives. Subsistence remains the way of life for the majority of Tanzanians, just as it was when Germany occupied this territory over one hundred years ago.

Off to the Post Office for another taste of Tanzanian bureaucracy.
"Can I have five stamps please?
I paid the money and waited.
"I want to collect a parcel!"
"Just wait." And he started browsing carefully on his computer screen
Oh good. I thought. He's going to find the parcel on the system.
After five or six minutes, he gave me an A4 sheet stamped with a receipt stapled to it.
"What's this?" I asked.
"Receipt for the stamps" Not a record of posting, just a receipt for the stamps.!!!!!!!
"And what about the parcel?"
"Just wait."
After another five minutes, a man appeared and asked me for my name and address and the date of posting the parcel. I waited another five minutes for him to return and say.
"Not yet. Try on Monday."
I turned to leave, hot and frustrated, to find all the doors locked and barricaded. The Post Office had closed, and I was locked in. I had to be led through the bowels of the building to a car park on the opposite block, to where Caroline and the bicycles were waiting, and then walk the entire length of the block to return to my starting point, with nothing more than a receipt for five postage stamps, worth £1.25 in my wallet.

Returning to Christmas and greenery, one of the greenest things we've seen so far is the vivid green grass snake that nearly tripped Caroline up on the College driveway this morning.

She had been concentrating on the large green lizard that had just scampered across our path and we were wondering whether the goats on the football pitch, now showing patches of greenery after the rains, were tethered and being legally grazed.

They reminded me that I must burn our rubbish, before the goats, that were merrily eating the contents of our pit, save me the job. At home, we're tracking the progress of snails up and down the walls of our house. They are large snails, the sort you'd find in Alice in Wonderland. They scurry rather than slide, and have such distinct markings, you'd want to name them. I'm beginning to turn my thoughts to what might be our Christmas delicacy in Zanzibar.

Monday, 13 December 2010

Ratty is dead!

In the interests of delicacy and some people's sensibilities, I shall say no more than, Ratty is dead. I had worked out over the last few days that he was almost certainly nesting under a wardrobe in the spare room. This morning he was swiftly dispatched by the college *fundi* and I was left to remove what can only be described as a comfy little pad for rats. He had dragged rags, plastic bags, pieces of plastic and amongst the food and the paper, he had built himself a snug little nest in the base of the wardrobe. With the help of the bravest man I've met this week, the college fundi, we now leave for Dar with a clean bedroom and a huge sense of relief.

At the staff meeting this morning, I was the subject of general ridicule as the *fundi* told the assembled staff the story of how I ran for cover as soon as the rat appeared, leaving him to execute the task single-handed. I didn't mind. I heaped glory on his head, calling for a pay rise and general applause. He was my hero!

The conversation turned to the question of husbandry and the animals grazing as a result of the fresh green grass that has sprouted since the rains. Apparently the fine bull, which was grazing outside our back door on Saturday – the College bull, no less, or as the Deputy Principal likes to put it – "we say in Swahili, half a herd," - has gone missing. There are boys out looking for it at present, because they hope it has just wandered off, looking for cows, but the suspicion is that it has been rustled. I decided that today was not the time to describe the beaten up car, surrounded by men, cowboys we thought, backing up to the butcher's entrance, the other day.

In preparing to leave for Dar, we passed one of our water filters to William, our neighbour. I learned that he drinks the tap water, even though most of the time it is brown and smells bad. We only use the tap water for washing our bodies, and the toilet, and we filter it before we wash clothes with it. Water filters are low technology ways of giving some level of water purity. We are the only people in college to own one.

Back to financial matters: the Deputy Principal was pleased with himself because he said he was able to solve the problem of my allowance.

"Excellent," I said. "Will you pay me cash right now?"

"Ah, no! It must be paid into a bank account."

"But as you know Deputy Principal, I have no bank account and will not have one until I get a work permit. That will not be until mid-January."

At this point, his face fell. I had heartlessly dashed his good spirits and sense of achievement, with my cavalier dismissal of his efforts. I immediately felt guilty and tried to make amends,

"But never mind. I'm sure I can manage until January."

His face beamed and we were, once again, great friends. It's only money, after all.

Francis will kick himself all the way back to Mtwara, because he went to Dar at the week-end whilst Radio Maria came to us this evening, to record us saying the Rosary. Twenty-five of us squashed into John's living room to say the Holy Rosary and other prayers, live on national Radio Maria. The average age, without me and Caroline, was probably eighteen, the youngest being about three. Caroline and I concentrated more on getting the words out than praying, but it was one of those humbling experiences which, when we recall it in years to come, will seem no less bizarre than it did tonight.

The roadside stall at the end of the driveway is stacked with pineapples and mangoes, so, to celebrate our liberation from Ratty, tonight, I bought a pineapple. We cut it into huge chunks and ate it like urchins, with great squelching of juice and great gobbets of fruity flesh dribbling from our faces. What luxury! Our sense of relief in being rid of that rat, is palpable. No more will we wake at night listening, Caroline too squeamish to go to the toilet, no more will we wake up in the morning, stamping our feet and whistling. Our house is ours again.

Thursday, 16 December 2010

The road to Dar

We had decided that we weren't going to repeat the awful journey down to Mtwara, when we went back up to Dar. We had learned that there is a faster bus, with air-conditioning and a toilet, had booked the tickets last week and paid the princely sum of Tsh22,000 each. (£9.00) People thought us very decadent but we thought,

"What the hell! You only live once."

I should have realised something was amiss when we received a call from the coach company at 6.30am to say that we should get to the bus stand quickly, as they had changed the departure time and that the bus was leaving in half an hour. The departure time was not the only thing that had changed,

"That's not our bus," I said.

"Sorry. There is a problem,"

What could we do or say? We were given seats at the front of the coach, an old Ngitu Express bus and we were seated next to a family with a mama, a young mother, a young girl, aged perhaps four years, and a hen.

It surprised us how, with a spirit of resignation, the hours passed. Each time we stopped, the bus was surrounded by people selling mangoes, water, fish, pineapples, most things you might need on a long journey, but mainly mangoes. Parcels of fruit, baskets of water, trays of nuts were hoisted above their heads and pressed through the open window. The hen clucked and then screeched as it escaped its bag and nestled under our seats.

After four hours we stopped in a small town for refreshments. The young family got off and returned with a large fish and chips in a black plastic bag and the little girl ate, silently, deliberately, one-handed, staring at me fixedly. This little girl never smiled once; just stared. Another young boy, screaming when he was put down, was held up to look back over the seat at me and fell instantly silent, the look of horror in his face replaced whatever had been making him cry. The bus wound its way through the green and dusty landscape.

At a moment chosen by the little girl at the back of the bus, who could wait for a toilet no longer, the driver was *"shushied"* (asked to stop) and most of the passengers then took this as a signal to alight and make their way a few yards into the long grass.

We arrived at the outskirts of Dar as dusk fell and witnessed the absence of order, horrific chaos. Daladala, buses, lorries, private cars and bicycles, nudged, peeped, veered onto pavements, edged across lanes, men leaning wildly from windows, calling, waving, all the time, creeping inch by painful, smelly, hot sweaty, infuriating inch along the road to the next road junction. Along the roadside, stalls selling shoes, eggs, steel rods, chips, trousers, everyone surrounded by mud from the rains, broken cars, bicycle spares – the chaos went on for mile after mouth-gaping mile. Prurient fascination at this poverty kept us transfixed as we watched a woman, barefoot, a baby wrapped to her back, a basket of bananas on her head, picking her way through mud and waste. The baby slept.

When we arrived at the budget hotel in the centre of Dar, we had been travelling for fourteen hours. I might have complained, but the little girl next to me had sat, stared, slept and never once cried or complained, so I didn't.

Monday, 20 December 2010

Zanzibar

First impressions last, they say. Zanzibar is not like Africa; at least, it's not like the Africa I've seen. It is an exciting mix of Indian, Arabic and African smells, style and architecture. You can see at a glance why *wazungu* flock to Zanzibar, why Italians, particularly, love the island, and why the main town of Stonetown is so busy. At times it seems to be awash with souvenir shops, souvenir shoppers and young African men trying to persuade *wazungu* to buy yet more souvenirs.

Stonetown is a place to mooch around. I'd like to, but am dissuaded because of the number of *ticks* pressing to be your guide or to take you to show you their brother's shop. One such young man, Simon, befriended me yesterday. He wanted to show me his shop. I agreed. He showed me several, including his brothers. I commented on how many paintings of the Masai had actually been created by his brother. There are so many, in so many shops, all virtually identical. I showed him my wallet and his face fell. He told me he knows England. He has a brother living in Brixton.

I said "What another?"

I thought, "Well, don't we all?"

I'm told that poverty on Zanzibar is worse than anywhere in Tanzania, but, in truth, I haven't seen it yet. We are staying in a fairly large apartment on the outskirts of Stonetown. There are many such concrete blocks, four storeys, dilapidated, more like East Europe than East Africa. Ours is set in an overgrown complex of concrete blocks, steel grilles on doors and windows pervade, concrete stair wells open from doors swinging aimlessly off their hinges, graffiti abounds, as does domestic waste. Were it not for the heat and, of course, the cows and the hens, we could be in east Leeds.

We have the same issue with water as we do at home in Mtwara. Water gurgles then thumps its way up to the huge tank on a concrete tower outside our bedroom and this is the sign to attach the plastic hose and fill your buckets. The water is clean but not drinkable and for one precious window of about an hour, you can shower in clean, clean water. What a treat!

The daladala here are even more exciting than in Mtwara. Two wooden benches installed on the back of a small Japanese truck can accommodate up to twenty-four people. Children then squeeze in the gap between our facing knees and daring men swing from the step on the back. Yesterday our conductor, holding on rather waggishly with one arm, as he collected fares with the other, allowed the 500/- which I'd just paid, to fly from his hand in the breeze. He was annoyed but too cool to let it show. I saved him his blushes and we split our losses.

Thursday, 23 December 2010

The monkey, the mama and the mad, mad driver

A day trip to the Jozani national park to see the collobus monkey involved another exciting trip on the daladala. First of all find the bus, then check that it's going where you want. Not all daladalas go where they say they're going. If they have a full load of passengers for part of the journey, don't expect them to take you all the way. Check first. For us, it was a forty-minute journey through some beautiful, tropical countryside. Twenty-three of us squashed into the back of this truck on wooden benches and with a roof, just high enough to bash your head three times as you kneel/walk your way down to the far corner. People are friendly. It's a good job, though, as you couldn't get any closer without committing an offence. We were squeezed out at the park entrance and registered with the ranger and guide.

Jozani national park is a protected site, a tropical rainforest of 5000 hectares and home to the almost extinct collobus monkey. The monkey, once almost rendered extinct, mistakenly, on the orders of a former British Consul and expert on Zanzibari fauna, has a reddish brown coat and uniquely has only four fingers on its hands. It eats leaves, un-ripened fruit and, when necessary, charcoal to allow its digestive system to handle toxins. It is, we are told, not aggressive, not curious and provided one does not go too close, quite harmless.

"Just take a photo of that one sleeping, Mike," said Caroline.

No sooner had she said it, than an adolescent male, too curious to see us, fell from the tree above us and landed on our friend, Mike's, face. The guide, as well as us, responded in the way one would expect. We all bellowed with laughter. Blood was pouring from his nose, but we only stopped laughing briefly to pass him a tissue.

The way home had the same number of passengers, but this time the passengers were predominantly women. Perhaps this explains why we were so much more squashed. When I thought we were completely full, absolutely no more room, one more, very large woman levered her backside between me and my neighbour. This was a miracle in itself, because I would have sworn that there was no space there; and yet her enormous behind eventually found its way to the wooden bench. The combination of the bumpy road, the heat, and the ample folds of the woman next to me, soon rocked me to sleep. I woke to the sound of boys banging the side of the truck,

"Mia moja na tanu ya fungu". That's about 4p for about six mangoes. Passengers filled their boots and their bags.

Our journey continued. One moment of tension was when we were stopped by the police. This happens a lot and I've yet to work out what they are looking for. It must be *al-quaida* terrorists, because it's certainly not unroadworthy, overcrowded, speeding vehicles, because they would be far too busy. Our conductor looked nervous. I felt nervous and I'd done nothing wrong, yet.

Our journey continued. Suddenly we were thrown to one side. At least other passengers were. I was just enveloped all the more deeply into the soft flesh of the woman next to me. A rival bus had cut us off and we were retaliating. There followed a dangerous game of cat and mouse all the way into Stonetown, the driver weaving his way in and out of parked trucks, past bicycles and in and out of the centre of the road. The bus behind chased, swerved and pressed up against us so close that the conductor was rather less cocky than he had been. He spent the rest of the journey looking sheepishly over his shoulder, as the rival bus threatened to crush his legs.

When we alighted in Stonetown, it seemed rude not to say good-bye. I felt I knew my fellow passengers so well.

Saturday, 25 December 2010

Gloria in Excelcis Deo

As I type this, the haunting chants from the mosque fill the room and drown the chatter and squeals of children playing outside. The odd motorbike tuttuts past but the prevailing sound is one of prayer in Arabic. This is Christmas Eve and there is absolutely nothing about our life here, our routine today or the atmosphere about us, to remind us of that. This is a Muslim country.

But what a treat was the Christmas Vigil in the Cathedral. First of all Mass was said by the bishop. He was in white, with mitre, staff and thurible . But nothing, nothing, could upstage the altar. Dressed in papal white and gold, the rear of the altar had Christmas trees in coloured lights and huge plastic trees in each of the wings, dressed in red and gold streamers. The lectern looked as if it had been lifted from a bingo hall and the altar, with a white twinkly cloth dressed in coloured flashing lights, would not have looked out of place in a Soho club. It was, however, all done in the best possible taste.

The choir sang, clapped, swayed and danced in Kiswahili, Latin and, for good measure, at Holy Communion we sang Silent Night in Kiswahili. A young boy in front of us slept through the whole service, while his mum and his aunty took it in turns to nurse him, to fan him and finally to wake him so that at midnight he could queue to see the crib.

Zanzibar town comprises the old town of Stonetown which is where tourists are concentrated, where restaurants serve poor quality and expensive European food and where the very expensive hotels sports plastic Christmas trees and coloured lights. The outer suburbs of Zanzibar town is where we live, alongside a few hundred thousand poor Zanzibaris. As we walked to the taxi rank late last night, women were still cleaning the street preparing for another day's work. Our taxi driver, Omah, knows about Christmas. He has been to England. He knows little of Muslim festivals, even though he is Muslim.

Jesus was not an African. He was mzungu. I know this because I also queued to see the crib. Bethlehem was depicted in accurate detail as a Palestinian townscape set in relief on the crib wall. Inside, the characters had been lifted from an English village scene of the eighteenth century. Even the sheep were Swaledale. Baby Jesus smiled beatifically through his golden locks as scores of Africans lined the church to kiss his feet.

Monday, 27 December 2010

The brides, the bishop and that Don Estelle look.

I've mentioned this before, but evidence is all around of a huge difference between Africa and Europe – things are expensive here, but time is very, very cheap. The evidence of poverty is everywhere in this country.

Yesterday, in the market, where women sit on the floor to strip and bundle spinach, for sale at 200 shillings a bunch, a man had set out his repair workshop. He had stripped an ancient, electric kettle and was painstakingly, with only a small screwdriver to assist, rebuilding it. It was the sort of kettle that is thrown away every day in the U.K. – virtually valueless, because a brand new replacement from Comet, Tesco or Argos is so cheap, we barely think about it. He might make 1000shillings for repairing it because its owner would pay that rather than pay the 25000 shillings for a new one.

More evidence of a country with time on its hands was yesterday's sermon. The bishop spoke passionately for thirty-four minutes. My bum ached, I was sweating and I had to work hard on concentrating on anything other than how much I wanted to get on with Mass; but I was in a very small minority, when he had finished speaking, a spontaneous cheer and some ululations erupted from the congregation. He clearly knows his audience.

It was the Feast of the Holy Family and for about twenty young people it was their first Holy Communion. The girls were more glamorous than the bride we saw on the beach later that day – shimmering white dresses, gloves, even ear-rings. It was clearly a big day and as the choir sang at the end of Mass and the clapping grew with more fervour, some women roused the congregation urging us to clap and sing louder. This was these young people's big day and it was our responsibility to make it a memorable one. It was always going to be remembered because the church was stuffed with cameras. As the young ones received the Host for the first time, a gaggle of photographers pressed close to the bishop, a camera with a huge light flooded the scene and for a moment communion looked like a film set. It was the young brides, and the cool, shimmying, bespoke and besuited young boys, though, not the bishop, who took centre stage.

We're leaving Stonetown today for the east coast and hopefully some quieter days. Life as a mzungu, with money in my pocket, amongst people who have so little, but where touts and ticks will initiate the most far-fetched conversations in the hope of parting you from some of your money, is irritating, tiresome and depressing. In Mtwara, we are used to children calling "shikamoo" as a respectful greeting to someone older than themselves. In Stonetown, young children approach us and say, "Give me dollar." This experience is challenging because of course we, the rich ones, the beneficiaries of the unjust trading relationship that separates Europe from Africa, are the ones who have created the injustice, and as a consequence have to accept responsibility for these small but ugly manifestations. Young people who see wazungu and think they want some of that money is hardly something we can fairly criticise.

But, for now, I've had enough. I told one man off the other day for haranguing me to visit his shop. I told him he was rude, that he had not been raised to act like that and that neither he nor I were personally responsible for poverty or peace. We are however both accountable for our actions.

I kept my hand firmly in my pocket; he grumbled at my parsimonious sermon and then quickly turned to approach a more cheerful tourist.

I wish I didn't stand out so much as such an obvious tourist. I thought that by wearing the wonderful and garish shirts, I might blend in. In fact, to blend in, I'd need to wear an Arsenal, Chelsea or Manchester Utd shirt. In my large white hat, loud shirt and big shorts, I look more like Don Estelle than Julius Nyerere.

Thursday, 30 December 2010

Jambiani

The east coast of Zanzibar is many people's idea of paradise. White beaches, a blue blue turquoise green sea, but always calm and clear; wooden dhows dotted across the lagoon; and, in the distance, a deeper blue line, flecked with white surf, as waves crash where they meet the coral reef. I'm sitting on the terrace of a small bungalow with a garden of palm trees, cactii and a flametree. The garden ends where the beach begins. For the first time in weeks, it's midday and I'm not sweaty. The breeze through the trees and the lapping of waves is cooling and relaxing.

Of course this is not paradise. It's just a scene from a Bacardi advertisement. Fifty yards from the beach, behind our bungalow, are the houses of the residents of Jambiani. They are not on holiday. They live here, many of them without work, some of them selling face-painting or massages to tourists; others, selling boat trips or tours; none of them living well. None of them, that is, apart from the Swedish businessman who owns the bar and the beach bungalows where we eat dinner and drink cold beers. It illustrates one of the challenges for development in Africa. This country is crying out for investment, but when it comes, it comes from Sweden or China or Italy and the profit goes back to whence it came. The investment creates employment, but often the jobs are short-term and unskilled. Last night, Hassan, our neighbour, entreated us to eat at his place. We had imagined another thatched *duka* (shop) with plastic chairs. We had not imagined that his wife would prepare a fish curry especially for us, that he would come to our house to check we are coming and to escort us; we had not imagined that we would go in his house, sit at a small wooden table and wait for him to serve us, elegantly, with warmth and almost too much enthusiasm. His house was a series of concrete rooms, separated by dirty corridors. Apart from our small room, there was no light and his wife sat on the concrete floor in the dark preparing our dinner over a *jiko*. The food, although salty, was delicious. Great chunks of *changu* fish in a rich curry, were served with a flourish by Hassan, his voice booming in the dark. After we'd eaten, he brought rose scented water with clean towels. He washed and dried our hands and when we asked for the bill, he said, "Pay what you think. I want people to know what we do." I wonder what Hassan might achieve if he could build the *duka* outside his home that will enable him to run a restaurant commercially. If he got the investment, would he have the business skills to make a profit and grow his business? We're not sure. Hassan is charming, loud, with huge energy; but is he as wily as the quietly spoken Swede running the bar on the beach. The Swede already has the cards stacked in his favour.

As the tide recedes, evidence of the local African enterprise emerges from the waves; small stakes in the sand used to trap and grow seaweed. The seaweed is collected at low tide by local women and sold for pennies. The two men, Peter and Musa, who took me out on their dhow to see the coral reef, spoke of what they need to do to make a living when the tourists are not there, fishing, cutting wood in the forest, repairing boats – odd jobs to get them from one month to the next.

As we leave Jambiani, young boys are waiting for low tide, so they can race their toy boats in the deep rock and coral pools left behind. Peter and Musa are off to fix their largest sail for Friday's dhou race, an event created for tourists, but taken very seriously by local boatmen; an old woman is selling massages, Hassam is inviting new tourists to his home for dinner and I've left a caustic message with Simba, the agent, about the fact that although he had promised us that the *fundi* would fix it, we were without water for most of the two days we stayed there. That's Africa.

Sunday, 2 January 2011

Daylight robbery

The Union Brothers beach bungalows at Nungwi are managed and run by a motley group of men, all aged between twenty and forty, all of them pretty surly at times but hard working all the same. As we leave for Stonetown I tip those who had cared for us – a tip which was 1/150th of the cost of one room for a night. We've shared the complex with our fellow VSO volunteers so last night was a warm New Year and farewell party, as some of them we are unlikely to see again. The party on the beach at midnight was a sweaty fusion of African rhythms and Yorkshire dancing in Crocs.

The next day, just before sundown, we watched the dhows return with the day's catch. Half an hour later a wooden table was brought out on to the beach laden with wet, shiny barracuda, tuna, red snapper, durado, calamari, lobster and octopus. We chose our fish and watched the chef slice them, roughly but expertly, for the barbecue. We then sat down to a candle-lit dinner on the beach, the freshest fish I've ever eaten. The uneaten fish is packed off to Stonetown at about midnight, to be served in the restaurants there the next day.

As we drove back to Stonetown, we came face to face for the first time with corruption in public officials, as we watched our taxi driver slow down at the police checkpoint and smile. The two greeted each other like old pals, "Asalaamu alekum,"
"Wa alekum salaam," and a hand is drooped from the window of the car in nonchalant appearance of greeting. No-one sees the 1000 shilling note pass from driver to policeman. It happens smoothly, without comment or query, just a fixed smile on the part of our taxi driver.
"It happens all the time- every road, every car carrying passengers, every day."

Meanwhile, traffic chaos reigns in Stonetown. For the want of a couple of traffic policemen, gridlock brings the city to a standstill.

"Does anyone complain?" I ask, naively.

"No. No-one complains. That would only bring trouble. We're used to it."

It means that policemen are making thousands and thousands of shillings each year illegally by charging a highway tax from passing drivers. This is no Dick Turpin story. The country is imploding with inefficiency and waste while policemen stand on the sides of roads taking bribes.

We tourists pass on by, immune. We don't notice the bribes and we don't really care. It's not our problem. There are two worlds here in one city. We are the only *wazungu* using the daladala from the concrete complex of Mchina into the market. We are always met with stares; sometimes hostile, but usually uncontrollably curious; and as we walk through the old town, we meet more and more white people, until finally, near the sea and the expensive restaurants, we outnumber the Africans.

European and Africans sit uncomfortably alongside each other here. You can't live day in, day out, in grinding poverty and all the time watching riches beyond your dreams, saunter past your doorstep every five minutes, without it turning your mood and affecting your civility.

We're going back to the mainland tomorrow and some normality.

Saturday, 8 January 2011

The Uruguru Hills

Where to start? Well, we finished up in a daladala, with me squashed in next to a gorgeous family of mum, baby and little boy. Earlier, we had come down the mountain at breakneck speed, on tyres which had their inners showing, with Jack, the driver, becoming more erratic as his embarrassment grew and the three of us shouting at him to stop. Amos really did not know what to do.

Amos, of the Wildlife Conservation Society of Tanzania, had been our guide and guru for the past three days. There is not much he doesn't know about the trees in the forest, the fruit and berries on the hills and the Uruguru people. There is not much he does know about the workings of a car or what might constitute reckless behaviour on the part of a taxi driver.

We arrived in the small mountain town of Kilone soon after ten o'clock in the morning. The town resembles a pioneering town from the wild-west a hundred years ago. Deep ruts in the red brown road matter little, as the only traffic is from young boys racing their pikipikis. The shops are wooden shacks selling everything from oil to biscuits, phone cards to bicycle spares but we can't find a tin of coffee for love nor money.

Our first walk of the trip took us to the small settlement nestled under a mobile telephone mast – the home of Kingaro, the chief of the Uruguru tribe, the fourteenth such chief, whose ancestry can be traced back three hundred years with great accuracy, thanks to the oral tradition of histories being recounted to visitors. Sadly, he was not at home. He was away staying with one of his numerous other wives. We did, however, meet his mother and his father-in-law, the latter, having been granted permission from his son-in-law, proceeded to tell us the story of the Uruguru people. The Uruguru people speak their own language and although times are changing, retain the tradition of women in the community being the landowners and decision makers.

The hills are alive with people. Tucked away, seemingly behind every small banana plantation is a small mud hut and a family growing what they can. Bananas are the most obvious, but there are pineapples, cassava, jack fruit, field after field of rice, black pepper, cloves, passion fruit - even coffee. At every field, or every twist of the hillside, another shamba, and more fruit to harvest.

As we traipsed, sweating up the hill, we would rest for a while whilst young men passed us going down the mountain carrying pineapples or bananas. Intricate baskets of pineapples and whole branches of bananas strapped together are hoisted onto men's shoulders. They run down the hill, presumably because to walk or to dally would hurt too much. We calculate that these burdens of fruit typically weigh between 50 and 70kg.

Taking photographs is often problematic. Many people are suspicious and superstitious. They often simply refuse. I have started tricking people into having their photograph taken by, first of all, inviting them to take mine. The magic of the digital camera, for young and old, brings gasps of wonder and usually great belly laughs of hilarity. A group of young men was flattered into submission as I admired their Herculean strength. They laughed as I tried in vain to lift the basket. A man in a distant field waved to us, called "Habari?" and had his daughter run two hundred yards up the steep hill to present us with five bananas. The poverty of subsistence farming is dotted across the hills – a small fire here, women working in iron-age fashion on a steep hillside over there, babies sitting in dirt in the shade of a great mango tree while their mother scrapes the land with an ancient hoe. Dash any thoughts of pastoral idyll, this is grinding, unforgiving, relentless hard work.

Once having made the climb in soaring temperatures, the magnificent beauty of the place unfolds. We climbed one small scale of the dinosaur's back to look down over Neolithic settlements. In the distance a jagged skyline of forest, buttressed by steep slopes of banana plants, encircles us, but lets us peer over into the great Morrogorro plain in the shimmering distance.

As we picked our way down through great Jurassic ferns, avoided treading on gardenia and orchids, we heard monkeys yelping and laughing in the trees above us – trees that had grown there since the earliest man hunted and gathered.

The Kingaro's father-in-law spoke of times when Nyerere had visited, when Arabs had come for slaves and when the British had shown them how to terrace the hillside. I asked what was good and bad about the British. They had helped with tree planting, they had stopped robbery, they had curbed unjust beatings and they had respected the role of the Kingaro. What was bad? I asked....and my camera gave up. Honestly. But in truth, he had nothing bad to say about the British. I was left thinking that like many old men he thought fondly of happier times when he was young and fit.

And so to that reckless taxi driver and a wacky races style descent on a rutted road. We broke down in a hillbilly village where men sat on upturned boxes playing draughts with bottle tops. For a moment the scene had tension, but I accepted the offer of a game, lost easily and laughed, and all was well. The huge man with the welding gear whipped out his torch and fixed the radiator. Jack and Amos looked on helpless. As we set off down the hill, young boys were still shouting after us to mend the *pancha* in the front tyre, but Jack was determined to get us home. We were determined to get home alive and eventually persuaded him to stop so we could jump on the daladala that had pulled up ahead. I squeezed in beside my new family, gave the thumbs up to my young boy and we headed for Morrogorro and a cold beer.

Monday, 10 January 2011

Home at last!

In the end, we flew down from Dar to Mtwara. All the garish tales of buses breaking down and impassable roads were irrelevant, as we waited, early Saturday morning, with half a dozen other wazungu in the domestic departures lounge. We arrived an hour later in the middle of a torrential downpour, called in at the shops on the way home and by ten o'clock our neighbours were popping round to see photos and listen to our stories from Zanzibar.

At first, it was almost an anti-climax, the journey on the bus had become so lurid in our minds; but we slipped smoothly into the Mtwara pace of life and our comfortable routine once again - a comfortable routine, that is, of no water, save the stuff that had been sitting in dustbins for four weeks, and no electricity. We really did not mind. It felt reassuring to be in our own rat-free home, washing floors, sorting out laundry and chatting with neighbours.

This morning has been a hectic start to the week. First of all, having seen the photos of the Bursar's wedding, we then went to the bank with my first cheque. He had not explained to me previously that I could present a cheque at the bank for cash without having a bank account. I was too polite to ask why it had taken three months for this option to be presented to me. Still, the queues at the bank were serpentine, so we decided to abort and return later. Imagine the scenes in Europe if customers had to queue for up to two hours to pay in or take out their own money.

Next, to the house. Francis was on fire this morning. We had given him some marshmallows from Pontefract as a New Year's gift and after we had explained that they are sweets, he became animated and tackled the deputy bursar with my list of household jobs zealously. An hour later, five wiry, muscle-clad students set to work dismantling the wardrobe that had been home to Ratty for so long. They had no tools and were amazed when I presented them with my multi-tool with a screwdriver. They were polite, tried it, then graciously handed it back before setting to work with the hammer and *panga* (machete-like blade) again.

The flame-tree outside our back door has grown over the last few weeks and the giant seed pods which look and feel like old leather scabbards have started scraping the tin roof of our house so that, at night, in the wind, the house is filled with the sound of a large bus with rusty brakes. Hamis, armed with a *panga* from next door, clambered and leapt barefoot to the overhanging branch and in minutes had hacked it off. He then directed the other students as they removed the broken wardrobe. They dumped it outside our back door,
"Please don't leave it there," I said, "You should place these in the tip and I'll burn it later."
"Yes," they said, smiling, then walked away.
Later, the Bursar, the Deputy Bursar and an assistant arrived in a Landcruiser, the College Landcruiser. They loaded the broken wardrobe into the back of the Landcruiser and, eventually, I had to ask,
"Mariki. Why are you doing this? Where are you going?"
"This wood will not be burned, Mr Strain. It will become a house for a dog."
A Landcruiser, three men, in the middle of the working day, to move six large pieces of smelling, rotten timber, so that it might be used to build a kennel. I did not say what I was thinking.

Returning to College has been a moving and quite humbling experience. Each of my fellow tutors greeted me with, "Habari za safari," (How were your travels?) and I was reminded of something that Philbert had said to us before Christmas. He had told us of Nyerere's plan to unite the nation, by engineering integration, by forcing large sections of the population to move around the country to be educated. This large-scale 'bussing' scheme had the desired effect of eroding prejudice between tribes, but it led to generations of people spending large chunks of their lives travelling home for holidays or back to college. People do not travel for pleasure. That would be an indulgence few can afford; hence, the polite but incredulous question from my colleagues.

So people in Tanzania, generally are too poor to travel for pleasure but they have enough time to move scrap timber around to build a kennel for their dog. Few things are wasted here, except time

Thursday, 13 January 2011

A touch of reality

Until now, Tanzania has been pretty exciting. The discomfort has been unusual, but knowing that we have only to put up with this for a year, makes it easy to tolerate and is humbling, as we see our colleagues, who live in much harsher circumstances year in, year out, tolerate these conditions without much complaint. Today however, it's starting to get under my skin.

I have had a niggling, gastric problem for the past two days which has left me weaker than usual. I drink water, but nothing else, and I find sleep even more difficult as I'm plagued with stomach cramps. I got up this morning, thinking that the worst had passed and dressed to go over to the staff room for the start of term staff meeting.

Mama Eliwaja, the Principal, directed Francis to be my interpreter. Francis is willing, but he is much too involved in the meeting to be an effective interpreter, so that every time I asked in a stage whisper, what had been said, he 'shushed' me and scribbled an illegible note. Eventually, rather like a persistent child, tugging at his sleeve, I managed to get from him the gist of what was being discussed. All the tutors were sitting with grave faces and with absolute concentration on the speaker.
"She is suggesting that something needs to be done about students' hairstyles," Francis whispered, impatiently.
"Hairstyles?" I said. Had I heard correctly?
"Yes. This discussion concerns students' behaviour."
A moment later, some tutors were laughing.
"What now Francis?"
"The Deputy Principal has reminded us that all of us – even you Mr Adrian – if we find students off campus at night, must take responsibility for punishing them."
"And what is he saying about his shirt?"
Maskat, a dapper man generally, stands about five feet four and weighs about fifteen stones. He stood to show the cut of his shirt.
"He is reminding us that we must dress correctly. Some shirts require their tails to be tucked in trousers. Others should be worn - like this – with the tails over the trousers."

Eventually, the Principal spoke gravely but in a reassuring tone, so that I knew she was drawing the meeting to a close. Everyone had been able to say their piece. One tutor complained about colleagues speaking about them behind their back. Another complained that the Principal had shown undue favouritism to some. Everyone was listened to politely and attentively. No disagreement was voiced and nothing was agreed. No decision was taken.

After the meeting had closed, I asked the Academic Tutor whether I could now have a copy of the timetable. I was aware that the only other English tutor has gone away on a course and will not be back until the week after next.

"Ah no. Mr Adrian. College opens next week and you will see the timetable then."

I have English Club to look forward to because I have already met a number of students who are looking forward to practising their conversational English. And I have the Primary School football coaching to work at with Maskat, the Deputy Principal. I also have teaching at the Secondary School to occupy me, as that school still has only one English teacher and approximately 400 students. As for teaching in College, the job I came here to do, well we'll have to wait and see.

On a more positive note, we have had new mosquito mesh fitted to the house. We are the only ones to have been offered this improvement. Apparently, there is no money in the budget for other tutors' houses, so although we are the only residents using an anti-malarial prophylactic, we are also the only ones to have our house protected.

Two men spent two days with a hammer and a broken screwdriver, prising off old beading, fitting lurid green nylon mesh and then re-fitting the old beading. New beading would have cost too much. They arrived with a homemade ladder on a bicycle and worked barefoot all day. At least it's good for the local economy, if it doesn't keep the mosquitos away.

As for the rats, we are now convinced that there is a growing family living in the roof space. They are noisy at night, scurrying and squeaking on the hardboard ceiling. I tried to suggest to Francis that they might be mice, or perhaps bats; "No. Mr Adrian. They are rats. We all have them. You must put all your food away at night and hope you don't see them."

Well I've fixed the catch on the bedroom door, the holes in the ceiling have been plastered over and so unless it's desperate – or one of us has a small gastric problem - we won't be going looking for them.

Monday, 17 January 2011

A new term, a fresh start and a clean sweep.

Well I seem to be over my niggling little problem. With the help of some medical advice by email and a short course of anti-biotics, I seem to be ready just in time for the start of the new term. Self-help is the order of the day. Caroline had to remove some stitches from my back this evening and although squeamish with a sterile knife, 'needs must' as they say, and she set to.

So at last, term starts. At 7.30, tutors gathered with "Habari?" "Happy New Year" and a review of the week-end's football results. I waited. I waited for the academic tutor who had promised me a timetable. I waited for the Deputy Principal who was to lead the student body in their first assembly. And I waited for all the other tutors to arrive. Slowly, none of this happened.

What did happen, was the methodical tidying of the whole campus by a well-ordered army of students, equipped with plastic buckets, pangas and hoes and directed by student leaders, reporting to none other than my friend, Francis.

Yesterday evening, I'd been to watch the Merseyside derby in my local and on the way home, I noticed how the students' return had transformed the neighbourhood. I had grown accustomed to the sleepy, shuffling pace of life and the students' arrival, as students everywhere will, made the place look a bit messy, but much more interesting. This morning, those same students appeared in blue uniform, lined in serried rank for inspection and morning assembly - quite a transformation.

The College grounds are extensive. They include a large area of shrubland where grass needs cutting with a simple blade. Weeds in paths have grown over the summer holiday and need picking and cutting. Hedges and shrubs are pruned and trimmed, grass verges cleared of litter, rooms washed, chairs and tables straightened and tidied. All of this was done by a volunteer army of students, whilst tutors watched and waited.

Having noted my timetable, I walked the short, beautiful walk through the shrubs and between the baobob trees to the Shangani Secondary school. This morning, the place was a hive of activity also, as students buzzed in and out of classrooms, sweeping, swilling, and straightening furniture and blackboards. Weeds were picked, sandy ground swept, litter collected and floors washed. Teachers were copying out the timetable while the Deputy Principal was busy registering new students. We were proudly told that over one hundred and sixty Form I students had registered in the past few days. I doubt there will be much teaching this week, but people seem happy and excited to be back.

For those of you who might think this inefficient or ineffective, remember that this happens in a place without computers, without administrative support, without even very much paper. There are no support staff, other than those women working in a rustic kitchen preparing food for over seven hundred students. And in the secondary school, there are not even enough chairs and tables for teaching staff. Under the circumstances, what we witnessed this morning was a demonstration of huge commitment to sustainable education in a country that is aware of the need to develop, but can do so in its own way and with very limited resources.

Tanzania is full of young people. Caroline and I are amongst the oldest and in our early fifties and in a gentle, polite society like Mtwara, are met with "shikamoo" wherever we go. Where a cheeky child shouts at us, a stern look can quieten them or make them run. Usually, when youngsters, particularly the four and five year olds we pass on the street, shout "Hi wazungo", they do so without malice.

Caroline, today, met for the first time, the new class of children at the Montessori nursery. Amongst them is Charlie, a five year old, who suffered a stroke at birth and is paralysed down the left side of his body. He held Caroline's fingers as he counted from one to ten in Kiswahili and showed her the correct way to count.

The children are encouraged to look after each other, helping each other wash and tidy themselves. Cleaning the school and college grounds, or, at nursery, children washing their own cups and plates, is part and parcel of growing up. There are no assistants, no support mechanisms and where there are services, few can afford them, so people do things for themselves. Needs must, as they say.

Tuesday, 18 January 2011

Medicine, Chocolate and that irregular timetable.

Well it started badly. We had an awful night's sleep of bad dreams probably brought on by the anti-malarial prophylactic and the sound of water rushing from an open tap. The irregular timetable for water means that sometimes water is available in the tap when we're asleep (except of course last night we weren't!). Frustrating, but the buckets must be filled whenever the water comes.

This left us in no fit state for work. I rushed unshaven, but still excited to my first class. Max was teaching my class! I asked later, why? He said that the timetable is still flexible at this stage. So timetables can be both irregular and flexible. This is Africa!

Caroline is in some discomfort, a recurrence of a painful condition she had thought had been sorted before we left UK. Whenever there is the scent of a medical complaint we become concerned because we have been told at every turn that medical services are just not available as they are in Europe. Truth to tell, our experience to date is quite different. We have been very lucky, we know, but still.....

First of all, it was the mole on my back that had grown and changed colour. Caroline insisted I had it checked. The medical support we get through VSO is first rate and as we passed through Dar last week I dropped in to the clinic for an assessment. Within the hour I had been given an anaesthetic and the mole had been removed and dispatched to Holland for analysis. I don't know how many patients it serves and I don't know how much VSO pays for this deluxe service but the clinic is smarter, more modern and much more efficient than almost anything I've encountered in the UK.

We felt today that for Caroline we needed some advice. Unlike in UK we have the mobile numbers for some good friends who are doctors working a few hours away. Hazel phoned us back immediately, gave her initial opinion and then prescribed medication. Where would we be able to buy it?

We went first of all to the largest Dispensary, the Benedictine Dispensary, serving the affluent district where we live. Helpfully, the sign told us it is open daily until 5.00pm.

Unhelpfully, at 4.45, it was closed. We moved on to the steel container which is Mama Mtupa's shop, an elderly Polish lady who seems to know everyone and everything. She stocks Cadbury's chocolate and as Caroline was in need of comfort food, we bought a Fruit and Nut bar. Mama Mtupa is something of a legend in Mtwara. She married a Tanzanian many years ago and has made Mtwara her home, building a number of successful businesses which her daughter is developing. She directed us to the Duka la Dawa (pharmacy), and we cycled across to an air-conditioned shop which stocked precisely the medication prescribed and we bought a week's supply for tsh3000 (£1.40.) So, in a country that has so many problems, for those with money, all sorts of things are possible.

Life is something of a roller-coaster for us at the moment. We get over one illness, then we realise that our visas are about to expire. We get our timetables showing that we will be busy, then we both fall ill. The one consistent element in our experience in Tanzania to date is the terrace at Southern Cross and the *bia baridi* overlooking the Indian Ocean, as the tide recedes and the wading birds peer and poke for pickings.

Tonight, as we left, the staff were preparing for the arrival of the Minister for Minerals – a pretty important portfolio in this neck of the woods. I noticed the four wheel drive in the hotel car park belonging to the large man I'd seen some weeks ago, the director of the regional water board. It took all my will power not to stop and ask him why his irregular timetable couldn't at least be restricted to waking hours.

Friday, 21 January 2011

A comfortable routine

Well, it started really well. We had had water yesterday afternoon and yet we woke to the sound of the cistern filling. That meant running water for the second day in succession and this time it would be clean water, as the dirt in the system had been washed through yesterday. A shower, clean clothes and full buckets before breakfast is a great start.

We had received notification, finally, yesterday that our application for the certificate giving us right to reside in Tanzania was ready, and I had an email to show the Immigration Officer. Everyone we told had laughed when I'd said that, as of Thursday, we would be illegal aliens and that we were presenting ourselves to the authorities on Friday morning, for them to do with us as they would. Everyone here thought it hilarious. I hope for their sakes that they never come into contact with British or French immigration officers in similar circumstances.

As it was, I had met, last week, the Regional Immigration Officer, Mr Mpota. I knew he was a charming professional man who saw it has his job to stick to the procedure but to help us through it. When we asked what would we do if Caroline had any need to travel before the certificate had been issued, he said that he could extend our visas, something which we had been told was definitely not possible. Clearly, a man worth knowing.

At school, there was to be a whole school assembly or *barasa,* in which the entire student body sits in the shade of the great baobob tree in the yard and listens to the school's plans for the year ahead. It is an occasion when a vision for students is set out, when expectations are raised and where students are encouraged to feel part of this new community.

In College, things are moving at a much slower pace. Of the one hundred students I should be teaching, only thirty-four have so far returned from their summer holiday. Everyone tells me they will be here "in the coming weeks." This morning's staff meeting was concerned with illegal roads that have appeared in the grounds around the college and the college's plans to dig trenches and place tree trunks in their way to stop through traffic. No mention yet of the examination papers I spent two weeks marking last November.

At the Montessori nursery, a strong healthy routine of play and porridge has been established. Charlie, the young boy who was paralysed at birth, has befriended Caroline and through gestures, tugging and half-mouthed words, he tells her what he wants and when he can do something for himself. He's still teaching her numbers in kiswahili.

We have a routine of sorts now. Ten hours or more of teaching in college, ten hours or more of teaching in school, after school classes and each morning spent in nursery and each afternoon spent preparing classes, we have barely enough time to cycle across for our *bia baridi* on the terrace at the big hotel. At high or low tide, the last hour of daylight is always spent looking over the ocean.

In the staff meeting this morning, I could tell Francis was not paying attention. He had been telling me how the girl he wanted to marry had got away and was now promised to another. I only realised at the end of the meeting that the woman he was referring to was Beatrice, sitting right next to me.

We will turn our attention shortly, to activities for the week-end. My colleague, John, and I discussed hiring a daladala to take a group of us to the beach. Now I know that Francis is looking for a wife, a day trip on a charabang becomes all the more convenient.

Wednesday, 26 January 2011

Winds of change

On Saturday, we spent the whole morning drifting about the beach with the tide way out and all the rock and coral pools exposed. Dozens of crabs scurried for cover at our footsteps and tiny fish darted for the shade of rocks. I discovered for the first time that sea urchins can move. I imagined them to be a plant of some sort, but I was truly amazed to see these balls of long black spikes rolling towards the deeper water. I had never understood why I never found them in the open, always under the water, usually sheltered on the side of rocks. Now I know. They know where they are and they seek the deeper water.

Our companions were women, bent double, grabbing handfuls of shellfish from the sand. They collected them in old buckets and paint pots and worked in small groups, kangas wrapped about their middle, their rears pointing skyward, backs straight, necks strained. It looked excruciating. I dived occasionally to see the blues and greens of fish, and the oranges and reds of coral, but, truthfully, I was too scared of the sea urchins to do it for too long.

Later at the fish market we bought two small cory. The men stood swatting aimlessly at the hundreds of flies, they scraped and hacked the scales and fins, and slit the fish open with a rough blade, the innards spilling to the floor. We fried them for lunch with spinach and potatoes.

By Sunday afternoon the weather had changed. The wind had strengthened and the swell of the sea with the high tide, sprayed up on the terrace as we sat and watched sundown. For a moment, the scene could have been Scarborough, as the sky darkened, the wind gusted and the sea churned grey. Except for the cloying heat. There was no let up through the night. We lay in bed willing it to rain, the tough seed pods rattled on our tin roof, sounding like small animals. Strange noises kept us awake, wondering, listening.

This morning, the wind was still gusting, the sky was grey and threatening, but still it did not rain. At 7.30, students were milling about the campus, my English class had only a handful of students.
"Where is everyone?" I asked one of the girls, copying from another's folder.
"They are performing their duties, sir."
"But I am to teach you English this morning,"
"Yes. They will come."
But they didn't. The entire student body was being punished for their failure to complete cleaning duties yesterday. Their punishment was to sweep the pavements instead of attending class. I was too irritable to stay and teach the five faithful students who did attend and I barked at them to be there at 1.00pm, when I would attempt the lesson again. The wind, the oppressive heat, and the grey dullness of the clouds were creating a bad temper I had not experienced before.

I cycled across to school where Form I waited patiently. For the first few weeks of term, Form I is not taught in subjects, but undergoes a cross-curricula induction covering basic skills in literacy, numeracy and science. For me, it was a chance to play some games, sing some songs and act the fool. We all loved it. I took my tea as children were still singing,
"Head, shoulders, knees and toes, knees and toes."

In the midst of all this a Form III student asked if he could interrupt our lesson to ask for "condolences". Students were asked for a small contribution and invited to write their names in a scruffy exercise book, in a list drawn up under the name of a fellow student, who had died.
"How did he die?" I asked.
"Tuberculosis, sir," and he passed on to the next class.

All in all, the wind has changed, the season has changed and with it, to a degree, our mood. We have started work, but the reality of life here, its harshness and cruelty, has today, crept up and hit home.

Saturday, 29 January 2011

Froggy!

The wind remained gusty all week. Most days were mercifully a little cooler and we slept a little better. Still, we have intermittent water and power, there being no warning ahead of the short power cuts and the even shorter bouts when we actually have water. It comes as a huge irony, therefore, to be threatened with disconnection.
"What are you going to disconnect?" I asked the man from the water board.
"There's no water in the tap, so you'll have to tell us when you reconnect it or we won't know the difference. And are you offering a rebate for the dirty smelly water we have stored in our plastic buckets?"

Fortunately, perhaps, Francis came to the rescue again and directed the smiling man with the huge wrench to the Bursar's office where arrangements for the bill could be agreed. We had the same issue with the electricity a few weeks ago, when Mr Mkonga stood firm and stopped them from removing the meter.

Mr Mkonga is the deputy Bursar, sometimes called the storekeeper, but never anything rude to his face. He has gaping holes in his ears, the result of an adolescent ritual in the Makonde tribe. It's not his ears that make him so impressively fearsome, it's the fact that he shouts at tutors for not punishing the students for not clearing the campus. When he met the two young men from Tanesco the other week, I knew they would not come back to disconnect us in a hurry.

What's strange is, that in a country where maintaining constant supply is a challenge, they are very efficient at disconnections. Well, come to think of it, not that efficient, because on both occasions, Mr Mkonga and Francis have managed to see them off, on each occasion with the threat of Mama Eliwaja, the Principal, in their ears.

The week has been a frustrating one for me in college. On each of the four occasions I have had classes to teach, I have arrived to find hardly any students present. There is no accurate record of who is in college and of those in college many did not attend my lesson, either because they chose not to – understandable you might say – or because another tutor had given them punishment duty. Whichever was the case I taught groups of fewer than twenty students on a course on which I am told over eighty are registered. They have teaching practice in four weeks' time and have never yet written a lesson plan.

I discussed this with Philibert the other night – that's Mr Ngairo, the former Chief Inspector of Schools to those who don't know him. We spent the evening sitting outside his shop, the Upendo Grocery, sipping beer and enjoying the best *chipsy mayai* in town. Philibert, you will recall, remembers nostalgically, the reforms of Julius Nyerere and sees the country in need of another educational shake-up. We reflected for instance on the difference between the state run teacher training colleges and the private Catholic university. We reflected also on the fact that whilst I haven't started teaching yet, he was back in work in the private Seventh Day Adventist school – King David's – on 4 January. It's the school where Mama Eliwaja plans to send her daughter once she has graduated from the Montessori nursery. Mama Eliwaja is a Lutheran and attends a popular charismatic church two or three times a week. As yet, this church does not have its own primary school.

Caroline and Charlie continue to spend productive mornings together, and it would appear that although he is a bit old for kindergarten he finds the chance to be with other children a healthy part of growing up. It was a shock to see him placed on the back of a bicycle when his older brother came to collect him. His legs were placed around his brother's waist and he was held on with one arm as they made their perilous way across the tracks to home. Usually, he is collected by his father on a motorcycle – much safer!

I finish today's entry with joyous news that we've had running water nearly all morning. We've showered and washed all the laundry. Caroline is particularly thrilled because having finally got rid of Ratty, we seem to have been joined by Froggy, a tiny, slimy, brown-green little frog who has made it up the waste outlet to take up residence in our bathroom. Each time we flush him down the pipe, he manfully struggles all the way up again.
Caroline is not amused. She's off to buy a heavy drain cover.
"Do I look like a woman who would have a frog in my bathroom?"

Saturday, 5 February 2011

The Regional Commissioner, staff changes and some family favourites.

More heat, no water. Well, when I say no water, I don't, of course, include the torrents that turned every path and road into a ruddy mire. We walked to Mass in our Crocs which made a particular impression on the smart gentleman getting out of the large shiny car with Tanzanian flags.
"Whose is that car?" I asked him when he approached.
"That's the Regional Commissioner's."
"Is he here?" I asked, stupidly.
"I am the Regional Commissioner."
The Regional Commissioner is the most senior civil servant in the region, reporting to the Prime Minister, appointed directly by the President, he is responsible for all state-run health, education and infrastructure projects. My mind whirred during Mass with all the questions I might ask if I got the chance.

I didn't get the chance, because, although he was keen to talk, offering us a lift home in his beautiful car, it was to present us with a token of Our Lady of Carmel. The Colonel, for, as a retired officer from the Tanzanian army, that is the title he prefers to use, wears the scapular at all times and was keen for us to do likewise. He has an official residence, rather like a stately home, overlooking the harbour, but chooses to live in a more modest house in the quiet affluent district close to college. He has soldiers at his gate who salute as you leave.

There have been developments in personnel at college, with new tutors arriving through the week. They are posted by the Ministry without consultation and with very little notice. I met Neema, a new English tutor, in my class as she had been given my second year diploma students to teach. She seemed embarrassed, so I smiled and laughed it off. I had previously attempted to reduce class sizes by diving teaching groups between available teaching staff, but that went down like a lead balloon as custom has it that when a new member of staff joins college, class sizes stay the same, tutors simply teach fewer lessons. I made clear my views on this.

The Academic Tutor, emollient as ever, tried to assuage everyone's feelings by suggesting I teach at the secondary school next door. I explained that this wouldn't be appropriate and in the end, I announced that I would now be the English specialist offering support to tutors and students alike in spoken and written English and preparation for teaching. My friend Roger, summed it up nicely when he asked,
"Very good, Adrian. But what exactly will you be doing?"
I'm not at all sure.

I am teaching a few hours each day at the secondary school, having great fun with Forms I and III. They have all completed a rigorous course in English language at primary school, which means that they know their adverbial clauses and prepositions, but their vocabulary is so frail, they have few functional skills. Like me with Kiswahili, we can read and write modestly, but become jabbering idiots whenever anyone speaks to us.

We have also started teaching in the Montessori training centre three afternoons a week. There are fifty students, all of them women, training to become nursery nurses and primary school teachers, using the Montessori method. The Centre is the work of the Sisters of the Holy Redeemer, an Order founded in Wurzburg, Bavaria, and active in Tanzania for nearly forty years. They run the kindergarten where Caroline works each morning, they run a dispensary caring for the destitute and have created a farm, offering self-sufficiency for landless people. The difference between this small, efficient, beautifully clean college and the Ministry-run Teacher Training College where I was placed by VSO, demonstrates much of what is so challenging here.

So we are busy. We have started doing something productive. The training centre offers us the chance to have some fun. The women love singing and this week, we were royally entertained with,
"Miss Polly had a dolly that was sick, sick, sick
So she called for the doctor to be quick, quick, quick."
We will be covering the Communications Skills syllabus and developing their proficiency in conversation, but we also feel compelled to teach them the words to "Michael Finnegan", "Deep in the heart of Texas" and, of course, "The Sound of Music".

Wednesday, 9 February 2011

Mud, Mr Mkunga and the movies

We're legally resident here. The piece of paper giving us permission to reside here has been issued. It is an Exemption Certificate and with it we can open a bank account, get a driving license and travel in and out of the country at will – pretty much everything that a Tanzanian resident could do. I had not understood why this had taken so long. I know everyone says, "Well you know Adrian. This is Africa." But I sometimes think that Africans get the blame for things which are not necessarily their fault.

Earlier this week we had lunch with Pieter, a Flemish man who has been the administrator of the Benedictine hospital at Ndanda for the past six years. Before that he was with the Benedictines in Namibia for eight years, so his experience of Africa is significant. He told us of the saga of his work permit in Namibia, where the Archbishop, concerned that Europeans without the right paperwork were being arrested and thrown in gaol, went to see the President.
"You have come to see me about a work permit, your worship? Really! "

And he picked up the telephone and barked at his Immigration Minister to make sure the paperwork was arranged.

"Excellent," I said to Pieter, "That's OK if you can call on the President personally."

"You don't understand, Adrian. It took another four months from that phone call before I received my work permit."

What is being done with ferocious efficiency is the closing of informal paths and tracks across college grounds. The college has extensive grounds from which, over the years, have evolved a network of paths and tracks which criss-cross according to human convenience. Mr Mkunga has decided that, for reasons of safety and security, all these paths must be closed. Accordingly, students have been dispatched to hack down trees and shrubs, dig crude trenches and in whatever way they can, block the route of the paths; this at a time when roads are thick with mud and Landcruisers speed past, splashing anyone unfortunate enough not to heed their blaring horns. As a result, small children on their way to kindergarten, students to and from secondary school and tutors going to church, now pick their way gingerly, or after rain, traipse miserably, along a route, three times longer and thick with mud, rather than take a five minute stroll through the baobob trees.

As far as I can tell, no serious research has been undertaken to establish whether these paths do actually constitute a risk to safety and security and even less work could have been done to determine that by closing them the safety and security of local people has been enhanced. It certainly hasn't improved mine and Caroline's safety, nor that of the little ones who live nearby, who usually walk unaccompanied to kindergarten. Little four-year old Salumu, on his way to kindergarten alone this morning, was turned back by an armed guard, and made to walk the long muddy way round.

What is really galling is that it is students who, in return for the tsh150,000 they pay annually for their education, are deployed rather like soldiers on a charge, to do this unpaid manual work. If the college paid 150,000 shillings a month it could build a marked path through the woods and police it. I don't think Mr Mkunga has made that calculation yet, but I'm going to speak to him. The bigger problem is that few public servants are encouraged or rewarded to think like that. They are required to fill in the forms and obey the rules and ensure that everything is shipshape for when the auditors call. Efficiencies and innovation are most definitely not valued.

The issue of students and discipline we find strange. Young men and women, generally in their early twenties, are made to wear uniform, prevented from socialising around town, made to do manual work, punished by removal from class for failure to attend class, and this morning, expelled for having an 'unsuitable' hairstyle.

What I think I learn from all this is that the college, if this is evidence of a trait in Tanzanian public life, is strong on visible signs of strength. Lacking so much capacity for real change; instead, it falls back on more visible and comforting signs of strength and purpose – parade, discipline, punishment and pointless rules. Significantly, at the private Catholic University along the road where we take lunch, there are no such outward signs. Students dress casually, sit and chat at leisure, and a small discrete sign advises students not to wear shorts or slippers at mealtimes.

I have found a data projector in college and plan to put on Film Nights for students. The Deputy Principal wants to vet any film I screen, especially when he saw the '12' certificate and noted scenes of strong language and violence. I asked my good friend Pascal what choice of film would students prefer.
"Something about the life of Jesus," he said.
"How about Mamma Mia?" I said.

There might be something of a cultural chasm to bridge in the days ahead.

Wednesday, 16 February 2011

The Feast of St Valentine and the birthday of the Prophet Mohammed.

It was Valentine's Day and Caroline had the idea of screening Sleepless in Seattle. The loudest, scariest thunder storm gave way to torrential rain and a power cut. Nevertheless, in Crocs and ponchos, we braved the storm and managed to get the 'picture house' ready. We started with about sixty students – all of them male. Clearly the women had thought better of paddling across campus for a foreign film. Valentine's Day or not, it wasn't their idea of a romantic night out. So at the critical point in the film when Tom Hanks meets Meg Ryan at the top of the Empire State and boys were chatting and some got up to leave, Caroline turned in a hoarse whisper and said,
"I'm going to tell them all to sit down and shut up in a minute."

Most seem to enjoy the film nights we have initiated. We're not sure whether it's the films they enjoy, or just the opportunity to sit and watch the images of another world and another culture. I've promised them the Sound of Music and South Pacific, but one guy has already asked for Rambo. There's obviously another cultural chasm to bridge. This cultural chasm shows itself when, in this audience of 19-30 year olds, at the first hint of romance, a man and a woman kissing or the suggestion of sex, they fall into uproarious, but nervous laughter. Later that week, in class with student teachers, we spoke of their ambitions. To pray and to have babies was a common response.

I cycled along to the nearby Pentacostal Church this morning to an interesting community development event. I had been invited there by my friend Deogratius. We call him Deo. Deo is a clinical officer in the Ligula hospital and is also on the Board of a local NGO which is trying to build awareness of HIV/AIDS and other actions, designed to strengthen local participation in community development. It was a superb demonstration of good governance development in action. Over fifty community leaders representing over a hundred thousand people from dozens of villages in Mtwara's outlying areas, were being trained in some of the procedures of good governance – consultation, community planning and accountability. I was welcomed as an observer and chatted to Mfaume who had taken the day off studies to represent his village. We spoke of the expectations his village has – school, water supply, clinic. Much of this is unachievable in the short-term, but the enthusiasm for change driven by local people was evident and was being harnessed by this new NGO, Sajaku, "Helping our communities help themselves".

The days, now, are often cooler, often greyer and usually involve at least one great downpour. This is a time for farming. All around this neighbourhood, stretches of what we thought were open, unused land are being fenced, dug and planted. In many cases, the rains have brought out the lush evidence of earlier planting; maize and rice seemingly sprouting and flourishing overnight. Two weeks ago I chatted with my neighbour William one morning, early, as he shuffled through the soil barefoot, dropping a couple of maize seeds every half a yard, kicking the soil nonchalantly to cover them as he passed. Today those maize seeds are already six inch green shoots. This land is so warm, now so moist, so fecund.

People have prayed for rain. Whether Lutheran, Catholic or Muslim, people speak naturally and openly of the need for God to answer their prayers. The Regional Commissioner has clashed with the Bishop over the business of kneeling as he receives Holy Communion. He may be an eccentric, but his very public display of religious observance is unremarkable here.

Today is a public holiday celebrating the birth of the Prophet Mohammed. The Catholic nursery and the Catholic training centre are both closed, as are all public buildings and public institutions. We're off to the market to buy cloth for suits, skirts and shirts and see the tailor. Birthday or no birthday, it's no holiday for those particular Muslims.

Sunday, 27 February 2011

Kiswahili and some creature comforts

We had a small taste this week, of just how dangerous a place this country can be. Typically, for wazungu, the dangers we face are relatively minor and more easily overcome with money. As we left the Msemo hotel late one night, we were advised not to walk. The dogs which accompany us on our bicycles each evening, apparently have been trained by the Massai to protect wazungu from ravaging dogs which collect in a pack down the road. We couldn't get hold of a bajaj and for a moment we felt stranded; but only for a moment, because as we hesitated, a large air-conditioned car pulled up and a kind man called Alan, with an African driver invited us to hop in and drove us to the door of our house.

Another dangerous aspect of life in Tanzania is travelling on public transport in the rainy season. VSO has taken the decision to fly volunteers between Dar and Mtwara at this time because the roads are liable to be flooded, and the buses unable to complete the journey in one day. So our journey up to Morrogorro was very comfortable – taxi- plane- taxi – to the spotlessly clean training centre where we are taking an extension course in Kiswahili. My neighbour, Mr William left for Morrogorro, coincidentally, on college business, the same morning, but he was travelling by bus. We live a cosseted life here, with three full meals a day, clean water in the showers, a beautiful landscape and warm friendly hospitality from the Mgolole nuns. We are also cosseted from the dangers of moving around the town, which has far more traffic than Mtwara and traffic which moves faster than in Dar.

As we sat in Elvis' bar the other night, we heard wailing and shouting from further up the road. Someone said there had been an accident and we stepped out to see if we could help. Hazel, our friend, a doctor, removed her shoes to run to the scene faster. I followed. In the thick black of a power cut and with people strewn across a busy road, amid children screaming and throwing themselves on the ground in shock, we found a young girl, motionless, lying on the roadside next to her mother; her mother, helpless and distraught. The child, a girl aged about nine, had suffered a major blow to her head and whether she made it through the night would be down to fortune rather than medical assistance. At the hospital, which fortunately was only a few hundred yards down the road, there were few facilities. The girl was seen by the staff on duty, but Hazel explained that, with few resources, there was little that could be done. We were not told, but Hazel's best guess was that the girl would not survive.

Apart from the awful tragedy for the young family – the girl was one of three young children seemingly walking with their mum, barefoot down a busy road at ten o'clock at night – it was the unremarkable nature of it all. Death, often violent and very often accidental and avoidable, is part and parcel of life here.

Our week of Kiswahili training is now over and we are staying overnight in the aptly named Econolodge in downtown Dar-es-Salaam. It's run by and popular with Asians and the lobby today is packed with cricket fans watching India play England in the World Cup. The rooms are sparse and clean. When I say clean, I mean there are no cobwebs, but that doesn't deter the cockroaches. The showers are functional, but the Tanzanian fundi, always willing to be generous with splashes of tile adhesive, grout and paint wherever it might fall, made no exceptions here.

When we arrived in October, I recall how Caroline, tired and tense after an overnight flight, slept squeamishly on the bed, making sure none of her body actually touched the hotel sheets. How things have changed! On the last time we arrived here, she threw down her bags, threw off her clothes, shouted "Yes!" and leapt into the shower.

We're off for chicken tikka and a few beers down the Badminton Club tonight, before setting off for Mtwara, bright and early tomorrow morning. It's been lovely to spend a few days in such comfort with friends, but I'm actually looking forward to my own bed and our routine. During our Kiswahili course we had to describe a day in our lives. I became a little homesick as I described mine - chapatti for breakfast, rice and beans for lunch, spending time with warm, appreciative people, bia baridi at the ocean and home for some telly.

Friday, 4 March 2011

Juju and babies and the men from the 'leccy'.

Last Sunday's papers carried the startling headline that over 60% of the population of Tanzania believes in juju, some form of traditional beliefs associated with witchcraft and superstition. The same survey revealed that whilst the overwhelming majority of the population is either Muslim or Christian, a significant proportion of both these groups of believers also believes in juju. Belt and braces you might say.

I might have considered this the stuff that Sunday papers are made of and left it at that had it not been for two separate conversations in the staff room over the past week or so. Luli, the physics teacher asked me,
"What is the word in English when someone throws themselves down on the floor trembling?"
"Epilepsy?" I offered.
"Does that mean being possessed by a devil?" she said......
Today, a young girl fainted in class and I had to carry her out to the headteacher's room and lay her on some cushions. I asked Dastan the Deputy Head what was the school procedure for this event.
"Just leave it to the other female pupils," he said. "There are so many cases nowadays – three just this morning."
"Well it is very close," I said.
"Many people believe it is the work of evil spirits and the baobab tree," he said

"And what do you say Dastan? Do you tell them that's nonsense?"
"Well it is strange that it only affects the girls."
"Have you asked if they are eating breakfast?"
"Yes. Of course," he laughed. "But still..."
Dastan is an energetic committed teacher, exactly the sort of person Tanzanian schools need. I see him at Mass most Sundays. He wears dapper suits and rides a trail bike which his wife has difficulty getting on. But still....

Neema, my colleague here in college is not someone who believes in juju. She is a young, caring and thoughtful woman, newly arrived from Arusha and newly married. She hopes to re-train at some point to become a social worker. When I first met her I asked her, in true Tanzanian style, when would she have children. She laughed and said
"Very soon, perhaps."
She was wearing a loose dress but I didn't risk it that time; but yesterday, I pressed the question and my hand on her belly and we laughed.
"It's due in August," she said.
She walks long distances to buy fresh milk, understands completely why so many women die through lack of good ante-natal care and access to a midwife at the time of delivery. She's ashamed of Tanzania's history of killing twins because they were thought to be evil. She'll go home to Arusha to a hospital and her mother.

I hope the medical services are better than the electricity company. I removed the cut-out switch from the meter the other day as it was faulty. I managed to mend it but called the fundi to see what should be done. The fundi looked genuinely scared as he told me to put it back. That is Tanesco's property and I could be fined. When Tanesco arrived they arrived in style – five men on the back of a lorry. All five of them looked at the offending part and started to dismantle it. I snatched it from them. They looked surprised.
"Have you got a replacement?" I said "Or are you going to repair it?"
"We take it away and bring you a new one."
"Not on your life," I said "Leave that where it is, bring a new one and then take the broken one away."
I stood firm, they hesitated, and then climbed back in their truck. Had they taken it I would be without power. That was three days ago and they haven't been back with the new part yet.

I'm talking to potential sponsors for an event to raise awareness of HIV/AIDS here in college. The bank manager was understanding, the Manager of the Port Authority would like to help and Vodacom's CSR person is getting back to me. They all agree that an event to target students with voluntary testing is a good idea. In class the other day, though, in a discussion with prospective teachers, came the question.
"Why does the West want to convince Africa to use condoms? Do we know for sure that it helps stop AIDS?"

The frightening thought occurred to me that there will be some in this new generation of schoolteachers who are as ill-informed and superstitious as the juju believers and murderers of twins.

Wednesday, 9 March 2011

Irony

As I sped through some of the poorest communities I've seen since arriving in Tanzania, on the pillion of a motor-cycle, whole families came to stand, stare and point; the children calling, with eyes agape, "Mzungu!"
I looked like some zealous claims adjuster clutching a battered briefcase, bouncing down dusty rutted tracks and dodging ruddy pools. We slid past families, where old men sat listlessly on a caked and cracked clay floor, children barefoot played with wire toys, women with babies wrapped on their backs and, sometimes, young men were cutting back whole fields of grass with wide steel blades. At the village – some thatched shops on the main road - most young men sat chatting and calling "habari" aimlessly; some were drunk, most without work or purpose. We were just east of Masasi, and whilst southern Tanzania is the poorest region in this country, here, sixty miles west of Mtwara, I could see evidence of some of the worst poverty yet.

We were visiting Mwena Secondary School, a collection of one storey classrooms without water or electricity, huddled round a neat, dusty quadrangle of flower beds and the Tanzanian flag, hanging limply from its pole, centre stage. I had come to assess four students on teaching practice and my first lesson was history- the scramble for Africa and the impact of colonialism. In this ramshackle classroom, with a pitted concrete floor and the government standard blackboard the only thing vaguely resembling a teaching resource, the deepest of ironies washed over me, as I sat at the back, awkwardly aware of these students' grasp of some of the reasons why I was the richest person they had ever seen.

I had assessed four students that morning and watched their faces crumple as I gave them honest but constructive feedback on the quality of their lessons.
"Can you say whether the students were learning?" I asked.
"Yes. They understood well."
"I'm not sure," I said gently.
"But you see, sir, it is their English. "And it's your English too that's the bigger problem," I thought, but, thank goodness, didn't say.

Tanzania has a lofty, but misplaced, goal of teaching across the secondary curriculum in English. It is the Government's view that the future prosperity of Tanzania is dependent on its people being able to speak the international language of business and tourism. There is a huge shortage of teachers, few of them can speak English well enough to teach in that language and when they arrive in secondary school they are faced with classes of sixty children who have studied English grammar at primary school, but have little, if any, functional English language.

That afternoon, after I had observed lessons on 'Sources of information for history' and 'writing a business transaction letter', I congratulated my students. The learners were reasonably engaged, many had understood the basic facts and in any case with a mzungu in the room, they could be forgiven for not listening as well as they should. What was disheartening was the brazen way in which most of the students had coached their classes prior to assessment. One boy conspiratorially whispered with the student teacher at the start of the lesson, as he looked nervously in my direction. They need not have been anxious. With no resources and a dry syllabus, it is easy to spot those trainees who have both the language skills and the presence to make effective teachers.

We're staying in Ndanda, more accurately the Benedictine Mission at Ndanda, a huge complex comprising the largest and best hospital in the region, workshops, printing press, a mineral water plant and much more. Guest houses for visitors are spotlessly clean, with heavy wooden furniture and plumbing that works. Breakfast, lunch and dinner - salami, eggs and wurst or schnitzel. We could be in Bavaria. The rooms have keys, showers, sockets and switches straight from Germany.

What they do have that is African is wildlife. A crocodile was found in the sewage system at the sister hospital twenty miles down the road; a monitor lizard patrols the lake especially dug by the Benedictines for swimming and last night, Caroline, screamed, ran into the bedroom and shut the door.
"That's it," she said. "You'll have to deal with it."
"What is it?" I asked.
"It's either a frog or a large hairy spider, about an inch high."
"How can you tell?"
"By the stripes," she said.
I was wondering how Caroline knew so much about hairy spiders. I found my slippers. I looked. A piece of sellophane from a plastic bottle drifted across the floor. For a moment it might conceivably have looked like a one inch hairy spider, but not for long.

Sunday, 13 March 2011

Bribery, the Benedictines and some big buttons.

We were squashed so tightly I was almost enjoying it. I had counted twenty-eight people standing in a bus with twenty-eight seats and we were stopping to squeeze more on. A young baby was tugging at my arm – the first white flesh he'd seen perhaps - and his mouth wide with astonishment left his mother's breast bare and vulnerable. His mother mouthed a toothless laugh. Few people spoke, few were animated, and when the bus stopped, the bus fell silent.

Two policemen, both in dazzling white suits and peaked hats, one carrying a smart cane, had waved us to stop and were making their inspection. One approached the driver and patrolled the bus, literally kicking the tyres; the other greeted the conductor at the rear of the bus, out of sight of most of the passengers. They didn't attempt to board the bus – now that would have been fun – and they didn't look at tax discs. They kicked the tyres, spoke to the driver and 'chatted' with the conductor. It happens every day, across Tanzania, on almost every main road, out of every town.

Before we become too self-righteous about this blot on Africa (and large parts of the rest of the world too) I wanted to share some thoughts about why the problem seems to be endemic in poorer countries. Tanzania pays its MPs lavishly, and is justly proud of its constitution and its robust democracy. The problem with democracies where eighty per cent of the population lives below subsistence level, is that the people tend not to be too worried about voting; more about who can help them get their next meal. When I asked Lucia why people didn't object to being stopped so regularly, especially when we all know the real reason, she just smiled, a little enigmatically, and said,
"Ah no. This is Tanzania."

A healthy village community can send its representative to meet other community leaders to plan for a new clinic or a replacement water pipe; but a policeman or a government official, who is paid little and has no connection to his masters who make decisions, is left isolated; alone, with only his capacity to wrest small payments from those even more vulnerable and isolated than himself. With bottom-up decision making, you get empowerment; with bottom-down decision making you get exclusion. This is really what politicians mean when they talk of a democratic deficit. Exclusion from the decision-making process takes the responsibility of citizenship away from individuals and we are left with lazy policemen kicking tyres and extracting bribes.

Not doing things the African way is what the Benedictines are good at. As they set about embedding themselves, about a hundred years ago, in a country riddled with malaria, they soon realised that too many priests were dying too quickly to live like Africans and they set about building a little Bavaria in this fertile land.

As we strode up the hill behind the Abbey, we could have been in southern Germany with the vegetation, the warm sun, but with cloudy skies, and perhaps most tellingly, the well-made road, carved through rock in places, boasting a paved water gulley on each side and with large heavy concrete slabs placed strategically at water crossings. It all shouted to us that this had been built by Europeans, intent on staying.

The road follows a steep sided valley, at the head of which the priests have dug a small lake. The lake, about thirty square metres, is lined with boulders, young trees and grassy banks. It was built as the header for a hydro-electric station, giving the whole Ndanda community a secure source of electricity, the only place in southern Tanzania that doesn't suffer power cuts. It's also a beautiful place for swimming, and as we know, few Africans can swim. It has steps to aid the swimmer and even has a small changing area with shower – not quite Baden-Baden, but almost.

Of considerable interest was our meeting with Jorg, a retired German surgeon who has been coming here as a volunteer for many years. He and his family first came here in the 1970s. They stayed for a number of years and had two more children here. I asked about the arrangements for delivering babies, as many of the European women we have spoken to have said that they would not have their babies here. Controversially, he snorted that if you are planning to live in Africa, then you should have your babies in Africa. We discussed the question of whether or not the supreme effectiveness of the Benedictines was in the long-term good for Tanzania or ultimately disabling. What Europe did to East Africa after the Berlin Conference and what the Benedictines have done here since would not appear to be comparable, and yet they are.

Of equal interest to us was our conversation with Francis, a Tanzanian water engineer, employed by a German company, working on improving water supplies across the region. He confidently predicts that, with the four new pumps he has commissioned, water supplies in Mtwara will be more stable by September of this year. Not the direct result of the Benedictines, but the German influence here all the same.

Back to Mtwara though, for some normality. You can be spoiled with fresh clean water, butter on the breakfast table and doors that close with a click. We were missing that homely feeling of geckos up the walls, surround sound cockerels and mucky brown water. We were, honestly, pleased to come home to friendly faces like Salamu and his pals, who come to the door at least twice a day, "Hodi?", and leave with, "Ahsante", and a toffee.

My first call was to Mohamed, the tailor. He was to have finished my suit and two new shirts. Before leaving for Ndanda, he had apologised for his tardiness. His father had died.
"You can only use that excuse once," I thought.
This time it was because he wanted to consult me on the size of buttons.
"Big ones," I smiled through gritted teeth. "And no sneaking off to the *msikiti*".

Friday, 18 March 2011

Lollies, dogs and the evil eye

We are very lucky to be living where we do, for we are surrounded by young people. Tanzania is a country full of young people, partly because people of my age tend to die. In church, young people from about four years old, sit silently for two hours. In school, the youngsters I teach are so well behaved, I often think they are just under-fed. They often seem listless. At home, on campus, children play, but have no toys, no games, no bicycles. My little friend, Salumu, was seen playing with a broken electric plug the other day and his friend Wengi, can be seen sometimes with a plastic lid from a bucket.

For less than a pound, we can buy a bag of lollipops, (fruity ones on a stick that double as a whistle). We wanted to have something to respond to the regular requests for something. We were conscious of what this looks like- white couple giving out sweets to African children- it doesn't get more patronising, but then we thought,
"No. They're children and they love lollies."

So every evening now, a steady stream of little ones comes to our door with a "Hodi," and all around campus you can hear breathy whistles from these plastic sticks. There is no particular age limit as to who calls for a lolly or who gets one. Two teen-age girls (we never see teen-age boys, so I don't know where they go!) often come to the door, sometimes to borrow a bicycle and other times for a toffee. But yesterday, when Tatu, the Deputy Principal's wife, came for her English tutorial, embarrassment left my skin crawling, as Caroline tried to give her a lolly. Tatu smiled graciously.

The kindergarten for those lucky children who get to go, is something of an oasis in what would otherwise be a desert of stimuli for children's development; however, even this Montessori nursery on Fridays succumbs to the African way. Children, no matter what age, are expected to do their duties – cleaning, sweeping, litter-picking. Children have to bring their own *fagia* (besom) to complete their duties.

Before the secondary school boys can play their football match this afternoon, they have to cut the grass which has grown rapidly in the recent rains. As I write this, a line of thirty boys, armed with scythes, are slashing their way down the length of the pitch. Teachers tell me that this is the African way. It teaches a sense of responsibility, a sense of duty of care for the environment. I'm not convinced. They get beaten if they don't do it.

I suspect campus can be a dangerous place; in fact, Mtwara after dark, is generally not a place to walk around. This is not for fear of muggers, although they do happen, but the greater risk of being attacked by the dogs that people keep to protect themselves from burglars. Lucia, the other morning at 5.30, crept out of her house where she's lived for fourteen years, and sneaked around to meet us and our taxi.

"Don't come here, please Adrian. The dogs will bite you."

They are kept inside during daylight hours, but are let out as a pack after about 11.00pm. As we lay awake last night at 3.00am, listening to two dogs howling at each other outside our bedroom, I wondered what would happen if I did have to venture out. I realised why the rats like living in houses – they risk being eaten by dogs if they venture outside.

A few days ago, I wrote about traditional beliefs and the fact that 60% of the population still believes in juju. Today, I read headlines describing how a Lutheran Pastor has discovered the cure for AIDS in the root of a 'special' tree. Neema, my colleague who is expecting a baby, spoke of her sadness that I did not believe the story about Pastor Masapila. She went on to claim that AIDS is spread partly because America and Europe have dumped faulty condoms on Africa. Reading about it on some wacky website is one thing, but when my colleague reports this as fact, then the true horror of the poverty which has bred superstition and ignorance hits home.

Of course, another reason for young people's good behaviour and deference towards *wazee* (older people) is that they fear being cursed by us should they cross us. If it's true, it's quite an awesome power. I thought Salumu and Wange were nice to us because we gave them lollies. Maybe not.

Tuesday, 22 March 2011

Gender mainstreaming

Gender mainstreaming was a term we learned in training before starting the placement. I think it means taking the question of gender – or rather, gender equality, from the backwaters of political correctness to an everyday role in one's work and professional relations. Simply, given that gender stereotyping tends to leave girls and women at a disadvantage, we should do all we can in our professional roles to undo this stereotyping, ensuring that girls, for example, receive as much attention as boys in class; or, choosing non-stereotypical roles for girls, in writing or speaking. In teaching the interrogative in English, one might use,

"Mary, park your HGV in the truckers' bay, will you."
 or, with the passive tense,
"Julie, those hods will need to be shifted before the girls can lay any bricks today."
That sort of thing, I think.

Tanzania needs some gender main-streaming. Tanzanian culture is one of fairly strict and strictly observed gender roles. And there is little deference paid by men to women. One could argue that this should be liberating for women. No more smiling demurely as doors are held open or seats offered. Women are expected to be at least as strong as men and it is normal for women to carry loads rather than men. In our induction training last October, we learned that 40% of Tanzanian men believe that it's right to beat your wife. That would have been alarming had we not also learned that 60% of women believe that wives should be beaten. There are some disappointed women out there.

It's complicated though, because, unlike in the UK, Tanzanian women never give up their names; professional women rarely give up work after having had children; command equal pay for the same work; and are reasonably well-represented, for instance, in Parliament. How much this translates into women's lives when it comes to the majority of poor, ill-educated Tanzanians, I am not sure. Boys are more likely to attend school; boys are more likely to stay on to Forms V and VI (A Levels) ; men are unlikely to undertake domestic duties at home; and so on, and so on.

It leaves us in something of a quandary sometimes, as to what to do for the best. Do I give up my seat on the daladala to a pregnant younger woman and risk derision or do I remain seated and accept the silent approbation of passengers unanimously respectful of age and wisdom? It is after all in these daily experiences, rather than in lofty policy pronouncements that we can truly change things.

This week, whilst walking in the hills near the Makonde plateau, we came across a small stream in which a group of people were washing clothes and collecting water. It wasn't wide and it wasn't deep, but Caroline is nervous and timid when it comes to taking a stride across water. I waited. She hesitated. I encouraged. She told me to help. I looked around and saw the enquiring faces. What should I do? Help her? Walk away? Shout at her to hurry? Risk being mocked by the onlookers?
"Just put your damn foot on that stone and step across," I said. "And don't be so ridiculous."
"Don't you shout at me." Caroline replied, in very un-Tanzanian fashion. Eventually, using my hand to guide her, she stepped gingerly over the one firm rock in the middle of the small stream and, with my help, crossed. Already the group of onlookers were talking; one woman laughed. As we said good-bye to them and strode up the hill, we heard them guffaw. My kiswahili is not so good, but I could swear I could hear them talking about us. What might they have been saying?
"You see Musa. The mzungu cares for his wife. That is the future for Tanzania."
I think not. More likely it was a pronouncement on my machismo which translates roughly as,
"No-balls Babu."

Saturday, 26 March 2011

The white man's burden

We've had clean water in our taps for over twenty-four hours now. Caroline has washed everything in sight. If that wasn't luxury enough, we are off to the market this morning to look at toilet seats. Without going into too much detail, we have needed a toilet seat for some weeks now, and, even after painstakingly learning what I thought would be the Kiswahili for it, I couldn't trace one in Mtwara anywhere, until, that is, the other day, when I found a small shop behind the market.

"N'omba kiti ya choo," I guessed.

The woman in the shop looked bemused, then a look of comprehension washed over the shopkeeper's face,

"Cover for toileti?"

"Exactly," I sighed with relief.

"We have three," he boasted. "One at 5000, a medium grade at 10,000 and a heavy duty one from England at 35,000."

"Can we look at them? I don't want to rush into this."

"Come back on Saturday," he beamed.

I can't wait. It is one sign of the luxury we expect in our lives, that not only do we have a flush toilet –that alone places us in the top twenty per cent of high-livers in Tanzania - but we have a choice of toilet seats.

An old man sat at a table near us the other day as we ate our rice, beef and beans for lunch. He looked sixty, but was perhaps only forty with one leg so withered that he could only move it by lifting the boney stick with his hand. He walked with the help of an old wooden pole, in broken flip flops and torn and stained shorts. His shirt flapped open, showing a sunken greying chest and his toothless mouth gaped. He mouthed pleading to women asking for the scraps from their trays.

With what I reflect now to be supreme mzungu arrogant patronage, I was able to say a couple of words, make a couple of gestures, agree to part with the equivalent of 40p and had a tray of substantial wholesome food served to him by one of the catering staff– enough to sustain him for the whole day and more. The woman who served him thanked me with a warm smile as he fed himself hungrily.

Every day, every time we go out, every time we meet an African, we are reminded of just how much more money we have than ordinary Tanzanians. Having disposable income fifty times that of my colleagues brings challenges which I wouldn't have to deal with in Europe. At least a couple of times a week, someone, usually a teen-ager, will say "Mambo" and then ask for money. It's disconcerting because it's done so casually and so often. Perhaps we would feel better if a destitute beggar were asking for food, rather than happy, healthy youngsters just chancing their arm. We have to remind ourselves each time it happens, that even these happy, healthy youngsters have so little and in their eyes, we have so much.

A parcel from my sister arrived the other day, a Christmas present that had done a tour of colleges across the region before it landed at my door – a testament, actually, to the Tanzanian postal service. I was excited, two books, wrapped in expensive Christmas paper. Instinctively and naively, I turned to Neema and laughed,
"Better late than never,"
She didn't smile. She didn't ask to see. Like a brick it hit me. I was showing off. Neema, as worldly, relatively, as she is, has no conception of just how rich we Europeans are. When a small gift, a bottle of soda or a plate of chipsy mayai represent luxury, I can't always pitch just how we are perceived – colleagues, neighbours, but, above all, wazungu.

Living as we do we sometimes we feel caught between the true mzungu life of four-wheel drives, safaris, air-conditioning and housegirls, on the one hand; and, on the other hand, counting every shilling, never travelling for pleasure, sodas as a treat, often being hungry, the African way. We will always be wazungu because we will never be poor. It affects every relationship we have with every African we meet. I don't look for sympathy but that's a white man's burden.

Well this white man will shortly be able to unburden himself thanks to a luxury, heavy-duty toilet seat, imported from England for just this occasion. Decadent or what!

Tuesday, 5 April 2011

Some old friends, some new friends and some keki

I feel it's time to tell you some more about the people we've met since we've been here. The peculiarities of daily routine are more or less accepted now and not so peculiar, but the idiosyncrasies of the individuals we rub along with, are what make life so interesting.

There's Philbert, the former schools inspector. Philbert and I meet about once a week over a couple of beers outside Upendo, on a dusty piece of ground outside the old steel container. He and I are discussing the idea for my next project, which is to deliver language training to secondary school teachers and to this end he has already met the District Education Officer. Money is tight but there is much enthusiasm for the idea and Philibert and I are hoping that he will be involved in directing and administering this small project should it get off the ground. Philibert lives modestly, round the corner from Upendo – but seems to know everyone and everyone I meet seems to know him. We spoke this week of the relationship between tribes in Tanzania, something which had been a focus of Nyerere's life and work in building this new country. Philibert explained that the tension and humour between tribes is very much present in human relations, but is managed through an acknowledged humour, or *watanne.*

Philibert explained that there is no direct translation of this word, but it describes the ability for the Makonde, the Matumbe and Machinga tribes, for example, to mock, laugh and patronise each other, but never fight.

Then there's Deo, a young firebrand who, when he's not singing and shimmying in the choir on Sunday morning, is a clinical officer at the district hospital and a director of a small NGO supporting AIDS sufferers. He is a very, very busy man, who has recently announced his intention to stand for Parliament. He and I have done the rounds of large local employers recently, asking for sponsorship. As we made our way to the Port Master's office, I asked should we not make an appointment.
"Ah no. That is not the African way. If he is in his office he will see us."
I doubted the effectiveness of this approach but in the event, as Deo had predicted, he met us and after one or two further short meetings agreed to sponsor our event.

We have new wazungo friends also. A young American couple, Christians from Arkansas, with a Landcruiser and a huge barbecue. Have you pictured them? Got it? You'd be wrong. They're lovely. A gentle couple with a sweet one-year old, they are here for at least ten years, supported by their church and have no arrogance as to what they might achieve, but instead seem to accept humbly whatever life seems to present.

Young Kelvin continues to study hard. He comes round for the odd lesson, some help with a letter-writing competition, but really he enjoys playing with every gadget we possess – camera, binoculars, laptop, solar charger - but is ever respectful of our time and space. He lives with his auntie, his mother being in Tanga with Kelvin's half-sisters. There is some tension here from time to time from which I'm eager to steer clear, but occasionally the role of the wazungu who take an interest in Kelvin's life, is obviously discussed between Kelvin's mum and her sister.

Then there's Paschal, the young man who was first my Kiswahili tutor, but whose taciturn manner and inability to speak slowly meant that I learned little. It didn't help, either, that I would never learn my vocabulary. We've dropped the idea of my learning Kiswahili now and instead we go together to watch football and spend time together. This week-end was his graduation party.

I've not quite understood it fully, but I think that, because there is such a lapse of time between the exams and the certificate, by which time all the students have scattered to the four corners of Tanzania, the end of term party is held before the examinations. One of the tutors had donated a goat, I had helped with printed invitations and the students had stayed up late washing the floors of the classroom to prepare for the most stunning dressing one could imagine for a dusty room with concrete floor and grubby windows.

The class of 2010-11 had clearly been working hard for most of the night. The room was dressed in burgundy and white, the pitted chalkboard covered, as were the splintered doors. The tables clothed and the staircase finished with burgundy and white silk bows. Paschal had been involved in much of the organisation of the event and when we arrived, we were shown to our seats, served our goat and rice and listened and laughed as the MC called people out for special praise. Everyone danced at every opportunity. No-one went to the microphone unless he or she was moving to the African rhythm. Some of the girls had had identical dresses made for the event, and dotted around campus were elegant young women in gold evening gowns and pink satin dresses. It could have been a tribute event for Diana Ross and the Supremes.

The highlight of the afternoon was the cutting and distributing of the *keki*, a brown sponge affair cut into minute squares. The purpose of the cake was to create mild embarrassment by calling people out by name and watching them feed cake directly into the mouth of another, a form of harmless courtship ritual, which was fun because those involved showed such authentic coyness. Mama Caroline and Mr Adrian were duly called to the front to feed each other cake from a cocktail stick "in a British way". We tried to appear suitably solemn and boring and failed. Much mirth ensued.

Friday, 8 April 2011

April showers

It started raining earlier this week and apart from the odd hour or two it has rained continuously since. Last night we lay awake for hours, listening in wonder to perhaps the most violent storm in months, the bed trembling, as thunder cracked above our heads, rain so heavy on our tin roof that we needed to shout at each other to be heard. Every road around the campus has been transformed into a ruddy river and anything other than a four wheel drive struggles to make progress. I came home from teaching the other day, having made the mistake of taking Mr Mkunga's forbidden shortcut and found myself ankle deep in thick cloying mud. People build houses with it and in the absence of cement, it makes a very durable and adhesive alternative. Try getting it out from your mudguards and chain! I traipsed into college in plastic 'crocs' and a poncho, dragging my bike with wheels which refused to turn. I was greeted with looks of bewilderment and many, many, "Pole sana".

It's annoying for us. It slows things down. It makes our sundowners less mystical. And we stay indoors reading more. But that's it. We don't have to work outdoors, we don't cook our meals over a charcoal jiko outside a hut made of sticks and clay; our fruit stall is not awash with thick reddish sludge.

On many street corners you'll find a group of men, fundis and labourers, working round a roughly made bench, using hand saws and chisels, no machinery in sight. Carpenters are numerous here, for wooden furniture abounds. I say furniture, but I really mean four household items – windows, doors, beds and coffins. Windows are wooden frames with steel bars inserted as protection against burglars, doors are plain and functional but rarely fitted well; beds are stylish, but there is generally only one style; whilst coffins are numerous and diverse in quantity and style. Wood is expensive, whilst labour is cheap; but, as a result, poor tools and untrained fundi work long hours to produce poor quality. In many of the properties I have visited, private as well as public, the quality of finish is very poor. Only the Sisters and the Fathers seem to have cracked that part of Tanzanian life and at the convent and the monastery, there is not an ill-fitted door or window to be found.

A good many students from college were taken to hospital last week after the strangest and most unusual of incidents. A football match between another College and the Saint Augustine University was played last Sunday afternoon. Crowds thronged around the touchline and the atmosphere was noisy with chanting and drumming most of the afternoon. As we walked past, however, we faced throngs of people running scared away from the pitch. Fighting had broken out between rival fans and the police were called. People were taken to hospital, not suffering from cuts or breaks, but from shock. They were scared at the sight of the violence and went to hospital for treatment. I hear frightful stories of the conditions at that hospital and yet people seek medical quite readily. I wonder sometimes if this is borne out of ignorance rather than wisdom.

Fighting on campus, bad weather nor the imminent examinations will deter Maskat, Deputy Principal, from imposing his will on the student and teaching body. You will remember that Maskat is the small, rotund chap who has an opinion on every aspect of college life. People don't fear him, but they do as he says. For the past week, since Maskat's return from Newala, where he had been sorting out a family matter, students have hardly attended class, but instead have been seen morning and afternoon, slashing, scraping, digging, sweeping and cleaning. When I asked him why students had been deployed with such vigour, he said,
"Yes, Mr Adrian. I had been away for only one week and tutors gave a bad report on the state of the college environment."
Every blade of grass has been cut, every weed plucked and piece of litter picked. Much of it is piled in our waste pit.

As we made our way down those muddy lanes the other night, I realised that there is a comfort to be had from riding confidently, picking one's way round the deep puddles, the muddy gorges and the slimy ravines. Caroline lacks some of that confidence and, as her bicycle slid from beneath her, she fell off. She was wet through and dirty. She later showed me the huge bruise on her leg, but stoically had waited until she had cycled all the way home before getting in the shower and crying like a baby.

A day at the beach and a night at the movies
The bus lurched perilously over a deep ruddy gorge at the side of the road and the driver dropped to first, as the engine chugged the last few yards to the top of the hill. The bus had fallen strangely quiet as we all concentrated. I've no idea what we would have done had the engine stalled. It was an old Chinese coaster and was held together in parts with bits of twisted wire. A young man, who looked about fourteen, was introduced to me as the electrician. I commented that I could think of many things we might need that day, but a young lad without a spanner was not one of them. He proved to be an excellent fisherman though, so that was OK.

We were forty-eight people squashed into a twenty-eight seater bus, out for a day at the seaside. Our optimism knew no bounds. We sang, we laughed and we shouted at young children as we passed. No matter if the bus couldn't make it; our energy, enthusiasm and happiness would give it the last heave it needed. Earlier that morning, we had collected two hundred samosas, doughnuts and *bagia*; one lovely lady from the kitchen had come in early to cook fourteen kilos of rice and three cabbages over her fire. It was all packed into deep plastic buckets.

At the beach, we found shady trees, we found weathered old tables for serving food and perhaps the most perfect sea and sand for swimming I have ever seen. I even found a young woman to serve me cold beer, which she retrieved from a rusty container. In planning the day, I had been asked if students were required to wear uniform. I had baulked at that, but had tried to sound supportive. In the event, ignoring my fashion tips for the modestly inclined, women and men took the plunge regardless. Most could not swim, no-one had used a snorkel before, but with much splashing and teasing, I gave lessons in breast stroke and how not to swallow too much water.

The young tool-less electrician was dispatched with a piece of string to the shore as soon as we got there and almost instantly returned with a large squid. For the return journey, the fish was tied to the wing mirror, and jiggled its way home on a length of string. Everyone else slept, squashed up against a shoulder, a seat or a bucket. We had sand in our hair and between our toes; our fingers were sticky with sea salt and oranges; but as we turned into the college drive, the bus came alive with singing and chanting – a celebratory call, marking a great day out.

We were up before the church bells on Sunday, which should have given us a clue, but in the event we were an hour early. Seven o'clock Mass was at eight o'clock and, being Palm Sunday, started with a winding procession, a congregation of over a thousand and a packed church with standing room only for a three hour service. I had half a kneeler and Caroline was offered a seat by a young man, who knelt by her side on the floor for the entire Mass.

The whole parish was there. Huge palms were blessed then waved aloft and five choirs sang luscious harmonies without organ or leader, as we snaked our way under the fierce sun. Even the Regional Commissioner was offered little deference, taking a pew at the back of church, as children squatted at the altar rails. The reading of the Passion was unrehearsed. The readers struggled with their words and twelve pages of Kiswahili in a hot church on half a seat, seems a very long time indeed. The ritual of kneeling, of singing, of blessing and chanting has a narcotic effect as the hours drip by. I thought about many things. I thought about Africa and why this Catholic magic is so potent and I thought about Europe and cynicism and money and materialism. I thought about miracles and my bad back.

When Pascal reminded me that we were to screen Mel Gibson's, 'The Passion' that night, I asked him, seriously, did he not think that we'd had our fill. He feigned not to understand, but deep down was a little wounded at my irreverence. Caroline had bought him a DVD of the blockbuster movie, which, on the cover, claimed to be dubbed into Kiswahili. This was Palm Sunday, but it felt like Christmas. Students trooped into the hot classroom. I was a little resentful of Caroline's and Paschal's success in attracting such crowds. Sixty or seventy was the most I'd attracted with James Bond or Ocean's Twelve. We had to find extra chairs to squeeze over a hundred and twenty into the room.
"You see, Mr Adrian," said Paschal, rather smugly, "We said it would be popular."

As we started the film I had to explain that, whilst the cover had said Kiswahili, in fact, the cheap Chinese copy was dubbed into Hebrew with English subtitles. Their fervour was not to be dampened. One wide-eyed religious movie fan at the front said,
"Let's see it anyway, Mr Adrian. We know the story."

Tuesday, 26 April 2011

Easter - "Kristo amefufuka"

It took almost an hour for the one thousand people to queue in two orderly lines to kneel in veneration at the crucifix; a crucifix featuring a life-size African Christ sculptured from teak on an ebony cross. We had been warned that the veneration of the Cross was so popular that people had been known to go up twice. No fear of that this time, as a burly man at the altar rails made sure no-one tarried; a genuflexion, a sign of the cross and "thank you very much", that was your lot.

For the Vigil, the ebony cross had been replaced by a Makonde-carved stand for the Pascal candle and once the lights came on, the choir came to life with infectious singing and ululations. Handel's Hallelulah Chorus with a Kiswahili text was the finale after communion after which the congregation burst into spontaneous applause and ululation. The Brothers led a celebratory dance outside with a brass band. All day long people have passed us with "Pasaka njema", rarely have I witnessed such fervour.

There are two images which will stay with me as memories of my time in church here. The first one is of children, perhaps about seventy of them altogether, all under nine years of age, crammed cross-legged on a raffia mat at the front of church. They sat silently for each and every service during Holy Week, only stirring to genuflect piously when told to do so by one nun or other. The other is from the Cathedral earlier this week; when the choir of children in Papal gold and white, shimmying round the church, led by young boys with spears, the centre-piece of the procession, being a woman, dancing slowly but rhythmically, down the aisle; on her head a wide bowl, in the bowl a young boy, holding aloft a huge Bible.

Ndanda this week-end has felt like a strange wazungo enclave, with European volunteers gathering there for the warmth of solid German hospitality. Twenty of us went for a curry yesterday lunch-time, at a scruffy guest house run by an Indian family. We wandered down the road amid families squatting on the roadside waiting for loved ones in hospital. The chasm between African and mzungo is gaping here; unavoidable as its starkness slaps you in the face every time a man or woman approaches and in the most matter-of-fact, yet desperate way, asks for money for food. With us were Dutch, Swiss and German families, each with young children. With child seats, big cars and all the same conversations about routines, afternoon naps and colouring books that young couples across Europe have about their children, it seems somehow strangely incongruous here.

One sad event earlier this morning, was the young woman who silently followed us up the hill as we climbed towards the lake for a swim. I asked her would she walk with us, but she wouldn't talk. Caroline had been correct in her first wild guess, that she wanted to walk with us for safety, someone having been mugged on this road only a few days earlier.

In the short-term the memories of our time this time in Tanzania will be dominated by creepy-crawlies and the various species of animals that we've experienced up-close and personal for the first time. This week-end, we've been bitten and eaten by unseen insects in our bed. We've searched, swept, cleaned and sprayed but each morning woken with itchy red weals on our bodies. Not a mosquito in sight, but whether they're ants, fleas or midgies, they're very small, very quiet and very hungry.

It's hardly worth mentioning the small rather aggressive herd of cattle that squeezed down the path with us and the small goats butting each other were an entertaining distraction. As we waited for our sodas yesterday, we had to raise our voices to be heard over the sounds of the hen being killed; and the screams and screeches from next door last night made us hope that whatever animal was being attacked, its end would come quickly. Swimming this morning, I had to keep one eye out for the lizard, which although small and rather sweet from a distance, allegedly has been known to bite. On the way home, another lizard, which at first because of its size, we mistook for a crocodile, crossed our path. Caroline did not wait to check what sort of lizard; the frogs, giant spiders and centipedes had been distraction enough.

Wednesday, 27 April 2011

Union Day

We saw a glimpse, today, of what a new, young successful Tanzania might be like. I don't know if aid organisations 'envision' the future for Tanzania, but I wonder if that picture includes a huge restaurant, the height of a cathedral, crammed with chrome furniture, bars made from fishing dhows and a menu of burgers and pizzas. The chef was helpful, if slightly patronising, of the two *wazee,* consoling us with word that Wednesday will be Swahili night (and lunch, he added helpfully). This is the new Makonde beach bar, a new venture by a successful African businessman, the owner of the local commercial radio station, Safari Radio. Its target market is not people like me; it's clearly targeting a younger market with disposable income. It will have live music and although, as its name suggests, it borders the beach, in reality, it turns its back on the sea and looks to town, and its large vehicles, with loud music and loud fashion statements. I mention all this because I wonder if these are the early signs of preparation for the next phase of Mtwara's development. Gas and oil are about to be exploited off-shore and I am told the character of the town will soon change with the arrival of many more foreigners.
I worry that I have a vested interest in the old Tanzania, the Tanzania without brash bars but with plenty of poverty. Perhaps I don't much like the look of economic success here because it challenges my quaint view of this particular world. Certainly, the best two places to eat are inefficient and too expensive for most Africans. Both hotels are run at a loss by philanthropic Europeans, but of course the main beneficiaries of this philanthropy, apart from the one or two Africans who get work, are the indulgent wazungu who bask in the lazy indolence of sundowners on the terrace.

Today is Union Day, a public holiday celebrating the union of Tanganyika with Zanzibar. Zanzibar is a unique mix of African and Arabian cultures, played out on a tapestry of neo-colonial indulgences revived for a modern western tourist. The Swahili coast is where those Arab influences, blown in on trade winds, meet African bantu culture. The remnants of the slave market in Mikindani still display the intricate carvings on doorways, typical of Arab settlers. Arab traders became settlers because the trade winds were so seasonal, changing direction twice a year, bringing traders each way in a nautical, annual cycle. Much of the bantu culture is influenced by west Africa as migration of slaves and slave traders brought people eastwards. So today we are resting to mark the union of Zanzibar, once made great on the back of slavery, with Tanganyika, once a German colony, then a British protectorate and a collection of dozens of separate tribes, unified and made strong under the leadership of Mwalimu Nyerere.

We didn't stay at the beach bar; we cycled on to Msemo for our own quiet, boring sundowners. As we sat in our usual place on the terrace, not needing to order as the staff know what we drink, Caroline was greeted with a smile and, "Good afternoon, mwalimu", as a little boy half hopped, half skipped towards her in gleeful embarrassment.

It was Valentino, of the gyrating hips and the suggestive shimmy, one of Caroline's fans from kindergarten, out on this holiday Monday, celebrating his younger sister's birthday. The family was pleased to meet Caroline and Valentino look suitably pleased with himself in his dark suit and oversize shoes.

Once again, public buildings are closed but small traders carry on as usual. There's certainly no holiday for our baisikeli fundi, but then there's not much work either. I waited patiently as he mended and re-mended his ancient broken bicycle pump. I wanted two-pence worth of air and he was struggling. I asked how much is a new pump. Five thousand shillings apparently (£2.00). Caroline thinks we should invest in new equipment for him and have free puncture repairs for life. She might be on to something.

Monday, 2 May 2011

Weddings

There were twenty-one of us squashed into perhaps the most dangerous daladala I've been in yet. The gears crunched and even the horn- usually the most effective device on these old vehicles – sounded in its death throes. Francis was next to me and taking calls constantly, sorting out problems for a wedding reception to be held in college that evening. There are many such events and students are deployed as free labour to clean and arrange. The noise keeps us awake at night and then the students have to tidy up the next day. Francis was fascinated by the guest list for the Royal Wedding, wanting to know why Catholics weren't invited. "There are many reasons why Tony Blair was not invited, Francis" I said. "But being Catholic wasn't one of them."

We were visiting Mikindani, the old slave port, a short drive up the coast. For many of the students, as they approach their final exams, this was their first visit to this historical site. Why? Because no student is allowed off campus without permission and no tutor had organised such a trip. This is not because it's Tanzania. Philbert has told me of the many and various trips his school organises. And it's not about money, as the return fare to Mikindani is little more than a bottle of soda. When I told Maskat about the trip, he said
"Ah. I wish I were a student again."
"Well you had your chance, Maskat," I replied. I felt angry.

I've been busy with meetings with the municipality over the past week or so, pitching a proposal for English language lessons for secondary school teachers, which, if the District Education Officer agrees to support it, will see the majority of Mtwara's two hundred secondary school teachers attend an intensive English conversation class over the next two years, improve their spoken English, theoretically improve their confidence in teaching their lessons in English and improve learning across the curriculum.

The idea is mine, but arranging the support of the municipality is entirely down to Philbert. We chugged up the hill last week, in Philbert's ancient and tiny Suzuki, to an eight o'clock meeting with the Municipal Academic Officer. Everywhere he goes, Philbert is greeted with "Shikamoo" from former colleagues, most of whom he seems to have taught. Certainly, the top man, the Municipal Director, is one of Philbert's students and he chuckles to himself as he tells me. He didn't say why and I was left wondering what memories Philbert had of his earlier teaching career.

We chat a lot about teaching and the differences between his school – a fee paying school, with the best results in the district - and mine, a normal state school serving a reasonably well-off suburb. I was complaining that schools couldn't seem to supply desks and that there always seem to be one or two boys at the back of class sharing a desk. I invariably separate them and make the offenders sit close to the front. Philbert sighed, and said
"Ah no, Adrian. Have you noticed students' names written on the desks?"
"Yes. I assumed this was graffiti."
"No. That is the desk paid for by that student's parents when he or she started school. The students sharing a desk have not bought their desk and will only get one if a school desk becomes free."
So I had been singling out those students, whose parents could not buy a desk, for chastisement and humiliation. Wonderful! Why had I not been told? I have questioned myself often over the past few days about what I might have done, what questions I might have asked and how much more could I have learned if I only spoke more Kiswahili.

When I first informed Maskat, the Deputy Principal, of our decision to leave, his face fell. He and I seem to have built a good mutual understanding. I certainly have great respect for him as he cares genuinely about the welfare of the students and, although his methods are unnecessarily strict, I never doubt the integrity of his motives. So when I told him we were leaving but would return in January to teach secondary school teachers, he showed me the resource centre, a purpose built classroom and office located at the rear of the campus. It has ceiling fans and the office has air conditioning, but it is filled with bin liners full of exam papers and has literally been gathering dust for over five years. I have written to all concerned suggesting I re-open it and start my teaching there. Maskat read the letter slowly and deliberately; no skimming or scanning, but reading and digesting every word. After a whole eight minutes, he looked up with a serious face, as though he had eaten a large meal, then smiled and said,
"The letter is delicious."

Tonight is film night again. I've been trying to broaden their horizons, with offers of films other than James Bond, but to no avail. Arnold Swarzenegger, Rambo and Bruce Lee remain firm favourites. Until today that is. I am living in the poorest district of one of the poorest countries in the world and what did Caroline and a hundred or so Tanzanian students spend Friday afternoon doing? Watching the Royal Wedding! Having initially been pleased to escape this wasteful nonsense back home, I was shocked and hugely disappointed to see how popular it is here.

"Mr Adrian. If you can show the highlights of the Royal Wedding," said Maso. "That will be better than James Bond."
I give up.

Monday, 9 May 2011

Geckos, Graduation and a good fundi

"Yes I know you live here too and I'm not jumpy, but if you come out of a room where I wasn't expecting you, it makes me scream."
Caroline has not, it has to be said, ever come to terms with the wildlife that she fears she's sharing her house with. I've told her she needs to tackle not just the creepy crawlies but the fear of creepy crawlies. There are perhaps three or four geckos in the house at any one time, but still Caroline screams. As we prepare to leave we need to decide whether, when we return in January, we will return to this house or find another. The frog, sadly, is not persuading Caroline of this particular location. He's black with red stripes and seems to wait until she's in the shower to pop his head up. I rarely get to see him.

We are preparing to leave and suddenly the things we will miss about the place are becoming apparent. High on the list are the students. Our recent visits to Msimbati and Mikindani, followed by the splendid graduation ceremony have shown us what a remarkably resilient, generous and good-spirited group of people they are. They danced all night on Wednesday and the next morning at 7.00am were there again at roll call, in spotless uniforms, preparing for revision as exams start tomorrow.

Graduation saw the whole campus come to life. It was as though the place had been sleeping and waiting for this day. Bunting was strung from the main teaching block, whitewash was used on the rough stones round the flower beds and every hedge in sight was trimmed to within an inch of its life. In the evening, staff moved to the library for their feast. Lucia had confided me earlier that she was hoping to sell the college one of her goats, but in the event Francis, sourced the goat from the market. Chips, rice, pilau rice, banana, goat, pumpkin, chicken and water melon – all on the same plate. The party went on until very late and Avit was at his most patronising when he told me the next morning how well I danced. One important lesson I learned from the day was not to judge too quickly, especially when I speak so little Kiswahili. The warmth and respect offered to tutors from students surprised me. There was no doubting the huge esteem in which Maskat is held. When his name was read out during the ceremony the cheer from the entire student body raised the roof.

Our comfortable lives have been upset considerably with the news that workers at the Southern Cross have come out on strike. It's unclear just what the root cause of the strike is, but suspicion of theft, a harsher attitude from management and some unreasonable behaviour on both sides, has resulted in an unofficial strike and the complete workforce being suspended. Asking for details of the action from the new Swedish training manager, revealed a determination to change things which suggest that hotel management is not as community focused as the hotel's entry in Lonely Planet suggests. This is a hotel which a tiny fraction of Mtwara's residents and visitors can afford, which claims to be run in the interests of community development and yet its workforce feel exploited and it is the wazungu customers who benefit most from this beautiful terrace on the Indian Ocean. The quality of service is perhaps the most truculent we've found in Mtwara, but whether that is the fault of management or staff, we are not sure.

We will be returning in January to start another two-year placement and we have decided to return to this house rather than rent another. Given the traumas we've gone through with noise and rodents, that might seem surprising, but in recent weeks, the sense of belonging here has started to permeate and to rent a smart house in Shangani would just place us alongside other wazungu and not earn any respect from colleagues here. Besides, for the money we'd spend in rent, we can invest in improvements to this house; in tiles for the kitchen and bathroom and a cooker and fridge. We're even going to build a small patio outside so we can enjoy the evenings more. We'll need to find a good fundi because most of the bathrooms I've seen are coated in thick clumps of grout and plumbing that isn't connected too well, but I have Mr Mkonga on the case and we are to meet one or two craftsmen next week.

We've started a list of the small items we will want to bring with us next time – things that add significantly to the quality of life, weigh and cost relatively little but are hard to obtain here. We will not need to bring clothes or cooking utensils, but we will bring witch-hazel, calendula and picture hooks. We won't need walking boots or paper or bedding; but we will bring Johnsons baby powder, good razors and IKEA light shades. Lastly, I will try very hard to remember a cover for the drain to keep froggy in his own place.

Saturday, 14 May 2011

Bad dreams, basketball and some bold children

The Larium had worked its wonders again, as I was woken abruptly from a strange, rather disturbing dream, featuring an unlikely collection of people from over the years, to the irregular thuds of the unduly zealous basketball player. I silently plotted some appropriate revenge for when I return. I opened my eyes to find a small, double headed centipede making its way painstakingly up the mosquito net. You might recall that there are frequent disputes as to whether this or a smaller cousin is the poisonous type. It certainly seemed to have heads at both its head and its bottom, so I urged Caroline not to use her fingers when removing it, just in case. It was her turn to go for breakfast, so there seemed no point in my getting up just yet and it is a measure of some progress, that, although she screamed and went to find rubber gloves, she did carefully remove it and placed it gently in the garden.

A second, strong memory from our time in Mtwara is the daily negotiation for breakfast with the kitchen ladies. We never know whether there will be chappati, mandazi, sambusa or bagia; we never know whether they will have *chengi,* but we do know that we will have to struggle with our basic Kiswahili with the morning greetings and suffer their laughs at all our basic mistakes. One regret that I have is my woefully poor ability in Kiswahili. For a variety of reasons –some would say excuses – we can still manage little more than basic introductions and greetings and simple shopping transactions.

Children will feature prominently as we reflect on our time here. Winston Wengi and, Salu; Witness and Joycie and Stella; none of them quite knows what to make of us. Salu has learned not to shout *mzungu,* but *mwalimu* as he asks for sweets, pens, oranges, anything....Joycie has not yet learned not to open our door and walk straight in without waiting to be asked. We don't have sweets or oranges for them, but they always knock and ask politely if they can take our empty plastic water bottles away. They play with them for hours. Where ever we cycle around Shangani we are greeted with "Mambo", "Good afternoon", "Good morning Mr Strain", "How are you Mama?" Ironically, it will be a relief in some ways to be back at home where people don't know us, or greet us every time they see us.

Whether people know us or not, at times they can be disconcertingly direct. Last week in church, the woman kneeling behind Caroline, slowly and deliberately plucked all the loose hairs from Caroline's back, rolled them neatly into a tight ball and passed it reverently forward. Caroline thought it rude to do anything other than carefully place it for storage in her basket. A young man, a teacher I know slightly, stopped me in the street and as we chatted and he learned that I was returning to the UK, said,

"So will you leave me your laptop?"

This last alarming question throws up the lasting pervasive memory of this first stay in this poor country. And that is of poverty. Poverty pervades every street corner and nearly every conversation; but poverty in the teeth of development aid. We have the impression that Tanzanians have become inured to development aid. There is just so much of it. 'Wazungu' means money. It can be debilitating. It offends my sensibilities, but, far worse, it corrupts Tanzanians' view of the outside world.

When we return in January, we will be much busier and hopefully, much more productive. Philbert has still much work to do in persuading Mama Mohamedi, the District Education Officer, to encourage the release of teachers. Mama Eliwaja is quietly confident that teachers will attend and the Centre will be ready; but as the dirty boxes of exam papers, which Maskat promised would be removed, are still in place; and the key to the Centre sits stubbornly in his desk drawer, I do not yet share that confidence.

When we return we plan to take a much fuller role within College, undertaking the same pastoral duties as other colleagues. We plan to expand and extend our excursions to local places of interest and try and understand better the thoughts and aspirations of this very religiously-minded body of students. The role of the tutor involves, amongst many other things, supervising early morning cleaning duties. The slashing and sweeping can be heard each morning from before 7.00am. That early morning basketball player is going to get to practice more cleaning and cutting, and less bouncing of that damned ball.

Tuesday, 17 May 2011

Leaving home and homecoming

The anticipation is almost painful. For the past few weeks, we've been fantasising about cool nights, tiled bathrooms and familiar faces. As the day approaches and we begin to pack, the excitement is palpable. We asked friends what they miss most about home and a common theme amongst the "things most missed", is people rather than familiar items. The thought of being able to understand everything and be understood everywhere offers an almost deliciously tangible prospect of normality and comfort.

This is not to suggest that living in Tanzania is unappealing; far from it. Despite the squeals and screams as we meet spiders and centipedes and cockroaches and frogs; despite the dirty water, the muddy streets, the fierce heat and the flooded paths; and despite the policemen, the bureaucracy, the slow service and the wazungu prices, we have fallen in love with Tanzania. Despite all the challenges, we want to come back to Mtwara - to students who smile and say "shikamoo"; to fundis who teach you Kiswahili; to the white hot beaches and warm ocean; to prawns the size of burgers; to barefoot babies playing with plastic buckets; and to harmonies and ululations from choirs that shimmy and sway. Despite the blaring music on a Sunday morning; despite the landcruisers that speed down unmarked roads; and despite taxis with bald tyres and bajaj that break down; it is the enterprise, the enthusiasm and the earnest courtesy that draws us back.

In fact, that enterprise is already changing the town in small but discernible ways. There are small shops appearing on street corners almost every week. The favoured design for a new shop is to lift a shipping container into position on the road side, construct a pitched roof from corrugated tin, cut two squares and weld into place two steel doors and with a ramshackle collection of different shaped shelves, stock your shop with anything from samosas to soap powder and when you're ready to trade, play some really loud music.

As well as enthusiasm for football and friends, there's an eagerness to please, to spend far more time saying hello than good-bye and to never say "no", but point your chin and say "ee" (prolonged ehhh). And earnest courtesy is important. In church when we give the sign of peace, it is done with gusto and vigour, care being taken to shake each neighbour's hand with that African handshake that has three distinct sections, "Hullo," "How are you?" "Stay well". It's more of a meeting than a handshake.

In truth, what we miss about home is quite simple. For all that Africa has seduced us, we are still visitors, looking in curiously. I yearn to be able to speak the language, but in fact what I miss is not the language, but the connections, the relationships, the friendships. For reasons of language and culture, the friendships we have made are with other *wazungu,* Europeans and Americans. They are important to us, but these friendships do nothing to bridge the chasm between us and Swahili people.

I looked on enviously yesterday, as Maskat, Willie, Lucia and others shared a breakfast of foul smelling beef soup and chapatti. I could have joined them. Their first greeting was "karibu". But had I done so, our conversation would have been stilted and forced. They would have been speaking of colleagues and allowances, of houses and animals and comings and goings. They know nothing of my world and even less of my motivations and anxieties.

Our immersion in Swahili culture will be placed on hold for some months now, as we fly home on Friday, to grey skies and traffic and a wet Bank Holiday. But first we must pack and the house must be cleaned. We have employed a young woman to help with the cleaning, partly because the place needs a thorough clean, as we leave for six months; and partly to find someone we can employ more regularly when we return. We have much to dispose of as well, clothes to be given to the Sisters, who will give them to the needy. A young woman knocked on our door yesterday having found a cracked and mouldy pair of shoes Caroline had left out as rubbish. Could she have them? Yes, of course. Today, she was wearing them proudly, cleaned and polished. We need to be sensitive in so much that we do.

Salumu will need to found first and then he must find our broom, the ubiquitous duster on a stick used for cleaning those awkward corners. He's taken it once and then returned it and it's disappeared again. He and his pals come round at least twice a day, asking for sweets, pens, or oranges or plastic bottles. Our broom is just the latest in a line of sticks and lids that make up their toys. But for now, I must tackle him,

"Nende kulete fagio wangu," I'll tell him. "Go and find us our besom, you besom."

Part Two

By January 2012 arrangements had been made for Adrian and Caroline to return to Mtwara, this time with an amended contract to teach English as an in-service course to serving teachers and students.

Saturday, 14 January 2012

Home again.

It really does feel like home – almost. An eventful week is finishing in homely style with the pungent smell of chillies, onions and potatoes from the kitchen, the whirr of the fan and the noisy shouts and bangs from the basketball court. I say an eventful week, because we've slept in five different beds on consecutive nights, met dozens of people, new faces and old, been disappointed and elated in equal measure and, tonight, wonder of wonders, we had a brand new fridge delivered to our door- on the back of a moped.

We arrived on Tuesday to find an inch of vivid reddish dirt covering every surface in our house that we had left so impressively clean. Depressing at first until I noticed that there were no footprints, no paw prints, no rat prints anywhere to be seen. The dust left virginal evidence of an empty house. Mr Mkonga, of the scary holes in his ears, seems a lot less scary now. He set four boys to work within the hour to wash the house and by mid-afternoon it was habitable. That evening we had no electricity, no water and no mosquito net. For the bursar, Mariki, it was a personal challenge to have the power re-connected. He returned just before dark with the missing connector.

The heat, the lack of water and the dirt has been challenging. Sarah and Andrew, our American friends, seem to understand without being told. They gave us a bed for the first night and the following evening in a heart-warming gesture of wholesome neighbourliness, delivered a warm tasty meal to our door.
"It's what we do back home."

We sped to Ndanda to say good-bye to one of our VSO colleagues. We raced through villages of mud and thatch houses, women lying listlessly under the shade of mango trees, children playing in dirt. We sped back to Mtwara the following morning as the sun was rising. The African dawn, here in southern Tanzania, is lush and eerie, so green you can taste it, with wisps of cloud wrapped round acacia trees and the low sun bringing shapes and colours into sharp relief.

Little has changed. The roads remain impassable after a heavy rain, policemen in crisp white uniforms still stop daladala arbitrarily to inspect papers, children still shout wazungu as we pass on our bicycles and we still laugh and slap hands in bonhomie as we are charged wazungu prices for a *pancha* repair. That sense of permanence, leaving aside the bigger question of development, is comforting. When Mohamed, my tailor, beamed the whitest smile at seeing I'd returned, I laughed out loud. Mrs Heman in the hardware shop asked where we'd been. And the man on the vegetable stall in the tiny ramshackle market, who insists we buy our provisions using only Kiswahili, greeted me like a long lost brother, offering his seat to Mama Caroline, scolding me for forgetting so much of the language, but pleased that his student had returned.

Some things have changed. Mama Ngonyani, my colleague in the English department, has had meetings to start the language project I have come to deliver. Of more immediate impact, having left saying I would plant seeds in the field outside my back door, I have returned to find she has planted the whole field with maize. She agrees that I have had two good ideas. Praise indeed!

The language project has been occupying a fair amount of Philbert's time. He has secured agreement from head-teachers to pay a small amount for expenses to teachers attending the course. He does this work in his own time at his own expense and for no reward. Although his son, Simon, attends the best private school in Mtwara, Philbert travels by daladala as petrol prices are so high. A litre of petrol is roughly £1, but wages are roughly twenty times lower than UK. Simon greets us politely with a "Good evening sir. Good evening Mama." Philbert has high hopes for him and Simon clearly has big ideas of his own. He has set his sights on passing the entrance exam for Ndanda Abbey School, opened by the Benedictines only five years ago and now the highest achieving school in the country.

The deep-set social strata in this society are all around. The best educated, best English speakers generally find secure well-paid jobs in the public sector. Ally Bashir on the other hand, speaks not a word of English, runs a dusty ramshackle electrical goods stall behind the bus station but has little difficulty in negotiating the best price. My lack of Kiswahili is embarrassing and does not help in bargaining. Still I was able to make myself understood. Deliver to my house at 7.00pm - "Nyumbani – saa moja – leo – sawa?" And it worked. At just after seven o'clock a dim light made its lonely way up the college driveway, the source of the light, a rusty red moped, driven by a grinning Ally Bashir who greeted us warmly, relieved to have found the right place and even more relieved to shed his heavy load – our new fridge strapped precariously to the back of his bike.

Friday, 20 January 2012

A new term

I had tried to concentrate on the staff meeting, but honestly my mind was on the electricity cuts. Two days ago, we lasted 'til 6.00pm on two bananas and a handful of nuts, as the rainstorms kept us indoors and the power failure stopped us from cooking. When I mentioned this to Mama Ngonyani, she laughed her belly laugh and asked why we had no *jiko* (charcoal cooker). I wanted to ask why the state-owned power company, Tanesco, had been given control of electricity services again, but instead asked about home-helps to show me how to cook. Cooking indoors, on the floor, in the dark, on a small charcoal cooker involves dexterity and patience which I lack. I remember Mama J in Morrogorro showing me how to alter the heat to stop rice sticking to the aluminium pans and how to use coals on the pan lid to cook the rice evenly. I wished I'd paid more attention. Despite our relative affluence, if we are to eat in a region bedevilled with long irregular power cuts we might need to learn.

There was a solemnity to this morning's staff meeting, noticeable in the absence of slapping of hands, subdued greetings and many younger tutors wearing ties as well as deeply polished black pointy shoes. It had the atmosphere of church or a tribunal or something significant. The telly wasn't on, so no-one needed to turn the sound down when the Principal started speaking. I sat next to Leonard, a tall very dark young man sporting a shiny red tie, black shirt, shiny black shoes and white trousers. He was told by the Principal to translate for me. I could tell he was nervous and after ten minutes or so, he gave up and I gave up.

We were twenty seven tutors altogether, almost exactly twice as many staff as the secondary school has teachers, with the same number of students. Maskat was sporting his most colourful shirt to date; clearly a shirt to be worn outside the trousers as to hide it would be a waste. Our Academic tutor, in the most vivid orange today, with sparkly cuff-links, led a litany of tutors' names and their subject areas, something I had thought all tutors would know. The topics ranged from photocopiers, to internet speed, to student behaviour and teaching practice. At ten-thirty the sweet tea and dough-nuts arrived, but who dare serve themselves? At one point Mama Ngonyani, instructed by the Principal, left the meeting to attend Court, where two students stood wrongly accused of theft. She returned shortly before the close of the meeting but the *mandazi* had already been eaten. When Aviti arrived two hours late, a murmur trickled over the meeting as the Principal listened politely to his explanation and chewed the inside of her cheek. Three hours later, the meeting closed. No decisions taken, the location of the photocopier undecided and the computers still riddled with viruses; but it was a solemn professional start to the new term and treated solemnly and professionally by all.

Inflation is taking its toll in many small but perceptible ways here. Our lunch, which last year included cabbage and meat, remains the same price, but comprises just rice and beans. When I remarked to Mr Moshi how tasty the potatoes are, he reminded me how expensive they are. To us they are half the price of UK, but then we have twenty times their money.

"But a kilo of potatoes is about the same price as a kilo of rice?"

"Yes, but a kilo of rice will serve a family two meals."

One of the reasons for the hike in prices is of course the new migration into Mtwara. Philbert had explained to me previously how the arrival of a thousand students at the new Catholic University had forced rents up and unscrupulous landlords had evicted local tenants in favour of newcomers, who would pay higher rents. I had lunch today with two students at this University. They came from Arusha and were derisory about both the government and local people's ability to change things.

"It seems they don't want to change and prefer to be poor."

Mtwara now has the new *wazungo* working for oil and gas companies. Many, many more Landcruisers, but never a white face to be seen at the market. They have people who do that for them. We have power cuts, water rationing, and the main highway to Dar still unfinished, but still the widening of the road down to the port, where so many *wazungo* work, is a priority and today thick clumps of red mud litter the roads where the lorries have trailed, and those of us on foot or on bicycle tread gingerly across this new gaping scar.

As we cycled home from a cold beer by the sea, we called in for tomatoes and a few chillies. The stall is owned by a young woman, who was caring for a young baby and cooking on a small *jiko* behind the stall. She had a few *fungua* of tomatoes, some chillies and some peppers. A few limp mangoes and bananas drew the flies from the tomatoes. As there were grey skies overhead and a gusting wind blowing, it seemed it might be a difficult night ahead for her. We bought enough for tea.

A new chipsy mayai place has opened down the road from us and Caroline had announced to me that, should there be no power when we got home, we would be eating out. Friday night is usually Philbert's night and this being Thursday I reminded Caroline that we are not here to live the good life. They serve a very good chipsy mayai at the Upendo Grocery. You will recall that Upendo is the rusty shipping container outside Philbert's house where there are some plastic tables and chairs on a dusty patch of ground next to a rutted road. The owner always meets Philbert, Caroline and me with a respectful *"shikamooni"* and wipes the dust off the bottles before serving us.

As we arrive home however, it's clear that there is not just electricity, there is also water. No need for chip omelette tonight, then, and our lesson in cooking on charcoal can wait for another day or two yet.

Friday, 27 January 2012

Niceties, names and necessity, the mother of invention.

In a ramshackle building, comprising four tiny offices, each with two desks, ancient computers, a whining ceiling fan and shelves carrying odd piles of dusty papers and flyers, posters for HIV awareness, notices of term dates and a banner behind one desk with the proverb, "Working together is a good start!" are where all state primary and secondary schools in Mtwara District are managed. Our meeting with the Director of Education, a small wiry woman, wearing a richly coloured headscarf, was to agree the start of an English course for teachers. This meeting was the result of the efforts of my friend, Philbert Ngairo. He has worked patiently and quietly. Mama Mohamedi knew the project, understood the need and pressed us to start.

The first weeks in College are proving to be a period of re-adjustment. I've had to re-adjust to the weather, to the stares and the shouts as we move around town on our bicycles and to readjust to a different pace of life. When someone responds, "Yes. You are right", to a complicated question, to which any answer but, "Yes or no", is preferred, then I have to remind myself to re-adjust. My accent, the speed with which I speak English and the unusual questions I ask, confuse many and, rather than offend me with a shrug, "Yes! or No!" is considered the most courteous option.

Caroline, on the other hand, has adjusted much quicker. She is quite assertive with our youngest neighbours, Salumu, Wangi, Joycie and Winston. They have grown another nine months while we're been away. They are cheekier, more talkative and beginning to say a few words of English and each afternoon come to our back door with calls of "Adrian" – no "shikamoo" or "habari", so quite cheeky. She has not been on a bicycle for nine months, but has returned, fearless of the ruts and the puddles. She is also more confident in Kiswahili. No more side-splitting mistakes. More often, her "Habaris" and "Maharabas" are met with an impressed, "Salama", rather than titters. The small black and red frog came to visit her in the shower the other day, but there were no shrieks, just a firm, "Get back in your hole, Mr Frog".

Mr Mkonga is a hugely important person in preparing my project. He controls the physical environment of the college. Nothing moves without his authority. No broken chair is removed, no path unblocked, no floor mopped without the chair, the path or the mop having first had Mkonga's nod of approval. Usually, it's just a nod. He wastes words rarely.

I am determined to learn as many of my colleagues' names as possible. I'm finding this quite challenging and the more mistakes I make, the more my colleagues laugh. As well as Mr Mkonga, there is his assistant Mr Mkunga, not to be confused with the fundi, Mr Munga. Then there are two Malubiches – John and Barnabas. Barnabas, is of course not actually Barnabas, but Ernest. The younger ones – Avit, Beatrice, Hassan and Siamine are much easier to remember. Generally, the rule is, if you're over thirty, you are known by your surname, unless like Mr William, whose first name is Simon and whose surname is Msiko, then William will do. Mr Maskat is really Khatib and his wife, Mama Tatu, is just Mama Tatu. So that's clear then.

I have begun clearing the Teachers' Resource Centre, making ready for English classes in the next week or so. A small team of students and I have been working all week in filth and heat, moving papers, books and boxes. We at first were plagued by wasps' nests with dozens of great wasps, the size of humming birds, with an ominous black trailing under belly. I've no idea how bad their sting is, but the students were clearly afraid. Caroline had bought an aptly named poison called 'Doom' and I earned instant respect from students when I was the only one to dare to reach up to the light fittings and kill them.

As we delved deeper, I found a carefully rolled rice sack. Inside, stitched on card, in red and yellow thread, was a tapestry showing the points of the compass. We found a great wooden chest of rice sacks covering everything from British rule in East Africa to the workings of the human eye. As we rummaged, we discovered abacuses made from bicycle spokes and bottle tops, maps of the Upper Volta, wooden clocks, blocks and boxes, all made by hand from sacks and sticks and cardboard- teaching aids that took someone weeks to make and now languish on a dirty floor. For every piece of bric-a-brac we found, one of the students would tell me solemnly its purpose and how it was made.

I've shown the teaching block to the Principal, the Vice Principal and most importantly Mr Mkonga. I have asked each of them what to do with broken chairs, papers and more significantly old obsolete computers, covered with years of thick red dust. Mr Mkonga at first suggested I ask Mr Maskat. Mr Maskat grimaced his most serious face and said he would ask the Principal. The Principal tried to appear non-chalant and told me to see Mr Mkonga. At one point, Mr Maskat attempted a more philosophical approach
"You know Mr Adrian, Tanzania is only just entering that period when computers can be seen as other than a piece of magic. In the 1990s if you said 'That computer is broken', no-one would have believed you."

So I turned to Mr Mkonga,
"Where is the best place to dispose of all these broken computers?"
He stared, pointed angrily at someone to do move some *panga*, then returned his gaze to me.
"You mean, where are we to dispose of these computers?"
I nodded,
"Yes. You are right."

Tuesday, 31 January 2012

Enterprise

Philibert thinks that Tanzanians are not as curious as they might be and this holds the country back. Enterprise is in short supply, some have said. There was no shortage of enterprise or opinions, however, at the market the other day, as we cycled from stall to stall, pricing sofa cushions here, looking for passion fruit there, taking time for a 'habari yako' with stall holders, where we buy cloth or plastic boxes.

"Utakwenda mbinguni, Mohamed," I said with a smile, but he detected my sarcasm.
"Pole sana," he looked quizzical.
I had cycled up the long, sweaty, dusty and ultimately fruitless hill to the market twice yesterday, only to find my tailor absent from duty and the various men, young and old, who seem to gather around his ancient and, on these occasions, idle, Singer sewing machine, were quick to apologise for his absence.
"You spend so much time at the mosque you're bound to have booked your space in heaven!"
He had my shirts and trousers ready, though. Although, it's a trail up the hill and although he is frequently not there, he is a skilful and honest tailor and I am reluctant to find another. In a country where it's normal for people to take a job there and then, he is unusual in that he will usually commit to take two weeks to make a couple of shirts and if he needs more time, offer an explanation by way of a quest for buttons, a measurement missing or a death in the family. Today, I went to collect four shirts and a pair of trousers. In the event I got two shirts and a pair of trousers, the blue piece of cloth, he claimed, was too small for two shirts. Better make a skirt for Mama.

The sewing machine sits on a step next to the hardware shop with the short fat man who sells paraffin in plastic water bottles. An ancient petrol pump advertises the store and the shopkeeper is often seen standing on his step perusing the market stalls, bajaj, delivery wagons and general hubbub of the market. He sold us our bicycles some months ago and I remind him at every opportunity that I know he over-charged me and I'll expect a good price from him when I eventually sell them. He is always charming, always offers Mama a seat, always guards our bikes while we go shopping and today, sat barefoot, trimming his toe nails with a knife better used to butcher a goat. As we sat and waited, we were ideally positioned to watch the rumpus which ensued.

A giant coach, belching black smoke and spewing thick dust, reversed up the hill back to the bus stand, in front of it a small but gathering group of men, young and old, at the centre of which were three policemen in crisp white uniforms. A soldier looked on impassively from the roadside, occasionally stopping and turning round drivers who thought they might sneak past unnoticed. The reason for the impromptu meeting was a minor car accident, but, having taken place in front of so many witnesses, was clearly going to be contested and one of the policemen duly produced a long yellow tape measure. Laying one limp end at an unmarked point in the middle of the road and strolling languidly up the street, he made his measurement at a seemingly arbitrary point some yards away. Another man, dressed in sharp shirt and tie, gesticulated and gestured as two policemen stood, hands on hips; less non-chalant, more, "Who's accusing who?"

Maso, my former language tutor and friend phoned the other day and asked me to post him some packets of cashew nuts, one of Mtwara's claims to fame if not fortune. They are a gift for his parents who he has not seen for many months, so I was pleased to oblige.
"How shall I get them to you Maso? What is your address?"
"Just put them on the bus to Dar and give them this number. The driver will phone me when he gets to the bus stand."
And that was that. No label, no names, no stamps and no queues. Maso phoned the next day to tell me he had them. A 'next day' courier service.

Talking of enterprise, I should introduce you to Mr Nuola, the builder, who I have asked to do some work on our house and on the Teachers' Centre. He's an older man; small, flecks of grey hair, and with an expression that rarely indulges itself with a smile. First of all, I asked him to provide a quotation for a small covered patio with a smooth cement finish. He gave me a price; then he gave me a price including materials; then he gave me a price with materials which actually finished the job. As we parted with him going to find some labour, we agreed another figure which included him being able to buy the bricks and cement this morning. At the moment I'm not entirely sure which figure I have finally agreed.

Enterprise like this seems to drive Tanzania forward. You'd be forgiven for thinking that in the long-term and at a very local level, it's Mohammed the tailor, the N'gitu bus driver, Mr Nuola, the builder and my fat friend selling paraffin that are the bedrock of this economy.

As for the builder: his cement, the bricks and a roof, there is a large trench full of rainwater preventing us from using the back door, the cement is parked in the front room, he tells me he's gone for bricks and the roof is sketched on the back of a piece of card. He impressed me yesterday when he took out a tape measure, until I discovered that the tape measure is only seventy-nine centimetres long. As with most things here, you have to pay up front as *fundi* don't have money for materials. He left me at lunch-time and told me he'd be back tomorrow. I said I hoped so, as, to date, I am the owner of the most expensive, 'hole by my back door' in East Africa.

Friday, 3 February 2012

Lions led by donkeys.

I nearly lost my temper. Nearly, but not quite. Instead, I joined scores of fellow Mtwarans and joined a crowd of earnest, expectant customers hoping to catch the eye a young bank clerk, in white shirt and a studied look of apathy. I had been to the bank the day before, waited in a snaking, sweating, shuffling queue for just over thirty minutes until I realised that, at that rate of progress, I wouldn't be served before the bank closed. So I left and returned this morning, ten minutes before the bank was due to open. It opened ten minutes late.

I arrived at the teller's desk in time to watch him indolently switch on his computer and stare aimlessly anywhere but at my face. I forced him to say "nzuri" to my "habari yako?" He looked at my cheque and told me to go to the most inaptly named "Customer Service" desk; actually a counter, with one clerk serving the pressing throng. A man came from behind, smiled at the supervisor and had his cheque approved over the heads of the customers in front of him. Against any principles I might have had, I did the same. In old-fashioned colonial style, I held my British passport aloft, smiled at the supervisor and had my cheque approved immediately.

After morning *chai*, I moved across to the dormitories to supervise the "cleaning of the environment", actually the slashing of thick, long grass and short, stubbly bushes which have not been cut since mid-November. Using a *panga or* curved, blunt blade, about a metre in length, sixty students worked in shifts for two hours to cut an area of about half a soccer pitch. Edison, my fellow tutor on duty, and I, supervised while the students laughed, sang and occasionally spoke to me, made gentle fun of my accent and gradually became bold enough to ask questions. Why was I here? Am I German?

Cutting grass is hard hand-blistering work and they have to take turns as there are more students than *panga*, but no-one times anyone. When one person is tired, he or she calls a colleague to take over. And they do, without complaint, often with a joke. This class of sixty students will spend every waking hour together over the next eighteen months; in study, in revision, in prayer and in duties around campus. Edison told me that he hoped that with Tanzania's development, it might not lose this spirit of kinship and community, a quality in short supply in the bank this morning.

There are more private cars in Mtwara nowadays, many more driven by Africans, white Landcruisers owned by NGOs, and big vehicles – lorries and diggers – presumably connected to the gas and oil installations near the port. There is some investment in roads. One, much needed near us, I am told, owes its existence to the planned visit to a nearby school by the President later this year. We mused today, as to how much of President Kikwete's itinerary we could foretell by tracing the route of new roads laid. But the more cars and lorries there are, the greater the chance of the odd accident or two. As cyclists we have grown used to a comfortable pace of life where a highway code, were it to exist, would comprise one rule,
"Try and read the other driver's mind."

For all the new roads being built or improved in Mtwara, there is still no talk of the road to Dar being finished. This is the main highway linking southern Tanzania with the rest of the country. The unmade road makes it impassable for many weeks and slow at the very best of times. The additional costs for transportation add a good few percentage points to the cost of living down here. Sofa cushions, for example, made in Tanzania, but bulky to transport, cost as much as they do in Europe. They are foam and come in one size only, because all sofas are the same size and design. They are nearly all gold, yellow or brown in colour, of various designs and sold in packs of ten cushions, costing the equivalent of two weeks wages for a teacher.

The cost of everything goes part way to explain why I have had such difficulty in getting anyone to throw anything away whilst I have been clearing the Teachers' Centre. Teaching aids made from wooden boxes and rice sacks are impressive for their ingenuity, but thirty year old typewriters offer this country nothing. Still Maskat looks at his most serious and wise when I ask him if we can throw them away.
"You see Mr Adrian, it's not just that they might be useful, but if we throw them away, that is exactly when the Ministry will come and ask to see our inventory".

Friday, 10 February 2012

Shopping

We had a list. We had priced all the items on the list and Mr Chiwembe said we merely had to go to collect and pay for the items on the list. Mr Chiwembe is a short elderly man, who has been the college electrician for many years. He owns a great iron bicycle, one of the Chinese imports, which he rides each morning from the north side of town, where he lives with his aged mother. He is not well and he finds the journey to college tiring.

We took a bajaj and I naively suggested the driver should wait as we only had to collect and pay. Mr Chiwembe smiled and said,

"Ah no, Mr Adrian. Perhaps it is better if he returns in a short while."
Wise words, as it happens. The electrical supplies shop is a small cavern of a store with two young women in full headscarves. As we produced our list it was obvious that two things were going to slow us down: firstly, every other person who came into the store seemed to be served at the same time as us; and, secondly, neither of the women knew where anything was other than bulbs or cable. A light fitting on display on the wall might have been in any one of dozens of unmarked white cardboard boxes. And so, in one of the more bizarre scenes this week, I climbed a broken stepladder as four or five people shouted instructions to me in Kiswahili, and I began a strange game of chance, until after a dozen or so unsuccessful attempts, I happened upon the right box. There was a general cheer of "Hongera", from the corners of the cavern. I doubted whether, when I saw it close up, it would be big enough, but, rather than disappoint an audience, pleased with itself, as well as me, I bought it anyway. To buy ceiling fan switches, a double socket, some trunking, a light fitting, some cable and a bulb had taken us about an hour and a quarter. Mr Chiwembe seemed disappointed and surprised that the bajaj had not returned. When we got back to College, I learned that Mr Chiwembe possesses two screwdrivers – big and small - and when I pointed out to him that the ceiling fan switches will need a drill, he looked downcast.

Nevertheless, as we finished for the week-end, four *fundis*, working almost in concert, had built a covered patio at my house, mended the electrical fittings, re-surfaced the floor and painted the walls in the Teachers' Centre. No mean achievement with no mechanical assistance at all, save four rough holes made with an ancient electric drill. The drill was used to fix the controls for the ceiling fans and both were fitted upside down for some reason, but no matter, they work fine. We have fitted electricity sockets in the floor under the teachers' desk to avoid trailing cables, something Mr Munga was skeptical about,
"Mr Adrian. Is it not dangerous, when it comes to washing the floor?"
"But Mr Munga, students know that. They will take care. Don't worry."
Clearly Mr Munga knows these students better than me, as when the completion of the Centre was marked with a final clean by class 1Dip3 last Tuesday, the first thing one eager young female student did, was to hurl a bucket of water directly over the sockets.

Next week, all students start teaching practice. At least, we think that will happen, because, although students are anxiously awaiting news as to where they will be placed, until the money to cover their expenses comes from Dodoma, no-one can go anywhere. No-one can explain to me why the expenses – equivalent to a few pence per student per day – are not available. There seems to be no shortage of allowances, or *chai* and *mandazi,* for supervisors of external private exams. Special preparatory classes have been organised and students are clearly excited and nervous, but nevertheless, neither teaching practice, nor assessment of teaching practice by tutors, will happen until such expenses are made available.

An air of normality is maintained as all six hundred students file past tutors in a uniform inspection. This happens every Monday morning, at ten past seven, immediately after the Principal has addressed everyone. Students are thanked for their work in cleaning the environment; tutors are asked to be vigilant in their supervision of such activities and then the sluggish, slightly embarrassed and, for me, quite embarrassing parade begins. A tie incorrectly tied here, an inappropriately garish belt buckle there, a skirt too short, or trousers too scruffy – a motley group of twenty or more students is yanked out of the inspection line and harangued by tutors. I checked my own dress code – open sandals, baggy trousers, loud shirt, – only a *mzungu* could get away with it.

Life is truly returning to normal for us in Mtwara. Children come to our *baraza* each evening to draw pictures with crayons, to show off their English words and to teach me the odd word of Kiswahili. Joyce, the Principal's six year old daughter – pronounced Joycie – is the least patient. She shouts at me in her rather shrill voice and when I gently, but firmly, ask her to say it again slowly, she raises her eyebrows, looks down her nose and sighs in frustration, and slightly threateningly, says "Ee", pronounced "ehhh".

And so the *wikiendi* is upon us already. First, to the barbers - a tiny shack of a shop, where an ancient computer plays a dubbed episode of Ironside. As I arrived, the man was taking the clippers to pieces with a large screwdriver. I looked hesitant,
"Karibu, babu." I thanked him and waited my turn, rehearsing in my head how I would ask for my haircut. In the event, my attempt to suggest a particular cut fell on deaf ears. I now know how, for next time, to ask for "Not too short," but with this haircut, that'll be a few weeks hence.

And so off to the hardware stall where I had learned how to ask for rat poison. Yes, Ratty must have told one or two relatives about the comfy *mzungo* home before his death, as one of his cousins has taken up residence in the second wardrobe, the one in our bedroom. The old lady, sitting on a plastic bucket next to the shop, was most helpful,
"Be sure to mix it well into a tomato or some flour. How many do you have?"
"Just one," I said.
She cackled and slapped her thigh. I felt chastened. If this doesn't work, I'll buy a *gifti* for Mr Mungu and see if I can talk him into another round of 'bash the rat'.

Friday, 17 February 2012

Domestic bliss

You see them all over town: old men, young men, sometimes boys, on bicycles; charcoal, packed and wrapped in sacks, the bicycle loaded with huge unwieldy parcels. Those struggling up the long hill from Mikindani, before free-wheeling down into Mtwara town, often resort to pushing these great iron mules.

Charcoal is the more common fuel for cooking, being significantly cheaper than electricity or gas and, in rural areas, the only source of fuel other than wood. Some research suggests that as urbanisation continues inexorably, the quantities now in use pose a serious threat to woodland and forests inland. Informal communities spring up around towns in every African city. They lack 'formal' services such as water or electricity, but they are removed from the rural area where they could be self-sufficient; hence, the demand for charcoal increases. At Staff House No 1 we have electricity and we could buy gas, but we wanted to try the most common form of cooking in Tanzania, the charcoal *jiko*. The great sacks of charcoal are to be seen all over town and one such trader arrived at our home last week.

Caroline bought one sack. A price was negotiated and a location for its storage at the back of the kitchen agreed; and then, rather than leave her the valuable rice sack, he emptied its contents on to the kitchen floor, leaving her in a cloud of thick black dust which covered everything in sight. He had wanted tsh2000 for his sack. William told us we should have a sack ready for him. Wise words, now. Instead, great billowing black clouds shrouded the pantry, leaving a dry acrid taste in our mouths and a jet black smudge on everything we touched.

It was a shame because it had been a good start to the week-end, revelling as we were in our killing of Ratty's smaller, but equally avid, nest-building, potato-nibbling, plastic bag stealing, ultimately, fatally, greedy, cousin. It may have been the rat poison or perhaps the wasp spray, but we awoke on Saturday to the fetid smell of dead rat behind the wardrobe. Cleaning the bedroom of rat remains and the rest of the house of charcoal dust occupied a fair amount of time.

At the small market near our home, we've found an old wooden stall, more like a covered rickety table, where perhaps twice a day, a toothless old man sells fish. He usually has just two fish, filleted into small portions, usually selling at tsh1000 each. Last week I bought two pieces of *changu*, the other night, tuna. When I buy it at about five in the afternoon, I know it has been out of the sea for little more than an hour and once its fried and garnished with fresh lime, served with local rice and spinach, it tastes delicious and the swarming flies, his bloody blade and the filthy market stall are forgotten when supper is served.

Philibert's mother died last week. She was eighty-one and died quite peacefully. Philibert made the two day journey to Songea by bus, his employer giving him compassionate leave but he still had to make the funeral arrangements with little access to money. Mobile phones now are the more common technology used for transferring money. One trip to the phone shop, to pay the money in cash, Philibert receives notice on his phone and collects the cash in Songea. Fast, reliable and cheap.

Life's daily cycle turns with a warmth and regularity that is comforting. We listen to the sweeping of the yard by Anna at 5.00am, the washing of clothes, the cooking on the *jiko*, occasionally the watering of the banana tree and then the return of the children from school and finally the return of William's hens and chicks as the sun goes down. William tells me he is lucky to have such hens, as they return, each evening, without need to chase them, to their bed in the back of his kitchen. Better to clean the hen muck each morning, than have them eaten by thieves or dogs.

"Your maize looks thin and limp, William", I remarked.

He looked crestfallen, but managed a weak laugh and said he would start going to church. He has commented once or twice that he would go to the Lutheran church across the road and for some reason chose today to commit to going regularly. Malibiche tells me his maize is poor because he has neglected to use good quality fertilizer. 'Biche's maize is certainly a lot stronger.

Sister Herman is unequivocal. She showed me her tiny notebook in which she has kept note, with a scratchy pencil, of daily rainfall measurements for the last twelve years. She explains that we should have had much more rain than we have had. People in south Tanzania will go hungry this year as the maize and the millet fails to thrive.

The Sisters of the Holy Redeemer have been in Mtwara for nearly fifty years. Originally from Germany, they have three areas of activity: they have built and are expanding the Montessori College where women are trained as primary school teachers in Montessori methods; they run a small dispensary for the poor and sick on the edge of town, where they give food and shelter to several hundred people each week; and they are developing a 200 hectare farm to the west of here, towards the Makonde plateau. There they have found a good water supply 200 metres below ground and now need money to pay for the solar panels which will power the pump to irrigate the area. In time, this farm will feed several thousand people in sustainable small-holdings. They have good support across the area but still need funds to make things happen.

We have rid our house of almost all significant wildlife now. First, there was the rat, then the frog. Caroline gave a shriek of resignation as she swept our red and black frog from his comfortable home in the shower on to the baraza.

"Enough is enough," she said. We watched as it sat, dazed, slow to recover, but then started to drag itself across the yard towards the large tree. Slowly, determinedly, as though it had been there before, it hauled itself up a metre of the tree to a fork in the stump to bask in a small puddle of water, which has escaped the harsh sun. Next came the over-sized cockroach, which although an asset in eating smaller flies and ants, is really too large and far too ugly to keep in the house. It was killed and swept into the yard. I watched the next morning as Lucas' cockerel ate the dead cockroach in two large pecks – well one peck and a gobble. So, life's cycle turns.

Friday, 24 February 2012

Paul McCartney, paternity and the Pope.

Just when you think you've settled in and nothing can suddenly bite you in the bum with its outrageous 'otherness', life here shakes you from your complacency. My slowness to understand just how deeply poverty and progress can drive great divides between us, was on show for all to see this week.

We sat with Philibert last night outside Upendo Grocery. It has been hot all week, hot enough to turn puddles into rutted ridges, then shifting sands; hot enough to twist the metal on our new tin roof and hot enough to find two days on a bus to Songea a trial of endurance for anyone. The road to Songea for most of its 600km is unmade and after the rains, filled with potholes and deep ruts. Philibert arrived in time for his mother's funeral and to lead four days of mourning with family members, many of whom had travelled much further than him.

One of the effects of Nyerere's social engineering which fashioned a nation from a collection of tribes, is for educated families, like Mr Ngairo's, to find themselves flung to every corner of this vast country. The journey from Kigoma to Songea takes four full days in the dry season. During the rains, no-one hazards a guess. Government posts are distributed according to availability and one's education. Candidates do not apply for posts; they are 'posted' and whilst account is taken of your preferences, there are many, many people in jobs, many hundreds of miles from their families.

"So your employer was happy for you take ten days off work, then Philibert."
Philibert had been away from Mtwara for twelve full days.
"Ah, of course I wrote a note asking for the time off, but if he had refused I would have quit. For him to refuse would be unthinkable."
And so we sat and compared the differences between Europe and Africa. I spoke of a teacher living here, from Germany, who is completing two year's paternity leave. And in UK, where generally an employee is given a day's compassionate leave to attend a funeral.
"So a man can have many month's leave for the arrival of his wife's baby, but one day for the death of his mother?" remarked Philibert.
The scale of these differences was left hanging in the air. We smiled and sighed and sipped our warm beer.

You would think I would learn. On our way out of Mass last Ash Wednesday I asked Malibiche about Shrove Tuesday.
"In England we make pancakes. It is a tradition we fulfil before we start fasting for Lent."
"Fasting, Adrian, is not so popular here in Tanzania."
I felt the hairs on my neck stiffen with embarrassment, but I persisted.
"So the Pope's new guidelines to avoid meat on Fridays have not been widely publicised here, then John?"

"Ah, I think if we are lucky enough to get meat on a Friday, few of us would reject it in favour of fasting. We fast most days you know."
My humiliation felt complete. For a moment, I felt that the church is not yet quite as catholic as God has planned.

I was learning to look for differences as the week progressed and as I have finally been given the green light to start teaching an English conversation class, I have tried to design the lessons to be fun, interactive as well as explorations of our respective cultures. I have been careful to try and select a good range of materials, balanced ethnically, across gender, age and interest group, when it comes to illustrating issues with film clips or excerpts of conversation. I decided that in each lesson it would be good to learn a song. My plans were dashed in the first lesson. Tanzania's exposure to, and awareness of, popular culture in Britain and America is very young. Little earlier than 1990 is known. In a country where the average age of death is 52, even if TV or the internet had permeated Tanzanian culture, few would be alive to talk about it. My films of 'Hey Jude', Cat Stevens and Tammy Wynette were going to have to be scrapped

"What is 'The Beatles' Mr Adrian?"
"Who is McCartney?"
Beyonce, Beckham or Britney - fine. The Beatles, Bobby Charlton or Bob Dylan? – not a chance.

Friday, 2 March 2012

Babies, books and bad time-keeping.

"Habari za asubuhi, Mr Munga?"
I started my week with the ritual exchange of pleasantries which involves asking everyone how was their week-end, their house, their work, their wife and often something else, which I ritually fail to understand. Mr Munga was busy in his workshop, a workshop which if it were tidy would grace any school or college but because there is so little space for storage, because the college is forbidden from throwing anything away and because there seems always to be something more pressing, the workshop looks more like an old curiosity shop of wooden oddments, guttering and broken chairs. Munga was speaking in a hushed voice with Edison; Edison was dressed for an interview in beige, sparkly suit and regulation pointy shoes. Munga had made a wooden frame of two pieces of two by three and had screwed them into place sandwiching an A4 notebook into place, rather like a flower press. I looked and pondered; I pondered as I looked and could think of no possible use for such a frame. It had been made with precision. Munga's tape measure is not only the full metre, but he was using a square to check the gap between the two pieces of wood. Eventually, I had to ask and interrupted the two of them. They seemed surprised at my question.
"I need to cut the notebook in half."
So Munga had used two pieces of hardwood (softwood would bend), four screws, the tools of the trade and an hour of his time, to build a vice for a cardboard backed book for the purposes of sawing it in half without it fraying.

"Why?" As I opened my mouth, I realised the frailty of my question.
"Because we do not need such a large book. We prefer a smaller one."
This scene was the opening exchange in a week of frustration, African time-keeping and eventually some elation as we both began to feel that we are doing something worthwhile. The English class starts at 3.00pm each day and on each day this week at 3.00pm there has been precisely one person sitting in front of me. By 3.45, most of the class had meandered in. Once underway, their enjoyment was palpable. One teacher, after finishing a particularly exciting round of the word game, "Pass the Bomb", asked if he could come again tomorrow. The lesson is as instructive for me as it is enjoyable for the teachers. They are unused to playing interactive word games; they start falteringly, showing great reserve and timidity; class discussions drag, no-one prepared to be controversial nor take the stage. The role plays, in contrast, are showcases of people comfortable with performance. Within moments, the story is set, the characters cast and a complex interweaving plot unfolds before us, using nothing other than an exercise book and a few plastic chairs.

Caroline, her friend Sarah, with my colleague Neema, have arranged to meet with one or two other women to discuss nutritional matters for nursing mothers. Doctors and mothers alike have spoken to us about the effect of poor nutrition on the cognitive development of young children. Breastfeeding, which I thought would be something we would be unable to teach African women about, it seems, is under threat - from pressures of women going to work and unable to express and store their own milk; from ignorance of house-girls unable to ensure hygiene in feeds; pressure from malnourished mothers, unable to produce enriched milk of their own, without a good diet. This group of mothers hopes to be able to share their experiences and learn from one another. They have ideas for the future to widen the net and work together to improve infant nutrition. I was just pleased to make the acquaintance of the woman with the coolest name yet,
"Mambo, Mama Kenny Rogers", I smiled, as they left.

Two young men, Mwakibe and Joseph, were waiting for me on my step as I returned one lunch-time. At seventeen, they have recently left school and spotted Caroline, a mzungu, hanging out washing. Following a brief chat, we agreed that they will come twice a week for free tuition, focused on passing their Form IV exams, with some English conversation thrown in. For my part, I will have an hour from them of Kiswahili conversation. I badly need practice. They have written letters for prospective pen-pals in England. Polite, diligent and so grateful, it's humbling. One of my neighbours is studying to be a primary school teacher at the technical college, next door. I naively assumed that the technical college would train young men and women in skills and trades.
"You are right," said Leonard. "They have many, many expensive machines. But, no, that was then. Now, they do not train plumbers or joiners, just teachers."
"On every street corner, there is a young man struggling to handle a plane or a saw. Surely we need trained craftsmen and women?"
"Again, you are right. But we need politicians and managers who will care about that."

I let the matter drop, but thought back to the beginning of the week where a trained teacher, now a college lecturer, stood over a joiner as he sawed a book in two.

Sunday, 18 March 2012

Fiery heat, some fish and another fundi.

The heat is unrelenting, building up like a great oven of a day until the tiny space between earth and sky fills to bursting and the rain pours in to dampen the bad tempers, itchy bodies and dusty paths. You'd think it would be a release, but the rain brings mud; bicycles choked with thick red cake, roads impassable for all but the great, smug four by fours, whilst mothers with babies wrapped to their backs, spindly schoolchildren in shiny black shoes and young boys laden with charcoal, struggle. With sandals slipping and shoes spoiled, no-one is grateful for the break in the heat.

The young man, Mwakibe, who works for us each day, has helped us smarten the land round the house. A small garden is emerging, the grass is cut, the rubbish buried, and the yard swept each morning. Mwakibe is a tall eighteen year old, with an infectious chuckle which gushes through his teeth, and turns into a snigger, too polite to tell me just how bad is my Swahili. He's six feet tall but with wrists and ankles which seem ready to snap and hips that can't hold his tatty trousers. He knocked on our door one day, having seen Caroline in the yard, and asked for tuition with his English. We decided to give him work and now he pays for his own tuition and is registered with a class that will coach him through to October next year, when he will re-sit his 'O' levels. He lives with his older brother, younger sister and his mother. His mum sells bananas on the roadside.

We eat together each lunch-time and slowly he has started to eat more. At first he would tell us he was full, unused to eating so much. Gradually we have introduced a balance of protein and carbohydrates and he is eating more, has more energy and more spirit. I've told him to be careful or he'll be fat like me but he just chuckles through his teeth, slaps his thigh, shakes his head and says, "Oh sir!"
"Chance would be a fine thing", we both think, but don't say.

We talk some days of what he hopes to do.
"Open a bank account", I urge.
"When should I do that sir?"
"When you have 20,000 shillings."
"When will that be, sir?"
And I take the notebook out again and show him our plan.
"Five thousand to your mum, five thousand for the bank and five thousand for tuition leaves you ...." I feel I'm turning into his dad.

So we turn to our next challenge. Tiling. Mr Ally and me, after a faltering start in agreeing a sensible price, seem to be getting on fine. Mr Munga had tried to convince me that the normal labour charge would be 45% of the cost of the materials.

I pointed out that Mr Ibrahimi would have been paid precisely nothing for two days painting had we used that method. So he and Caroline went off to buy the tiles and cement. Once we had paid for the wheelbarrow and loaded everything into the bedroom, Mr Ally smiled. He has an angelic smile.

"So Babu (he calls me grandad). Where is the sand?"

"Sand? You're the fundi and you've just come back from the building suppliers."

"I wouldn't call it that," said Caroline. "More like hardware from hell. And I'm not going back."

Maskat came to the rescue. He seemed surprised that we would ask.

"Sand, Mr Adrian? Of course you must use the college supply."

"Of course," I said. "Why didn't I think?"

So college may not have a bull anymore - you might recall that it was stolen; it may not have many books, nor enough chairs in classrooms, nor enough money for teaching practice. But it has a limitless supply of broken chairs, from which Mr Munga will make my bookcase, and enough sand to supply all our building needs for years to come.

Tiling with Mr Ally is a messy business. It has to be. Sloppy mortar, no spacers and no cutter - just the wooden blocks left over from Mr Norla's baraza to hold them in place. This morning, as I watched his truculent lad sitting, legs akimbo on the kitchen floor, surrounded with broken tiles, as he laboured with a rusty nail to score them, I realised that without my patronage, this mess would become a catastrophe.

"If I buy you a tile cutter, Mr Ally, you can pay for it week by week."

"But I have no work, babu. How will I pay?"

"But with a tile cutter, you shall find work,"

And with that, we cycled to the market to buy the tile cutter. Once home he whistled, and kept turning to me with a grin, saying "Safi", and then started phoning his mates. My kitchen is still a mess, but at least there are fewer broken tiles and the job is part finished. On Monday he starts on the bathroom. And when I say bathroom.........

Last night we were the guests of Mama Koka, a large woman of about forty-five who I had originally and rather embarrassingly taken for over fifty. She and her husband – a retired army officer – own a couple of bars and guest houses around the town. We were royally fed on goat, then boiled fish, the goat having been hit by a car earlier in the day and slaughtered by Baba Koka. I asked what will happen to the driver,

"He made off, but not without telling my boy that he knows me. So he will find me this week and it will be OK. Do you like the fish?"

The changu was a small delicately flavoured fish in a bowl of thin tasty soup.

"I bought thirty five of them for twenty thousand shillings."

I had to share with them my experience at the fish market the week before, where I had misheard the price and thinking I was getting a bargain, bought a huge kolekole for twenty five thousand. But we cut at least ten large fillets from it and the massive head, with eyes like gob-stoppers, made a greasy soup which I shared with William next door.

The heat bakes everything. Yesterday, small lizards were scampering for shade, huge cartoon-sized snails had slid up the wall of our house after the rain, fooled into thinking that the damp will last, but the rain stopped and they were slowly baked in the sun, before falling off to become snaily dust in the sandy soil.

Travelling around is as exciting as ever. Our journeys by bicycle are invariably a trail of "Mambos", "Shikamoo" and "Ee wazungu". Today's was momentarily even more exciting, as Caroline ran over a snake as it slithered for cover. She squealed, her voice momentarily rising an octave, but she didn't falter. We raced for the shade.

Friday, 30 March 2012

Dangers of the daladala

Last week we made the trip to Lindi. The daladala should have taken two hours; long enough for some, but the expectations here are of another order. When we arrived at the bus stand at 7.30, that familiar feeling of being out of place washed over us like a rash. Two white *wazee* carrying too large and too expensive a hold-all, gingerly avoiding the russet puddles from overnight rain, peering into empty buses, looked a soft target for 'helpful' daladala boys.

After a surge of excitement as we bumped down the road, we soon stopped and two ample women squashed onto the ledge behind the driver's seat. Where there is just room for one set of knees, here three were accommodated. I spent the next hour with my knees cushioned in a warm, soft bubble wrap of a lady's thighs. The little girl, face peeking from a garishly coloured scarf, spent her next hour with a look of petrified fascination. When two wiry, muscly men replaced them, I forced a smile.

The visit to Lindi was to be brief; a short talk to the hundred or so head-teachers, gathered there for a two day meeting of the region's schools. The entire meeting was conducted in English, in a wooden hall, perched on a stony bluff overlooking the Indian Ocean at Lindi bay. We were given jipati and soda, a prompt speaking slot and a bumpy bajaj back to the bus station. After a re-run of the jostling and one-upmanship of the boys working the buses, we managed to catch the slow bus to Ndanda.

The fast bus covered the eighty miles in about two and a half hours. Ours was to take four, stopping at overgrown lay-bys, where small mud houses poked through the cassava and banana plants and an old man in plastic sandals, a richly embroidered white kufi, holding his flapping skirts, waddled, in the most ungainly fashion, avoiding the mud and the detritus to struggle on to the empty bus.
The bus was empty but for two hungry *wazungu*, bouncing about on the back seat, waving at curious children and smiling a gentle refusal at the offers of maize, coconuts, samosas, nuts, water, oranges, bananas and every size and shape of dried fish.

My hunger got the better of me and I munched on nuts and maize for most of the way. We saw many strange sights but perhaps the most intriguing was the small man, wearing vest and sandals, wheeling a tractor wheel, twice his size, on the main road, down a very long hill, risking life and limb every time a vehicle passed. We wondered which was stranger- that he had the strength to wheel it up the hill prior to rolling it down the hill; whether he was returning to or taking it from a three-wheeled tractor; or that he had access to such a large tractor in the first place. Certainly, it would not go unnoticed in this neck of the woods.

Ndanda, or rather the Benedictine complex at Ndanda, is a strange place. Green, cool and often with a dampness in the air that with the food, the landscape and of course the architecture, you'd be forgiven for believing it to be Bavaria. The electricity sockets make no allowance for fifity years of British rule and are doggedly German. Stranger still, seems to be the effect of very obvious European patronage and benevolence. Unlike Mtwara, where we Europeans – particularly old British ones on bicycles - stand out as curiosities; in Ndanda, the European is the source of skills, of employment, the best healthcare, the best secondary school and doubtless the purest water in Tanzania. This is perhaps part of the reason why five young boys, the ring-leader daring to be cheeky, mimicked us with a "gibbledy, gabbledy yackety yak" and turning to his friends with a boastful grin, said,
"Good afternoon," and made to shake my hand.
Such forward behaviour from young boys – without a shikamoo or a "Good afternoon, sir." is most uncharacteristically rude and, as I approached him with a stern face, his confidence ebbed and, with it, so did his friends.

Our journey home was uneventful. Four hours, with the roof leaking on to the seat next to me and a young boy made to sit there. I'm not sure which made him feel more uncomfortable, sitting next to me or his damp backside. As we passed the salt flats near Mikindani they were sweeping the remnants of glass from a lorry-load of soda and an entire bus load of people was trying to pull a daladala out of the soft salty soil in which it had become embedded to its axle.

Bus travel is the only option for over ninety per cent of the people here and the dangers are common and obvious. I walked back from town with Malibiche the other day and he stopped momentarily pointing down at a concrete slab.
"Someone died here yesterday, killed on the back of a piki-piki, hit by a daladala as it sped round the corner."
Unremarkable and unmarked, the incident was barely worth the comment, but we stopped for a moment then walked on.

Saturday, 21 April 2012

Kitere

It was still dark and I was up before the dogs had stopped howling, with a Land Rover at the door to take me to Kitere. My hastily arranged visit with Sister Brigita was to see first-hand the large tract of land below the Makonde plateau which the Sisters are cultivating and to take photographs, in readiness for some wider publicity.

The road to Mikindani at that time of the morning is an eerie place. Figures loom suddenly from the darkness – women in head scarves with large buckets, bowls or baskets on their heads; young boys or older men on heavy iron bicycles, heading towards Mtwara laden with four great rice sacks of charcoal. As we rounded the bend to drop down the hill into Mikindani we saw the tell-tale sign of broken branches lain in the road. A hundred yards further and in the shadow of a bend, a great red truck lay on its side, surrounded by broken glass and spilt oil, the windscreen shattered with bright gashes of fresh metal glinting in the headlights, a lone man, like a marooned survivor, perched on the driver's door.

Dawn was breaking. One minute, startled faces with bright eyes and teeth were glaring from the dark, and the next minute the roads had come alive with truculent schoolchildren, women and babies and white shirted policemen. A dirt road with deep ravines and potholes had become a busy thoroughfare and as we sped through the scruffy hamlet of Kitere, another working day had begun in Tanzania. Boys with broken bicycles, women sweeping their yards, old men rubbing their boney heads – all stopped and stared at us, in our bold white car, high and mighty, ahead of a great swirling train of dust.

We were six. Two nuns - Sisters Brigita and Toma, two women, Halima and Mama Augustina and Morris, our aptly named driver and me. Before I had removed my sandals the women began laughing. They seemed to consider it unnecessary to attempt to talk; to stare incredulously and then giggle was sufficient. I grinned, pretended I was enjoying it and laughed back. The more I laughed, the more they giggled. We began our trek to the farmland above Kitere and the tiny hamlet of Kidule, an hour and half's walk, mostly barefoot, through mud, knee-high at times, and at others, wading through thigh-high flood water. Bright orange birds, tiny aqua blue birds, great black heron-like birds – all swooped and swirled around us in the moist, early morning air. We passed mud huts, with straw roofs drooping to the floor, a thin wisp of smoke and some foul smells escaping from one and as we passed, we heard
"Jambo?"
And the exchange of greetings, now reassuringly universal and repetitive ensued,
"Salama. Shikamoo."
"Marahaba. Salama mama. Habari?"
"Nzuri. Na wewe?" and so it went on. We were returning travellers, unremarkable, but warmly welcomed.

The village came out to help the Sisters with their work. There were young men, muscles shimmering with sweat through torn tee-shirts, *panga* slung casually, toothless women, straight-backed, great backsides horizontal, shin deep in a rice field, deftly cutting and plucking, never raising an eye, never mind their heads and a gaggle of children sitting on a makeshift bank of weeds and grasses, laughing uproariously, as I slipped and slid and adjusted my hat and mopped the rivulets of sweat. They were so comfortable, so happy. Even though I could not be more out of place, they made me feel at home.

The children do not attend school. There is no clinic within three hours walk and the only water before the Sisters drilled their well was taken from a natural spring, two hours walk away. They live on the maize and rice they grow and a few chickens and goats they keep. We tried to speak but they could not understand my strange accent. We joked about my hat, the colour of my feet and the pictures on my camera. Kidule comprises a thin string of mud houses with old and weathered straw roofs. As Sister Brigita and I wound our way up the gentle slope though the village, we greeted elders respectfully. An old woman, lay prone on the baked mud outside her door, her grey and balding head cradled in the crook of a bony arm, her knees bent and as she craned her neck to speak, she smiled and croaked a toothless "salama" to our greeting as we passed. Hens pecked, some small children played with sticks in the dried mud and two younger women paused as they swept, to stare and then smile at their visitors. There was nothing to see, the village existed, that's all. It isn't developing. Its children don't attend school; its mothers rarely make it to the nearest clinic three hours walk away. Its men and women farm the land in exactly the same way that their great-grandparents did. Sister Brigita sighed and suggested we turn round and take lunch at their house, a newly built house, built for the Sisters to develop their farm. A newly sunk deep well needs a pump and then the whole of this area will have good clean water and many hectares of land irrigated.

After a lunch of maize with pumpkin, we made an incongruous looking party making the return trip to the car – an old man with leathery feet carried a basket with twelve huge pumpkins; another, the toothless bwana from the shamba, carried a branch of bananas; a wiry young man with a clipped moustache and a great iron bicycle, had two squawking hens strapped to the rear and then the six of us. In the heat of the day the muddy paths had, in parts, been baked into sharp ridges and lumps. My soft mzungu feet were cut and sliced and the women laughed louder each time I winced. Eventually I hung back, pretending to wash my sandals, but in truth, avoiding their mockery. And so for the last mile or two I cut a solitary figure, with a florid kikuu draped over my head, picking my way barefoot, alongside ditches where boys fresh from school, sat, hopefully, with short sticks on the edge of the wetland, waiting for a bite. The chuckles from the mud huts as I passed, were predictable and sometimes tiresome, but an old woman still ran to fetch me a chair as I arrived at the car.

Home today in Mtwara and it all feels very comfortable and modern. Caroline prepares the house for visitors, I have to go to 'Modern Cutz' for another haircut and we have meetings in restaurants over the week-end. Kitere is classified as 'Mtwara-Rural' - its schools used for teaching practice by the College here. It's two hours away by car if you know the way, but it feels like another century.

Sunday, 6 May 2012

Graduation Day

The week started brightly enough. The weather has changed and each morning, with a sheet to stay warm, a cool breeze prompts me to turn over and stay in bed a little longer.

College was preparing for graduation. Teams of students, directed by tutors, slashed, cut, cleaned and swept. The trunk of a huge flame tree, which has lain sleeping for at least a year, was being cut and made ready for removal. A man with a chain saw had been hired especially for this task and so impressive was it, that a dozen students and tutors stood and watched the sawdust swirl in the wind. The area was being cleared and prepared for the graduation ceremony to be held under a canopy. He spent two hours cutting great blocks off the massive trunk, but then spent five hours stripping the saw and re-assembling it – chain and nuts and metal plates strewn across the grass. In the event, Mama Ngonyani's instincts were sound, safety won over imagination and the great ugly concrete hall was used rather than an airy space shaded by trees. It rained solidly for the next two days, so safety was seen as the right choice.

As the season changes from summer to winter, the rain is more persistent. I had asked about preparing a small plot for planting but was told not to bother as it won't rain now until December. The day the rain started every bajaj driver wore a pained expression. You'd have thought they would be pleased to be in such demand. Usually every street corner is littered with these three-wheeler taxis but in the driving rain, motorcycles are not wanted and bajaj could charge the earth, but they don't.

Thankfully on the morning of graduation day, there was a cheery breeze, some fluffy clouds and a warm sun. Two days of rain had delayed the programme of preparation and Maskat was bowling round campus with a fixed stare. Many hands make light work and by lunch-time, students were enjoying a soda as tutors and guests started to emerge in their best attire.   Still, Maskat didn't particularly want to hear me complain that the power sockets in my classroom were fused.
"Yes Mr Adrian. Fundi will come."
"But Maskat, the sockets in the office block are out too and your visitors arrive in two hours."
His face changed as he realised that the ICT presentation and the whole of the evening reception depended on the use of those sockets. A car was dispatched to find Chiwembe.
"It's Friday, Maskat. He won't be here for another half hour."

I have got to know Chiwembe. He has been the college electrician for donkey's years. He is a slight man, who cycles to work on a great iron bicycle, twice his weight and occasionally and quietly, he will tell me of the unusual pains he suffers - numbness he calls it - in his chest and arms.

The fault was quickly found in a cable located below a rusty junction box. A pick-axe was summoned, flag stones smashed and slowly with the help of one of the students, some great black cable, as thick as my wrist, was drawn out and pared and with some pliers and black tape, work began.

With bunting waving cheerily in the breeze, the steps boasting a fresh coat of paint and people nervously adjusting new shirts and sporting stiff shoes, an air of nervousness crept amongst us.
"Fundi. You will have this work finished by two o'clock?" snapped the Principal, It was less a question than a statement, but Chiwembe smiled and said, "Yes," but without conviction. As the guests of honour went past, we formed an impromptu welcoming party. The Minister stopped to shake my hand. He is a large man, forties with a winning smile, with expensively fashionable hair and bold gold-framed glasses. He could have been a seventies TV detective. As we were introduced, he glanced over my shoulder to see Chiwembe struggling with the last of the cable. A warm grin broke into his face,
"Mambo, Chiwembe."
Chiwembe grinned back. Across the rubble and between the shoulders of the worthy guests, the Minister stretched to shake Chiwembe's hand. Only then did I learn that Minister Kasim had been a tutor here over nine years ago and remembered staff like Chiwembe well and with much fondness. This chance meeting set the tone for the rest of the afternoon.

We took our seats in the hall in time for a soulful rendition of the national anthem. When important guests were introduced, the students reserved the biggest cheer for their own VIP. He was seated immediately behind the large frame of the Minister. As he stood, his squat body belied his great heart. Maskat was the crowd's favourite.

For the next two hours we were entertained by rappers in pumps and t-shirts, young children with drums and skirts and Form IV students performing a 'jive' - more like line dancing with African rhythm. But what rhythm! After the Minister had spoken for fifteen minutes, I thought he had been on too long, but then with a slight change to his tone, a huge roar of applause would swell the room. Every word was devoured. And after forty-five minutes, still the crowd were calling, "Kweli!" and "Kabisa" (quite right). It was a politician's speech to a crowd he knew well. I understood not one word but I watched faces. And their faces told me that I was in a community of people bound in common cause with a common spirit.

That night, as Kasim spoke again, this time as a former colleague and friend he asked for Chiwembe by name. Chiwembe moved to the front of the room and smiled, enjoying the attention and the memory as Kasim remembered old times. I said to Chiwembe later,

"You go all year Chiwembe, and no-one notices, no-one asks. And then on this special day, whether it's blown fuses or Ministers of State, suddenly everyone wants to know, 'Where's Chiwembe?'"

We laughed like drains.

Saturday, 19 May 2012

The Great Debate

The weather has turned cooler. Each morning, we wrap up in a cotton sheet, as an early breeze keeps the mosquitos at bay and allows a luxurious lie-in – til 6.30 at least, when cocks crowing, prayers calling, students sweeping and basketballs bouncing, force us to rise and start the day. Often it's a relief from a night of sticky sweat as howling dogs tear bits out of each other, not five yards from our bed. Frustratingly, when I try and find a neighbour to join in common cause and complaint I hear,

"Ah yes Mr Adrian. But you know, with the dogs we are safe from the robbers."

"But are there robbers?"

"No. Of course not. Not when the dogs are out."

Our armed guards are two young women, each shouldering guns that look like toys, who spend the night sheltering from the dogs and keeping close to college - not much deterrent for Maskat who has twice had bananas stolen from his back garden. I had once foolishly left old sandals out to find them missing in the morning. The shoe and banana thieves are the same thieves that Mkonga wants to deter from crossing the open land between college and our church. This open space of shrub and bush, with baobab trees standing in massive isolation as dusty paths criss-cross their way between Shangani in the north and Mtwara town to the south, is a favourite haunt for every scoundrel in town – according to Maskat and Mkonga, that is. They've never caught anyone, but then Mkonga thinks that's because they are deterred by the dogs at night and the tireless work of students to cut trees and dig ugly channels to block the shortcuts to school and church. Each Sunday, a small army of brightly clad men and women, pick their snake-like way round broken trees and bushes, jumping gingerly over thorns and sticks, thwarting Mkonga with every step. As a silent rebel, I drag the smaller branches to one side, a strong wave of chivalry surging through my veins, allowing worshipers to pick their way more easily,

"Do your worst, Mkonga. We shall not be moved," I think. And I try to remember to tell him the next morning. When I do, he smiles, rubs those holes in his ears and for a moment, tries to look interested before returning to his lists.

It's been a quiet very ordinary week-end. We went for an early morning swim on Saturday, having checked the tide tables and for an hour or so basked in a warm sea and then lounged on a deserted beach. We then set to work tidying the land around the house. There is a clear difference between we wazungu who aim to create order where there was natural growth and where there is natural growth, allow it, under controlled conditions and marked by white stones; and our African neighbours who, to deter snakes and inhibit mosquitoes, remove all natural growth close to the house. This morning there was an inspection by the Housing Committee, chaired by Maskat. He warned us yesterday, helpfully advising that no livestock should be allowed to live in the houses and that all poultry should be vaccinated. As if to prove a point, Caroline for the first time found hens in our shower this morning. The committee came by this morning as she was shooing them out and I was gathering stones to make neat borders,
"Do you think that these borders will deter snakes, Mr Adrian?"
"No, but then we have cleared our house of goats, chickens and cows."

The highlight of my week was the inter-school debate at Shangani Secondary which I was invited to observe. When I got there they asked me to be a judge and when I sat down to judge they asked me to be the "Overall Judge", choosing winners one, two and three. Pupils from Masasi had travelled by bus all morning to do battle with Shangani – first with words and later at football and netball. It is one of the many innovations introduced into school by the dedicated headteacher, Mama Shaibu. She was not present but her assistants, Kibakaya and Julius organised the day well.

My good friend Kelvin was one of the proposers, showing much presence and maturity as he took centre stage under the baobab tree, confidently putting his case. Another contributor from Masasi Secondary chose an American ghetto style of delivery, littering his argument with "mothers" and "brothers" and posing in a gangster stance, which went down well.

We're feeling tetchy because we have had a week of sleepless nights. For the first half of the week, dogs howled and fought outside our bedroom. Philibert tells me that it is the mating season and dogs travel long distances in response to the howls of bitches. They all seem to meet outside our house and force Caroline and I to lie, angry and helpless, listening to nocturnal couplings for hour after hour. For the latter half of the week we have listened to the tedious beat of a rattling bass from a beery bar about half a mile away. I asked Mkonga the other day if anyone complained,
"Yes. They need permission."
"And does the council ever refuse"
"Refuse permission to play music? No."
And so this morning, as I read the morning paper at 4.30am, the music finally stopped. Today a huge PA has been erected on the field across from our house for a sports competition later this afternoon. For half an hour we listened to,
"Hallo, hallo, hallo, one two three, hallo, hallo, hallo." He's just too far away for me to run over and pull his plugs out.

Friday, 28 September 2012

Night life

All week, each day, many times a day and most nights they pass, slowly, stoically, unsmiling; carrying their coloured buckets on their heads – a truculent, multi-coloured parade – bearing water from the well to their homes, or rather to their employers' homes. The fortunate ones share a heavy steel pushcart on bicycle wheels. For two weeks this has continued. There was respite briefly yesterday for a few hours, when water flowed through our taps and filled our buckets, then a return to the slow, rainbow caravan. When I received our water bill this morning, it was unsurprisingly small, a few pennies for the small amount we received and no apology, not even a wry smile for the bold irony of a 'Service Charge'. Lucia reminded me that I had promised 'a much improved supply' when I returned in July. It was no good blaming Francis, the devout, whispering water engineer from Ndanda. He would only blame his Chinese contractors. Lucia blamed no-one. She just found it funny that I was wrong.

We have returned to the comfort of home. Like an old shoe, it fits. It feels very comfortable. It feels like it belongs. Even the return of Ratty – or rather a great nephew of the beast himself – only spurred Caroline to fit a screen door. This simple frame with wire mesh was made with chisel, plane and, yes, screws. It even fits the door frame and hens that formerly marched in here at breakfast, looking startled when they were shooed out, now squark resentfully on our porch. We open it respectfully, though, for Tigger, the sleek, indolent ginger tom that has laid claim to the sofa next to me.

We did not need to rush back from England as it happens. We could have stayed for a few days longer in Lushoto in the north if we'd known. When I asked why so few teachers appeared for my class for the first week, one headteacher explained "Adrian. This is the first week. Better start next week."
"But that will mean that next week will be the first week?"
"Exactly."
I was concerned that the water pump out at Kitere had still not been completed. I phoned Deogratius trying to express just the right amount of impatience in my voice.
"I have had some problems, Adrian. I will come on Friday."
"That will mean he will come on Monday," said Sister Tadea, gently.
A code of courtesy exists here, the rules for which I was still learning.
"Africans say they will come on Friday as a polite way of saying they expect to start on Monday", explained Philibert, tactfully. The delays in starting teaching have given me chance however to establish a friendly working rapport with a number of artists – carvers, mainly, producing intricately beautiful figures in ebony; and, crucially, the Chairman of the small group of streets and alleys called an '*mtaa*'. Mr Abdulmajid is a quietly spoken, reflective, former engineer, now retired.

He heads the small committee which meets regularly to discuss local issues affecting the street – a new culvert was recently installed; a sandy alley will soon become a paved street and the most vulnerable families are listed for him by neighbours and the municipal social workers. Caroline went with him last week to the market as he patiently and vigorously bartered the best price for the cloth we were buying with money raised by Mtwaralinks (www.mtwaralinks.com) – cloth for the school uniforms for some of the children from his *mtaa*. Amid the easy comfort of shopping and swimming, there are families living close to us who exist each week on what we spend on beer. One elderly woman curtsied, her humility shaming me, as she greeted me, thanking me profusely for the help we had brought.

Our son, Martin, has been staying with us for the past few weeks, quickly establishing himself as a friendly newcomer, as he cycles to the beach and back. "Good morning, Baba Martin," someone called to me from a stall in the market the other day, where he is already known for buying seeds as well as fruit and vegetables. He has laid out a garden and set a mesh fence around it to keep out the hens and the dogs. Already the first healthy leaves of spinach, tomatoes and beans provide a splash of green against the red earth, painstakingly watered each morning by Mwakibe. It is the only visible sign of life in the earth as everywhere is parched brown and dusty. The grass has turned to crisp brown stalks and beneath them are bald patches of caked soil. All Mkonga's best plans for blocking the paths and byways between here and church have come to naught, as without vegetation, the area is an open desert, but for the mbuyu trees, stark, grey monstrous scarecrows guarding a ravaged land.

Tonight, in the night, the heavy thud from the music in the hall shakes the roof and rattles my nerves. Thirsty and hot, I creep to the kitchen for water. I've worked out how to open the door without it creaking, a feat, which, since Munga the Fundi 'fixed' the door and left it squealing each time it is opened, is no mean achievement. I wondered if the small rat which had scurried across our living room as we watched telly the other night had found a home in the kitchen. It was a much smaller, slower rat than its great uncle.

I had nearly cornered it the other night in the pantry but had not the courage to go to my knees to find it and kill it. Instead we left out poison and hoped for the best. It hasn't been seen again so tonight I crept even more gingerly, apprehensive. As I stepped towards the bedroom my foot pressed down into a squashy slime. Had a huge gecko left its doings? Had the cat been in during the night? Worse still, had I found the rat? I groaned out loud as a too-vivid picture flooded my mind. It was Freddy, now spread-eagled outside our bedroom. He must have grown tired of waiting for that damned water, or Caroline to find him and move him and was making his own way out. And now he was squashed under my foot, a lonely prone mush of a creature, not dead, not yet; and after some minutes, as though he'd decided he could play dead no longer, he stretched one slimy scrawny leg after a painful other and dragged himself towards the door and freedom.

Friday, 5 October 2012

All in good time....

The road to Dar is still not finished. A stretch of about forty kilometres remains unmade, sandy earth and stone will be compressed before finishing with tarmac – but not yet. This stretch has been waiting for many years to be finished; so long, in fact, that other stretches in need of maintenance have now been dug up and are awaiting resurfacing. The effect has been to extend the length of road currently under construction and make the journey between Dar and Mtwara even more perilous. Not that this deterred our driver with the curiously named bus company 'Butti ya Zungu' – literally, the White Man's Boot! This small quietly spoken driver hurled his huge vehicle up and down embankments, through potholes and overtook everything in sight with all horns blaring. The statistics for road deaths in Tanzania make grim reading. Europeans, cosseted with safe cars, safe roads, safe signage and a culture of compliance to regulations are justifiably shocked at dangerous driving, the poor condition of vehicles, the absence of markings and signs and the poor quality of the roads. Even more surprising is the absence of any serious voice of complaint. It's as though, having accepted that life is short here, that death can come from unexpected quarters each day, to start with road safety would seem indulgent. I heard a story the other day of a bus that careered off the road and into a roadside village, killing at least three people. Local people were understandably enraged and consequently the bus driver made a dash for the main road to try and avoid their anger and perhaps violence. As a result of government policies in the sixties, to force social cohesion between tribes, people were sent to college, university and employment in different parts of the country. Today, people criss-cross their way, by bus, to every part of Tanzania's huge territory, to attend a celebration, a funeral, a graduation or just to go home and see mum. At 6.00am, on the dot, each and every morning, the huge concrete sprawl of Dar's main bus station - Ubungu - erupts into a maelstrom of diesel fumes, smoke and the most awful cacophony of engines and whistles and horns as one hundred and fifty coaches tear and scream their way onto Tanzania's roads.

One safety measure which has been introduced is to ban bus travel in the hours of darkness. A consequence of this law, is this hellish cauldron where buses nudge and bump to their starting positions, edging perilously close to each other, horns blaring, as though the starter's pistol has signalled the first crack of dawn, and they must each win their race. It is perhaps pressure to reach destinations before nightfall that, in part, causes drivers to take such risks.

Closer to home, last April, the good metalled road leading to the port was dug up, supposedly as the first stage in widening the road. Trees were uprooted and the broad grass verge in front of the University, ruined, to be replaced with great heaps of soil and stones. Through the dry months of June and July, the sand has blown and the road now resembles a bleak desert where once there had been a grass verged street. This 'new road' will join the new 'ring road' planned to snake round the town centre as traffic flows are expected to increase as the benefits of gas and oil start to trickle down. Currently a swathe of beach front road has been churned by diggers, leaving a reddish scar wrapped round the coast, dotted with piles of stones. Women in shawls, squatting on haunches, surrounding great steel diggers, as they smash stones with their hands, leaves an incongruous picture of modern day Tanzania. People tell me that the road must be finished before the rains come in January, but if the road to Dar is anything to go by, I'm not holding my breath.

Thinking of the prospect of major projects, I saw an unexpected sight the other night. Returning from the classroom after having screened the weekly movie, I crossed the car park to see an old van being unloaded. Scattered in front of the main office were many brand new pieces of very expensive gym equipment, a donation from Finland apparently. Complicated devices to help with push-ups, press-ups, squats and thrusts in the pursuit of perfect abs, pecs and bi-ceps, littered the college, there being no arrangement for their storage. I thought this strange, not least because three times a week, we are woken each morning at 5.30am to the chants of young men and women jogging in time, part of their weekly regime of health and fitness, sustained each day with games and exercise each evening. All this is done with no equipment, just raw enthusiasm.

As this expensive European fitness equipment had arrived by road from Dar and had clearly been packed badly, many of the pieces had been damaged in transit and Adolph, the tutor in charge, was anxious to put them somewhere safe.
"Where's the gym, Adolph?" I asked.
"It will be over there next to the football field," pointing to a grassy area, amid trees and shrubs.
"So you weren't expecting this equipment so soon then?" I pressed.
Adolph smiled wryly.

Of course if you need to store something quickly, a teacher's college is a good place. It has lots of classrooms, empty of any books or teaching aids, and therefore an ideal spot to keep expensive weight-lifting machinery where it will remain untouched. Adolph assures me that the gym will be built in two months. A sod has not been turned yet, but then this country is full of surprises.

Friday, 12 October 2012

Homes for heroes

Still no rain, but Mwakibe's garden – for it is his now – is a luscious green oasis in a brittle brown desert. Lettuce, spinach, tomatoes, passion fruit, chillies and some herbs are spreading vivid green leaves and, watered twice a day by Mwakibe, are the only sign of vegetation around here.
"Are you sure it would not be cheaper to buy your spinach at the market, Mr Adrian?" Samwelli enquired.
"Quite certain. I'm sure it would be a lot cheaper," I replied.

After buying fishing net to keep out hens, imported seeds, twine, tools, not to mention Mwakibe's wage, this is entirely a labour of love. The investment is already paying a dividend, as Mwakibe now tends it tirelessly. Whereas formerly he had complained about the heat, had to be reminded to get on with his jobs, or turned up late on some pretext or other; now, he is at our door before we are dressed, fetching water from the well and cycling home in the dark after using his new watering can, his transformation into dedicated gardener is almost complete.

We have no rats or frogs, but no more welcome is the thick dark sash rippling on our bedroom wall. A shimmer of shook foil, glistening black like a horse's neck, what at first sight is one organ, on close inspection is a million, perhaps a million millions, eager ants marching in strict formation from the crack above the door jamb to the rear of our wardrobe. Perfumed sprays have little effect; the troops just fan out and against the garish yellow of the wall, take on a polka dot formation. Time for the wasp spray, a pungent sickly toxin that permeates all. Best cover your nose and your eyes. "HIT" is an understatement; it under-sells itself; for it is the final solution for the insect world. Nothing lives in our wardrobe this morning, but the floor of the bedroom and the hallway are littered, covered, with small black casings, the collateral damage from last night's carnage.

When we first moved into Staff House No 1, I remember the sinking feeling we both had as we closed the door and looked around at bare floors, bare walls, a concrete stall for a shower and a kitchen with one narrow shelf for a work-top. We had not prepared ourselves mentally for the shock of this hardship – the absence of windows, doors that close, cupboards or drawers, taps, water, flushing toilet. All seemed basic and harsh. Today, we have a ceiling fan, a patio and a tiled wall in the shower. We have a book case which wobbles and whose shelves are too narrow to hold many books, but it is furniture nonetheless. So we feel quite smug; particularly as I visited Mwakibe's new house last week-end as we begin to help his family move from their rented house near town to another property, slightly further afield.

Asha is perhaps forty, a small woman with bright eyes and an olive skin. She is mother to Mwakibe, his older brother Jaribuni and his younger sister Tamasha. Her husband developed a problem with his eyes, which kept him off work, so he went to Dar-es-Salaam some years ago to stay with his children by an earlier marriage and hasn't been seen since. Asha had been selling bananas on the road side; currently she works as a cleaner, part-time, and doesn't make enough to feed the family and pay the rent.

On the land she bought some years ago, she has built a simple traditional house, with sticks and thick mud – wattle and daub – and a corrugated tin roof. The house has three rooms, three metres square and, at present, only the earth for a floor. The toilet outside is a deep pit. No water, no electricity, no drains. It will have a cement floor, a wire mesh window in each room and a door which locks. It has no ceiling. As I entered the house, I realised for the first time just how cramped, dark and dank are these houses. The floors are red mud and the walls are perhaps eight feet high, with a gaping space below the tin roof. The family moves there in less than a month. Asha and Tamasha in one bed; Mwakibe and Jaribuni in the other room. Mwakibe sleeps on the floor at present, so he needs a bed.

"You know this house is too hot in the summer and too cold in the winter," says the fundi, who will make the floor. "A tin roof lasts a long time, but they are not good in this climate. The straw roof is best, but it needs replacing every two years."

I couldn't think about the roof. All I could see was the damp, clay floor, the dark caves for windowless rooms and the great pit of a toilet.

It will be fine. All around the house are Asha's neighbours. She is greeted by all with a friendly "Karibu" as children are fed, clothes are washed, hair is braided and all the household chores of everyday life are carried out. The small patio under the tin canopy is the focal point for so much of Tanzanian life.

In contrast to Mwakibe's place, we have had fitted the last piece of plastic guttering to the front of our house. I was left wondering why the fundi had measured the house leaving the gutter eighteen inches short, then why the fundi had fitted the final piece with a ten inch length protruding at each end, and why we had used nails instead of screws. No matter. Mwakibe sighed in wonder, "Ah. This is a fine house, sir."

And of course, with a toilet linked to a sewer, a shower with a drain, a kitchen sink with a tap, and four walls that won't wash away in the next heavy rain, it most certainly is.

Saturday, 20 October 2012

The best days of my life....

A weak whistle, soon after the first call to prayer, marks the start of another week. Its 5.30am. A ragged trail of track-suited shapes, runs past our house. Sometimes testosterone-fuelled young men run in time to their war-like chants. More commonly, there's the slap, slap, slap of flip-flops and sandals, as the reluctant ones jog sullenly in the dark. Later, at seven, the serried ranks of blue-shirted teacher trainees stand to attention below the Tanzanian flag. A series of military style parade duties are acted out, as women and men, some of whom are too old and too wise to be made to march on the spot, are harangued by their student council or teacher on duty. The student in charge stands on a small concrete dais from where a report of the previous week is read. The report includes whether the meals were served and whether classes were held as planned. Each day's report is written by hand and signed by the teacher in charge. Students who arrive at roll call late are punished, usually made to clean toilets or sweep the open spaces with a besom.

We discussed our memories of school days this week, students recounting their experiences good and bad, of their time in school. Consistently, amongst those bad memories were tales of punishments and beatings. Consistently amongst the fond memories of those who went away to school was the 'timetable'.
"The timetable?" I asked. "Why would the timetable be such a good thing?"
"Because we got good food and chance for social interaction," some said.
"Good food," I pressed.
"Ugali," they all shouted with one voice.

Ugali is eaten almost every day in every family across east Africa. It is made with maize flour and water, blended to a thick consistency then heated until it forms a coagulated mass and can be eaten in gob-sized fists, sometimes dipped in a weak vegetable sauce or with beans and local spinach or leaves. In college the kitchens prepare huge vats of ugali using great paddles to stir it, students traipsing each day with plastic plates and boxes for their serving which they eat on benches or sitting in the shade of a great flame tree. As we took the short-cut past the kitchens the other evening at supper time, Caroline and I were greeted with the traditional courtesy of, "Karibu" by small groups of students eating ugali and beans- literally, "Come and join us."

Philibert entertained us last evening with an account of how he prepared his lunch for school – a serving of ugali and beans wrapped in a banana leaf and tied with twine, the parcel slung over his shoulder. Without food for the day or at least a few shillings to buy chippati, a child might stay at home, carry out chores around the house, but at least be sure of a meal. School attendance is not just about teachers and books.

The other feature of life in school or college referred to in the most glowing terms is the social interaction. In college, given that the day starts at 5.30am and finishes at 8.00pm with an hour of religion, there would seem at first sight little time for socialising. Today the normal timetable of cleaning has been suspended in favour of an inter-form football and volleyball competition. Every goal and every point is greeted with great whoops of joy, the pitches being lined with men and women in impromptu chants and dances. As one young student, David, explained to me, "There are few chances to have enjoyment, so today, people will sing and dance."

Although the guttering is in place and a new water vat has been bought, still there is no rain. Last week-end with an extended power cut, even the tank above the great well was dry, there being no power for the pump. House girls and boys from across campus were sent on excursions to sisters and aunties to find water. Mwakibe's new wheelbarrow would prove a valuable asset.

The *mkokoteni* or wheelbarrow is a heavy metal box, iron grills welded together and fixed to a heavy steel frame on iron wheels, the rubber tyres punctured long ago. After a lengthy negotiation with the bicycle fundi, we agreed a price for new inner tubes and wheels. The fundi is severely disabled with twisted withered legs and works on the floor with his legs folded under him. He has a specially crafted three-wheeled cart which he drives with a hand powered crank, his wooden tool box strapped behind the seat. The wheels are bought without spokes and the fundi exacted a high price for the three hours it would take him to fit each wheel. It was good work for the fundi, the huge benefits expected from the gas bonanza having not reached him yet.

Amongst the topical issues we discussed last night were numerous government commentaries and media statements concerning the anticipated benefits from gas and oil finds in the ocean off Tanzania and Mozambique. The District Commissioner and everyone around him talks of how the local economy will be transformed. Philibert and I are less convinced. Certainly, Mwakibe's family's move to a traditional house without water or electricity – never mind gas – seemed to fly in the face of such optimism. Instead, we talked rather of the smart cars, the foreign workers and higher prices that have arrived now that gas is here.

"If a gas pipe passes by my house, I will not be any better off. My wife will still cook my ugali with charcoal. " said Philibert with a resigned sigh.

Friday, 26 October 2012

No English, no service!

Sundays are the laziest day. It's the only day when we need an alarm. As in most things there is a comfort to be had from a comfortable routine. Each Sunday we pass the women cooking jipati and mandazi on their open fires. They call "Salama" to Caroline and "Habari za jumapili" (How is the Sunday?). On the way home it will be "Habari za kanisa?" (How is church?)They sit or squat on haunches, usually a young child wrapped to someone's back.

The walk to the church these days, before the rains, is less of a trial. We have to remember to amble or we'll spend the first hour wiping the rivulets of sweat from our necks and arms, but the paths are dry and clear. We take a pew half way down the church. A door mid-way down the aisle is always open and if we're lucky, a breeze catches us from time to time.

It's Mission Sunday. I look around and see a church full of missionaries. They wear the most eclectic clothes, often bought from a branch tied to a tree and it's often emblazoned with the name of a baseball team or 'Rooney' or 'All Stars'. Others, including me, wear garishly coloured shirts made from kitenga, women wear big dresses, students wear blue trousers, nuns wear white. Each according to their station, women to the left, men on the right! The service last two hours. Whether there is a long sermon and few announcements or a short sermon and numerous announcements, Mass always finishes just before 9.00. The 'late' Mass starts at 9.00.

College is shaking with sport, as the week is scheduled as the inter-class tournament in volleyball, basketball and football, to select a representative team to compete in first the regional and then the national finals. Students, if they're not practising their shots at the basket, are rehearsing drums and dancing. Our house looks over the sports field and all week, the entire college population has been camped there each afternoon, cheering, chanting, drumming and dancing. Maskat takes a strategic position under a large tree. The morning after the victory the day before is another story. Men and women, are unable to hold their heads off the desk at nine in the morning, some fast asleep, all docile, no-one interested to play games or learn new words and my entreaties to start role plays are met with stony stares.

At pre-Form I however, they can't sing enough. After an hour of pronouns or adjectives, a hundred children call out to sing. And so we go through our repertoire, the words memorised. The skin-clad workers in the builder's yard next door, look on grinning, as the class bellows, "You are my sunshine". The class teacher Jenny and I work well together. She interprets my every word so I teach as though I were in England, joking, chastising, calling on the boy dozing at the back to read out his work – all possible only because each and every word is translated into Kiswahili. Without Jenny it would be impossible, as my Kiswahili is limited to "write this down", "say it again", "be quiet" and "open your books". The children, although they know all their irregular verbs and their pronouns, have little functional spoken English. And my accent is incomprehensible.
Nearly every staffroom door in Tanzanian schools has the slogan, "No English, no service." Thirteen year olds will start secondary school in January and see that each and every subject, save Kiswahili, is taught and tested in English; yet, they will not receive tuition nor be tested in spoken English. Should they succeed and so wish, they might go forward to do 'A' Levels and some, the Diploma in Teaching, without their competence to speak English having ever been tested.

Once they start teaching, however, they will be expected to teach each lesson and set each examination in English. Little wonder that many teachers pay lip service to the requirement only to use English in school and little wonder too, that there is a widening gap between the high-achieving schools, where fluent English is spoken throughout, and the government schools where competent English speakers are in short supply. Educators, policy makers and government spokespeople maintain that for the country to advance and develop, the commitment to retain English as the medium of instruction as well as the medium of government must be maintained. The fact that the emerging economies of China, Brazil and Russia have no such predilection seems to cut no ice.

Mwakibe's house is nearly ready for his family's move there. His mum, Aisha, looked on silently earlier this week, as Eric the fundi explained how he had changed the arrangement for the toilet. Eric is a successful fundi. He has a laconic stance and from his motorcycle or his garish four-by-four, his voice on the phone always sounds like he's firing someone. Still only thirtyish, his knowledge of the building trade has brought success to him early. He smiles rarely and unusually for Tanzanians, spends little time on small talk, but as he explains that the cement path around the house offers a path directly to the toilet, it is clear that he has taken a pride in his work. The wattle and daub shed with a tin roof, has a cement base leading to a deep pit; but this is all more than Aisha had planned. I ask if she's happy. She has used rouge on her face for this visit and her cheeks shine as she grins, "Yes. I am happy." She curtsies and tells me how happy she is for our kindness.

Mwakibe's garden is being harvested just seven weeks after the first seeds were sown. Luscious green Chinese leaves are now ready to cook, tomato plants are in flower and soon there will be chillies and onions. Mwakibe spent hours yesterday, carefully making teaching aids for me but he is not an enthusiastic worker when it comes to hard labour and the maize field has been awaiting his hoe for several weeks now.

"Today is a good day, Mwakibe", I suggested this morning. "It's grey and cooler than usual."

"But it's a holiday, sir." he reminded me, today being Eid al Adha.

"But yesterday you couldn't work after you fell off the motorcycle, and you're not even fasting."

He sniggered as he often does, trying to understand my sarcasm and taking the safer option of ignoring me. He watered his lettuce and left the digging for another day.

Tuesday, 13 November 2012

I'm lovin' it.

For as little food as they have, most Tanzanians are keen to eat what's healthy. Starch in the form of maize flour or rice is the staple diet. Protein is added through beans and local spinach is a tasty source of vitamins. So if enough food were available, I suspect Tanzania would be a healthy country.

A bench of old ladies, draped in every colour of kanga, waited toothless and patiently to be seen by the doctor. As I bent my head round the door and smiled at the long tired line, they grinned as one, beckoning, "Karibu". Celina called me through, ignoring my awkwardness. I had come to see this dispensary for myself, as I had heard so much about it since I arrived two years ago. It was created by the Sisters of the Holy Redeemer and one energetic German nun in particular, serving a poorer district of this already poor swahili coastal town. A large white block tucked behind the enormous white block which is the Catholic Church at Majengo, the dispensary is clinic, pharmacy and emergency feeding station in one. Built in robust German style, full of high quality polished wood and spotlessly clean floors with incongruously lurid paintings, and random Swahili paintings and Makonde carvings, it's unlike any Tanzanian health centre I've ever visited.

The centre treats more patients in a day than any other clinic, partly, because of the district it serves, but mainly because of the prices it charges for treatment. At TSH1000 for a consultation and perhaps TSH1000 for treatment, it's one of the cheapest around but still unaffordable for many.

Celina is a large cheery woman, the daughter of a Polish woman and a Tanzanian man, who speaks English like a European, with a touch of Polish impatience in her voice, as I quiz her as to the way the clinic functions. I had gone to see the emergency food given to the hungry and as we talked, three old ladies approached us, holding their stomachs. They were hungry and had come for maize flour and beans. A carefully kept register listed their names in blue ink and confirmed that they had each come here for food four weeks ago. They would each be given enough for a few days.
"Could you use more flour and beans?" I asked naively.
"The more we have, the more we would give. There is no limit. The need is here.

Every day, it's the same."Sunday Mass is usually an uplifting experience and this week we were graced with the dancing girls in papal gold and white, performing a graceful line dance on the altar steps and then shimmying the length of the church ahead of the offertory procession. Elf-like in size and stature, they provoked spontaneous ululations from around the congregation. And yet, perhaps the heat is getting to all of us. A whispered conversation behind Caroline, led to the cheery old man next to her, leaning forward and pointing out to the lady in front, that her bra strap was showing. As she tucked it away, she turned and thanked him demurely and then yanked the arm of the small boy to her side.

After communion, a man in front of me, clearly tired as well as prayerful, knelt too long and the creaky old man with glasses many sizes too large, sitting in front of him remonstrated with him to move away. For a few moments we were offered relief from the tedium of the reading out of offertory collection figures, as the prayerful man insisted on kneeling and the wizened old grump waved him away in theatrical whispers.

In Maibras' modest living room Philibert, Maibras, Doctor Mrope and I met to discuss community health insurance. At present, if you work for any arm of the state – teacher, doctor, nurse, policeman or soldier – a health insurance premium is deducted from your salary. Many complain of the inefficiency of the service and resent the charges, but for those in employment, it at least guarantees consultation and treatment. If you're poor, work on the land or in your own business, you pay as you go and it can be expensive. If you're poor and you get malaria, you to have to hope that a friend or a member of your family will lend you the money. So a community scheme, led by the local Council, offering insurance for a whole family for as little as TSH10,000 seemed too good to be true. It yet might prove to be so, and we are awaiting confirmation from a local dispensary before we agree to pay for the twenty poorest families in Kiangu B to join the scheme.

Today, after two weeks of disrupted lessons, while a lengthy sporting tournament ran its course, and just as we thought we could squeeze one week of undisrupted teaching in before lessons are suspended next week for terminal examinations, two hours were taken from us as representatives from the government health insurance scheme addressed all 700 students in a packed hall; so packed many of us found shade and rest under a nearby tree. They had details of a scheme costing TSH27,000 a year, a figure few here can afford.
"Why have they come?" asked Janet.
"To sell us insurance we can't afford," said Vaileth. There was a hubbub of disgruntlement near me. Students were cynical and suspicious, resentful of time taken from studies and annoyed at what they saw as well paid civil servants intruding. If Dr Mrope's plans come to fruition, we will be able to offer students a plan, costing them little more than TSH2000 a year. I explained as much to Moshi who as Dean of Students will meet Mrope to discuss the scheme.

Moshi's a fit man, proud of his physique and trains often to stay healthy. He was wearing a smart, beige shirt this afternoon, with a small yellow 'M' on the breast pocket.
"So you chose the shirt for the letter 'M', Moshi?" He didn't.
"Have you ever been to a Macdonald's?" He had never heard of them.
"They sell burgers and are perhaps the biggest burger chain in the world."
His face, usually a permanent smile, fell almost imperceptibly.
"What's a burger Adrian?"

Miracles

Two small girls, in broken flip-flips and dirty torn dresses approached Maibras with a sheepish smile and graceful curtsy.

"Shikamoo," they each said and Maibras beamed back and bent to shake their hands and greet them. Maibras and I made an odd couple, wandering from house to house, calling "Hodi". Old ladies sitting in the shade of a mango tree, peeling cassava, sewing or plaiting a grand-daughter's hair, stopped what they were doing to call "Salama" or "Shikamoo".

"Shikamoo" is the universal greeting of respect for older people. Maibras and I hear it all the time. Maibras is greeted with "Skikamoo, Babu." He is pleased and proud to be known as grandfather and tells me so as the two young girls, usually at his house picking mangoes from the great tree by his front door, skip towards him, slowing coyly, as he strokes their heads.Our task that hot Saturday morning was to meet each of the twenty families registered as 'vulnerable' by the municipal social worker, note the dates of birth of the family members and photograph them for their health insurance cards to be issued. As we meandered down dusty tracks, paths littered with debris, broken cars, scruffy hens and washing lines, we spoke of the hidden needs in this very ordinary quarter of Mtwara.

"None of these families has a man in the house, Adrian. Different fathers, different families, women holding it together."The community health insurance plan we were promoting on behalf of Dr Mrope might at least help each of these families get access to treatment and medicine. Theoretically, it will save lives. The old ladies who greeted us, knew what health insurance meant, even if some of the younger sulkier ones didn't. They greeted us with toothless smiles and broken chairs, entreating us to sit and talk, holding their arms out in gratitude. Around us were girls washing clothes, girls carrying buckets, girls holding babies. These last few weeks has seen the town become a web of women in every colour of kanga carrying every colour of bucket. There has been a radio announcement to tell us that each district should get water once a week. I wanted to say that knowing that it would come once a week, but not knowing which day or at what time was unhelpful, but then I remembered my conversation with Francis many months ago and him explaining that a timetable can be irregular. I scoffed then but nothing has changed. People accept it stoically. Well, most people accept it. Maibras went on local radio last week, berating officials for their incompetence as well as the insult offered when we learn that the Member of Parliament's street and the Regional Commissioner's house are never without water.Maibras is a clever man. He is humble, astute fiery and measured at different times. When I asked him about disturbances in Dar the other week, following an ugly incident between a Christian, a Muslim and a copy of the Holy Koran, he became angry, waving his arms as he called on the police to act and use the powers they already have. He claims to have little faith in politicians and yet he is one of the most effective local politicians I have seen. When I asked him about his houseboy, he speaks calmly, shows me the money that is left around the house, with which this boy, who he found on the street, can be trusted completely.

"See, Adrian. He stays here, he eats and sleeps here. He is like my son. I believe God will reward me."

Maibras speaks proudly and animatedly of his achievements in building a local police station on the opposite side of the road. It took him three years to collect the money and build it, but now there is a regular police presence in his neighbourhood and he often boasts how he took some 'foolish people' to be locked up for the night.

Perhaps people are looking for a miracle. End of term examinations start this week and church was full to bursting for Mass on Sunday. No coincidence here. For most people, success in life, including examinations, is secured through faith in God. Plastic chairs were brought out as the congregation squeezed more and more on to long wooden benches that bowed and creaked. As we wait for rain, each day becomes hotter and stickier and as we were squashed too close for comfort, I feared the two hour service might test my resolve. The choir, however, seventy students in blue shirts and trousers, raised the hairs on my neck and brought tears to my eyes. The choirmaster had an exaggerated, animated style – mouth wide, eyes glaring, arms searching and legs bent, sometimes leaping and stretching, he inhaled more volume and bellowed more passion than seemed possible. The choir, responded, transfixed by his passion, swinging, swaying, ululating; a Fantasia of musical animation. At the Offertory procession he led the choir down the central aisle in a slow rhythmical mesmerising shuffle, as the entire congregation joined in their harmonies. The collection boxes, sacks of maize flour and bottles of oil were carried by children, old men and fat women. A sombre mzee, with grey hair and bent back, slid his shoes in time as the young child to his left shimmied her way to the altar, led by the dancing dervish at the front.

Miracles are what people are looking for. In church, in the examination hall or waiting at a tap that has no water, people believe in miracles. A German doctor working in this region had explained to me recently that her project aims to place higher value on the birth of babies. A mother often is denied the right to a funeral for her baby, if it dies at under four weeks. She is left to bury it herself. As Maibras and I sat with Fatuma and her children, explaining the health insurance scheme, we remarked how few people remember or have been told their date of birth. Many mothers would recall the month their child was born - and this after a discussion with their sister or neighbour – but few could remember the date. The date is often not noted. If you need to recall your birthday, choosing a good date might help.

"So Fatuma, your birthday is 25th December?" I checked. She smiled.

"And the birthday of your young son?"

"25th December." she smiled again. "We are very lucky."

Thursday, 14 February 2013

Life goes on

It was as though we hadn't been away. Only the rich verdant spaces round our house that had crept from the red earth and softened the crisp parched stubble, was a clear sign that time had passed. That, and the maize field. Before we'd left, the maize field had been marked and fenced, a naked brown gash among the stark trees. Today strong young green plants wave gently in the breeze. In this part of the world, the New Year brings new growth; green rich fecundity where last month it seemed barren – a veritable new beginning.

Our friends and neighbours were eager to tell us of recent events – it was unclear which they found more significant – the floods or the protests. The floods had been as severe as they were sudden. New Year saw a downpour that lasted almost twenty-four hours and left low-lying areas in three feet of water, families homeless, family possessions wasted and ruined and the town reeling from the ensuing disruption. A nearby primary school had its roof ripped away by a strong wind, neighbours' houses were filled with mud, roads closed and traffic diverted. Maibras was in the thick of it from the start – emergency meetings with officials and politicians. Ultimately, little could be done, other than the community supporting those in greatest need.

As the waters receded, news of the government's announcement, that the gas, currently being recovered from the ocean off the Mtwara coast, would be piped to Dar es Salaam, filtered through to local communities in town. The reaction was violent disbelief. In many people's views, the government had reneged on a public pronouncement made some years earlier – that the gas would be processed in Mtwara, delivering jobs and investment. A pipeline carrying away the precious resource, seemed to symbolise years of perceived neglect by the government in Dar, leaving Mtwara to many more years of poverty. Further demonstrations are planned for the end of February, although it is unclear who is behind them and how well 'planned' they are.

This hiatus was played out while we were away and since our return, a strange calm in both the weather and the political climate have prevailed. College is beginning to return to normal classes, but this country seems obsessed with examinations – testing and certificating interminably. So, as one set of papers are marked, so another set of tests begins, leaving tutors and teachers with no time to teach. These breaks in the timetable lead to alterations with no notice. This morning, for instance, without warning, it was announced that special classes to teach 'lesson planning', 'classroom management' and other aspects of pedagogy were to be held. Seventy students brought their wooden stools to sit under the trees and wait for their tutor. They waited quietly for an hour and a half before anyone appeared

This 'gap' in the timetable has given me time to distribute the hundreds of science and maths books donated by schools across the north of England. The boxes each weigh about 25 kg and having travelled 6000 miles are a bit battered. I urged teachers to take care as they carried the boxes carefully to a waiting motorcycle, where they were perched precariously on the pillion.

"Let me get someone to carry that box, Sister."

Sister Auxilia, headteacher of the local Catholic girls' school, was having none of it.

"We were taught to carry these loads as young girls, Adrian."

And with that she swung the box up, to rest on her head and with the lightest touch of her hand to guide it, she strolled casually down the path.

On Monday morning, as happens every Monday morning, the college gathers for its assembly at 7.00am. The national anthem is sung, the national flag unfurled and the report of cleanliness, food and sports was read by the student leader. No outstanding events were to be noted, other than a baby was delivered on Saturday night. A baby, whose mother had tried to hide her pregnancy for many months, was taken by a tutor to the nearby hospital. So scared was the mother that she convinced the doctor that the baby was dead. The doctor was convinced and advised the nurses of the imminent miscarriage but the nurses examined the mother and realised the baby was alive. They were housed in a college house overnight and today they are both doing well.

Mwakibe's small-holding is thriving. He now wears blue polyester overalls, green wellington boots and thick industrial gloves for his work in the garden. He has built a hen coop from broken chairs and desks retrieved from the back of the college, after special permission was granted to me by the scary Mkunga and he plans to be selling eggs and chicken very soon. He has money in his pocket nowadays.

There are the usual comings and goings, the disruption caused by weather and riots, the road-works that are almost finished and then have to start again because the rains come; the babies born, weddings to plan, clothes to wash, tests to mark, seeds to plant, punctures to mend, rice to sell, and sometimes, sodas to sip, under the shade of a great mango tree. Always, the price of everything goes up and life around Mtwara goes on.

Saturday, 23 February 2013

The spirit of enterprise

Under the shade of the canopied mango tree, on the hard brown dirt, sits the bicycle fundi, Yusuph Lukanga. He repairs bicycles and shoes. He squats on a wooden folded stool called mbuzi or goat, with his withered legs, almost certainly a result of polio earlier in his life, folded beneath him. He moves around town in a huge, iron hand-cranked tricycle, with a small wooden box strapped to the back in which he keeps a tidy array of tools. He is a charismatic man, unshaven with a round head, and deep, black skin that glows. His teeth are all the whiter though he rarely smiles. He views me quizzically, perhaps suspiciously, as I take my place on the wooden bench that serves as a pew on which we wait our turn. His apprentices and acolytes are younger men, chatting too loudly sometimes, ever conscious of his ministrations. Two of the group depart briefly to return with a large aluminium plate of ugali and spinach which they lay by his side, while one brings a jug of water with which to wash the fundi's hands.

In broken English and Kiswahili, he asks if I have bought him the welding machine he wants,
"Bado", I reply. (Not yet). He shrugs as if he had anticipated this and I try to distract him with talk of the wheel which I need him to mend. It is quite badly buckled and as he spins it nonchalantly in his calloused hands, he quotes a figure which is far too high. We barter. He doesn't smile, but we agree on a price about the equivalent of the cold beer I'll sip at the ocean later that day. Before he starts work on my wheel, he lets one of the young men wash his hands and slowly he rolls the ugali into small gobbets and having dipped it in the fiery sauce, pops it in his mouth, watching me all the while, as I exchange greetings with the numerous bystanders who love to be seen with the mzungu.

It would seem that there is a crying need for money and training for many prospective self-employed fundi, shopkeepers, and salespeople. Maibras tells me that the banks are hopeless at meeting this demand. The process is slow, bureaucratic and at times corrupt. Many people have little faith in it and prefer instead to go to family and friends. Someone suggested to me the other day that for many Africans, their ambitions and capacity to plan for the future are blighted by the uncertainty of future government policies and by the demands from family for a share in their fortune. If it is likely that you will lose or at best have to share your wealth, then perhaps, it's less attractive to work so hard to acquire it. I'm not sure though. It seems that there is something in some people which drives them to make money; which drives them to work hard and look for every opening. Some have that drive- some don't.

Maibras and I went to see Mama Zuhura last week. She is a large woman wrapped in a kanga and a colourful scarf round her head. She lives in a collection of small rooms round a dirty yard where children are playing with some plastic lids. The cleanest room, empty of everything save a large fridge, has a small window cut into one wall. The window is framed with a steel grill into which is cut an opening, the size of a large plate. From this room, with the help of this large gleaming fridge, Mama Zuhura serves mutton soup to the workers from the small industrial estate close by.

Last week I visited Emmanuel in his stationery shop. It's half a container with a cable providing power to two old computers. Emmanuel is a slight man with a neatly trimmed moustache. His wife works for the council in the neighbouring town, so they can afford the rent on the container and their house. They have one small child. He shows me the broken copier which he hopes to replace.
"With the new printer-copier I can buy from Dar, I can charge only two hundred shillings per page and compete with the others," he boasts. Tanzania's bureaucracy means that everyone needs a copy of every official document and there are dozens of documents covering every aspect of everyday life. In the short-term there will be a heavy demand for copying and office services.

Mwakibe's mum has made a success of her shop so far. She sells flour, rice, beans, sugar, soap, pens, razors and a selection of sweets, tea and small novelties - an eclectic range of whatever she thinks sells and she can afford. She writes nothing down and when I ask her about margins, she looks puzzled,
"Sir," Mwakibe translates, "She doesn't always write things down," I suspected she didn't write anything down, but, on the other hand, since she'd moved with Tamasha and Mwakibe, from her rented house, she'd made the repayments and fed her family.

And then there's Mwakibe, who has just bought nine small hens.
"Any eggs today, Mwakibe,"
"Bado, sir. They are still learning about their new home."
The work on his hen coop was completed last week and yesterday he went with his mum, Asha, to their family's village and returned with a great basket of hens. Mwakibe still wants a driving job in the army or the Port. He thinks that such a job would have status and a steady wage. He's not wrong. A job in the public sector would also be a job for life, assure him of a pension and holidays.

I sat and watched my buckled wheel take shape. This man had never claimed a per diem in his life and no-one was about to offer him a pension. His thick powerful fingers had been working like this for years and if illness doesn't take him he'll do it for years to come.

"So you didn't bring me a welding machine from England," said Yusuph "If I had one, I could build many more tri-cycles like this one."
Maibras and I have a scheme that will lend him the money for the welding machine and see him repay the loan within the year.
"Is there a large demand for such machines?" I asked.

"Ndiyo," he grinned "There's lots of work for welding machines if you look for it, especially these," handling his great iron beast of a tricycle." And with that he span my new wheel with his thumb, cast an expert eye down the rim to check it was true and without a second glance handed it to one of his young assistants. "It's ready," he said over his shoulder. He didn't look at me, just returned to the small child's shoe and picked up his six inch steel needle.
 "Give the mzungu his bicycle."

May 2013

Sad times

The last few months saw Maibras and me working more and more closely together; patrolling the area, chatting to those families we had identified as in greatest need and meeting frequently with Philibert to ensure that our local actions were transparent and recorded. By March we had met with the local authority and drawn up a list of names; Maibras had organized a meeting of the local community and explained our work to them. We would be helping seven families with food and school uniforms; we would be registering as many local people as possible with a community health insurance scheme and employing four local people as litter pickers and street cleaners.
It was decided some months ago, one evening with Philibert at the Upendo Grocery, that something very local and very practical could be achieved and so Philibert introduced us to Maibras. Since then we have met each day in his small spotlessly clean house where a young man is always to be found cooking and cleaning. Gulshen, his wife, is often to be found sitting in the shade of the great mango tree, catching some fresh air in the last breeze of the evening.
One Sunday lunch-time, Maibras' living room was hectic. Five of us sat on chairs, the floor and a small wooden bench and agreed a work programme for the coming weeks. Maibras coughed throughout the meeting.
"That sounds like a bad cough, Maibras,"
"I know. I will go to the clinic tomorrow."
One feature of Tanzanian life that we still find surprising is the speed and ease with which people who can afford it, go to see a doctor. Where in the UK we would self-medicate with a paracetomol or a good night's sleep, Maibras will go to the doctor – a doctor he knows and trusts – and take a prescription for medicine.
Gulshen came through the room,
"And you will ask if there is anything to be done about the sores on your legs,"
Maibras' legs had red weeping ulcers on his shins.
"If they are not better tomorrow, I will see the Polish surgeon at Nyangao."
As I left, I felt more alarmed than I would back home. I met Caroline for lunch and there by coincidence sat the very same Polish surgeon. He had lived in southern Tanzania for many years, and was widely respected. I told him about Maibras and that he should perhaps expect a visit.
"I know the man," he said. "And truthfully, what you have described doesn't sound good."

I was even more alarmed. I called round to see Maibras the next morning but Gulshen informed me that he had left early for Nyangao. I phoned him that evening, but there was no reply. On the following evening, Tuesday, Philibert phoned,

"Very sad to say, Adrian, but Maibras died this afternoon."

I was stunned. We had become accustomed to death, of neighbours and the mothers or fathers of colleagues, of people we didn't know, dying suddenly and inexplicably. But for Maibras to be alive, not well perhaps, but alive and lively in his sitting room on Sunday and to be dead by Tuesday, seemed unreal.

The funeral was held the following day. A huge canopy was hurriedly but expertly erected in front of his house and a great carpet laid for *imamu* and dignitaries to come, to sit and pray. Scores of people crammed into his yard, women huddled at the front of the house, men in the large garden to the rear. After prayers and blessings, followed by huge plates of *pilau,* we made our way by car, bicycle, foot, coach, even police vehicle, to the huge unkempt cemetery on the edge of town. By the time the body was gently lowered into the earth, the number had swollen to hundreds.

The weeks sped by. Our days were filled with meetings with officials, endless conversations with local men and women wanting small loans for their businesses and establishing a small office in Maibras front yard, where a local council official, Justin, would continue the efficient administration of our small charity. Mwakibe quickly established warm friendships with each of the mothers we were supporting. If I approached them to see that all was well, a visible tension filled their faces, but on the mention of Mwakibe, their faces softened and a warm movement of their heads nodded their approval.

As the rains eased and the cooler weather arrived, talk of trouble from amongst younger militants filtered into our conversations at Upendo. Speeches by Ministers designed to appease communities about the future of gas and the benefits that would accrue to the local area here, seemed to inflame people and soon there was talk of strikes and violence. We were due to return to the UK but as the rumours turned into road blocks I began to enquire about flights.

After several days of rumours, the start of the strike came suddenly. All shopkeepers were told to close and all travel was stopped. In college, we heard only gossip from Chiwembe who cycled in on his great iron bicycle.

"The army is moving in," he said. "There will be fighting soon."

Later that day we heard the first explosions followed by rapid gunfire. Plumes of smoke billowed into the sky above what I thought were the shops near Mwakibe's home. Mwakibe seemed to be able to cycle in and out of college at will, but Maskat insisted that we should not venture out.

Later that day, the first stories of deaths – a woman killed by soldiers – darkened our mood even further. Whilst we were safe in college, Caroline and I were scheduled to return to UK and I was worried that we would not be able to make it to Dar. Buses were being stopped; there was talk of the bridge at Mikindani having been blown up. Our friends from America had hurriedly packed and driven to Dar the previous week. When I called them they advised us to leave Mtwara as soon as we could. There was talk of the airport closing and in any case the road to the airport was blocked.

In the end, we acted quickly. Confirmation from the airline that a flight would leave that afternoon, a hurried negotiation with the neighbouring college for transport and with luggage squeezed into the old Land Rover, we set off along deserted roads. We passed shops shuttered, car tyres smouldering by the roadside and occasionally the blasted remains of a business bombed for defying the strike. As we left the town to take the road to the airport we came across a road block, something we feared most. A dozen young men and boys sat astride a huge flame-tree cut down for this purpose, lying across the road. They waved their *panga* at us, shouting at us to stop. Our driver looked at me. He was scared, but he changed down a gear, swung the great rattling beast of a car down a rough track and sped along the roadside, skirting the road block. The crowd of young men were angry; one or two made to chase us, but thankfully the rains had stopped and the roads were dry. We left the road block in a haze of dust and smiled and clapped each other on the shoulders as we sped off to the airport.

We returned in August to a town where the strikes and the killings were talked about as history. Shops that had been destroyed were re-built and life had returned to normal. The gas would still be piped to Bagomoyo and the road to Dar had still not been finished.

Whales, a water closet and a wedding.

In the dry winter months, as the dusty breezes cool each night and sheets are used to wrap up from the cold, Mikindani bay becomes the scene of occasional sightings of huge hump-back whales. We took a motor boat out into the bay and drew alongside the great black length of the creatures, at a distance of about fifty meters. The engines were cut and the ten of us fell quiet as a hushed respect lapped over us. There were three of them – two adults and a child; the smaller whale seeming to gambol excitedly, its great tail swishing and splashing alongside the dark, sleek bulk of its mother. As the whales spouted their plumes of spray then dived into the depths, we started again our chugging pursuit - a pilgrimage of cameras.

Noel, a large Zambian with a long, long lens on his Nikon camera, had been with us to see the whales. We spoke about his business, which is looking after the security and other logistical issues for about eighty-six visiting white men, all involved with the gas industry. Mtwara is changing fast as the trickle down of gas exploration begins to have a visible effect. Metalled roads, razor wired compounds and smartly dressed armed guards are signs of a new investment from which local people seem to benefit very little.

The violence and fear that marked our departure from Mtwara in May has left few signs. The soldiers have left and the burnt out shops are being re-built. The conflict has always centred on the government's decision to pipe the gas north to Bagomoyo rather than process it here. Local believe people that processing the gas here will bring investment. Many still threaten disruption if their demands are not met; yet, all the way along the road from Dar, at intervals of perhaps one hundred miles, are great scars gouged out of the vegetation on the roadside and hundreds of eerie back pipes, piled high and deep, are the silent looming indication that the government would always have its way.

One indication of the new money that the gas has brought, is the soaring price of land and rents. Mwakibe and I cycled out to the neighbouring town of Mikindani last week, and took the unmade dusty road from Mikindani up the escarpment to the plateau, some five miles inland. Our destination was the aptly named Mjimwema – peaceful town, there to meet a self-made and successful farmer, Ima, short for Emmanuel, who owns and farms two hectares of land. We joined him at his small house of mud and sticks at the centre of a large field of meticulously planted pineapple plants, edged with orange trees and teak. We sat under the swooping mango tree, drank citrus chai and nibbled his freshly shelled nuts. We were interested in government demarcated land as it becomes available and how much it will cost. The cost is high – at least for us. The whole area is to be developed and ought to be good land for local people to settle and develop, but if the prices are forced up, speculators will move in and local people will be worse off not better. I didn't share all these thoughts with Ima. Ima was more keen for me to see his pride and joy. I thought it would be his 40,000 litre cement water tank, but no, just next to the house, with their own doors, roofs and locks, stood two fine toilets, tiled, plumbed and padlocked.

Mwakibe has become a central figure in the work we undertake in the local neighbourhood of Kiangu. Since the sad death of Maibras, Mwakibe has taken an increasingly visible role around the families we are supporting. He takes the small party of women to the big market each month to buy the flour, beans, soap, oil and whatever else is on their list. As Mr Ngairo drilled them this week-end on the effectiveness of the assistance they are receiving, they answered nervously, afraid of his piercing questions and his scrawly notebook; but when he mentioned Mwakibe, their faces softened and their eyes smiled.

We're trying to distribute four thousand books, donated by West Yorkshire schools, but a combination of transport, teachers' nervousness to take responsibility and their lack of familiarity with books, is making the task take longer than it should. Mwaikibe and I will attempt to start a mobile library service for schools next week, using as a pilot the handful of schools within a ten minute cycle ride of where we live. Our first task is to design and build a box for the bicycle which Mwakibe will take from school to school.

Last week-end's wedding between Chiwembe and his bride from Arusha, Mary, offered me another new and hopefully, unique, opportunity. The format we have grown accustomed to now, starts with the invitation card for which we all make a financial contribution. That pays for the glittery lights, the maroon and white draped curtains and sashes, the booming PA and the master of ceremonies and perhaps his suit with tails. This particular MC sported a huge glittering ring that he was adept at sparkling at every possible moment.

Sadly, much of the Tanzanian tradition has left the ceremony to be replaced by pale imitations of a flimsy western habit. So we have the cutting of the cake, the first dance and the interminable photos. What we have in Tanzania which I think is missing from our western ceremony, is the formal presentation of one family to another, together with speeches from both families – sometimes from mothers as well as fathers and always with a sonorously impressive blessing. What we have in Tanzania and what we happily lack in western weddings is the formal presentation of the sparkling wine. Two bottles of odd coloured sparkling wine were brought to the front of the room by Haule and Malibiche, using a slow seductive African shuffle. I had been enlisted by the MC to assist with opening them and in the same soft shuffle took over the teasing dance. We stroked the bottles, we held them aloft; we sloped over to each family inviting them to stroke and bless the bottle in turn; we teased the guests, the MC sliding forward shaking the bottle all the while, shuffling backwards with the bottle held high. Eventually, as the guests could contain their excitement no longer we prized off the corks and with an inevitably disappointing spurt of froth, poured the plonk for the bridal party – one of the stranger examples of public service I have performed.

Sunday, 29 September 2013

Warm ugali

Life in Mtwara is changing fast. Three years ago, bread was hard to come by. Now, a soft tasteless bread is available in most small shops, whilst the Sisters have their heavy German style bread on sale in at least two shops. Strange, then, the reaction to the proposal to sell goats milk.

"People in Mtwara won't buy it, Mr Adrian."
"Why not?"
"It's not the tradition."
Tanzanian's affection for claiming that things should not change because they are traditional, defies logic, at times. For example, I can point out that it is traditional for men and women to die young, for children to be malnourished and for girls not to go to secondary school, but most would agree that these are traditions Tanzania should lose.

Our plan to try and secure a sustainable source of nutrition in the form of goats' milk is facing some resistance – mainly because "people won't buy goat milk". We'll see. For an investment of ten goats, each of the fifteen most vulnerable children in Kiangu could be given a large glass of milk each day. Cows are preferred. I asked Mama Koka, who has goats, why she does not sell goat milk. "Because I have cows." The logic is insurmountable.

In discussing animals this week, the topic of wazungu and their pets came up. Why would you keep an animal in your home, we asked? My group was trying really hard to be cooperative and enlightened.
"I keep a cat because it catches rats," said Pendo
"Hens are easy to keep and provide fresh eggs." said Arnold.
"Dogs are good for security. They deter thieves and chase away witches."
"Witches?" I checked.
"Yes. Have you never noticed that if your dog barks and you go outside to see what's there and there's nothing? That's because the dog has chased away the witch."
Again, I thought, insurmountable.

And yet, times are changing here. Francis is home from Dar while he waits for his course professor to call him. He has nothing to do each day but wait. But it doesn't seem to worry him. He has marriage on his mind. He plans to marry next year, once the bride price is agreed and the festivities paid for. As we prepare to sell all our worldly possessions here, before returning to UK, I remember the first days with Francis. I recall explaining to him as he listened in wonder to the concept of an electrically powered implement for heating water. His eyes widened and then smiled as the idea dawned on him. Back then, we went to the great hardware store and queued for half an hour to buy an iron stick with an electric element and a plastic handle, the closest thing Francis could think of as an instrument for boiling water. Today the small shops next to *soko kubwa* (big market) are full of cheap Chinese kettles, called *jagi*, or jug, in kiswahili.

Mwakibe, Mr Ali and I went out to Mbae to look at a piece of land. The vendor had told us a good price for good land so I squashed into the bajaj with Mr Abdul Rahman and bounced along a dusty track for about five kilometres until we came to a hillside that defeated our valiant three wheeler. We continued on foot, across two small hills, along a dusty dry valley and finally up a small escarpment to the start of a steep sided hill. This was the 'good land' he had brought us to see. I left it with Mwakibe. Even the ever-optimistic Mwakas could see the futility of this journey. Land that a year ago, perhaps a few months ago, would have been sold for less than £400, Mr Abdul was asking three times that price. As we drove home, hot and bothered, the large and hitherto silent Mr Abdul nevertheless managed to ask me for payment, for 'disturbance'. I smiled, shook his hand, wished him a pleasant Sunday and left him outside his mosque.

There are thirteen children in the small district near us who are listed by the council as 'vulnerable.' These six families are supported by friends and family with a small monthly grant to cover some rice, flour, oil, soap, school fees and whatever other basics can be bought for £40. A health insurance card is paid for too which covers the whole family; but the insurance card does not include transport to Dar, to the only specialist paediatric hospital available to treat young Sharifa. Sharifa is nine and has an abnormally swollen and deformed knee, perhaps a genetic malformation or perhaps TB. She has been referred to Dar for assessment and treatment. She has something wrong with her left eye and the hospital in Dar can also look at that. In the main regional hospital here there is not even an x-ray machine. Philibert and I have drafted the letter to the council to ask for help for the bus fares for Sharifa and her mum but we need to create our own emergency fund for when this sort of thing happens again.

I met Chiwembe the other day. He's been on leave following his wedding. He told me he was tired and he looked it. Just before the wedding, he'd driven all the way to Arusha to attend the bride's 'send-off' party, then all the way back via Dar to make all the plans for the wedding. Now he has the task of setting up home on the newly bought plot in Magomeni, a significant and valuable wedding gift. Chiwembe is a softly spoken man with a demure smile and natural shyness. I asked how he was enjoying married life. If he could, he would have blushed, but instead, a raw belly laugh rippled round the table as Malibiche explained,

"Mr Adrian. Now, you see, every day, he has warm ugali." Ugali is the stiff porridge made from maize flour.

This obviously could be a crude euphemism or it could literally be one of the major benefits of married life here. After three years, I'm still not sure.

Thursday, 24 October 2013

Sports Week

I haven't been one to criticise my hosts here. I have tried to understand a different culture in a different part of the world with a very different history. I particularly try hard to see the country in the context of its colonised past; a history of abuse and exploitation, of stunted growth and development and isolation from investment, prosperity and all the social and education benefits which flow from such economic growth. To see inefficiency or lack of motivation at work as a sign of Africa's innate inadequacy is to misunderstand what led to this state of affairs in the first place. But to ignore the lost opportunities, to turn a blind eye to the wasted time and resources or to forget the lack of care taken with anything in the public domain is to ignore what one might see as this country's future. It's my view that like it or not, for Tanzania to lift itself from poverty, it will need to do some of the things, belatedly, that the rest of the world takes for granted. It must educate its young people to think rather than just pass examinations; it must empower its communities so that they can take pride in the public space around them; and it must nurture a sense of urgency so that people understand that to do tomorrow what could be done today is to let someone else do it, take the credit for it and get richer than you as a result. Mtwara Teachers College is a government funded training centre for about five hundred students, each of whom is supposed to have passed 'A' level to study for the Diploma in Secondary Education, qualifying them automatically for a salaried position in a secondary school. On graduation, after a month or two, each graduate is 'posted' to a secondary school somewhere in the country, usually according to their stated preferences. So, if you want to work in Mtwara, you will probably get to work in Mtwara; and if you don't, you won't. Arriving as a European in a teachers' training college, it takes a long time to rid yourself of those European pre-conceptions of what might motivate students and teachers to work here. Asked what are the factors which persuaded students to come to study for the diploma here, all agreed that money or a vocational drive to teach were low priorities. Access to higher education and job security were the most important factors. In the public sector, increases in salary are linked to academic qualifications and paid study leave is an entitlement after three years' service; hence, many teachers, tutors or government workers are often away from their post. Most students here have joined this course, not because they are personally driven to be teachers, but because it is the only route to higher education available to them; to others, already primary school teachers, it is a route to a higher salary; and still to others it is a route to a job for life which they can keep whilst pursuing other private interests. Foreigners, imagining that what the place lacks is motivation or modern management, are overlooking the much deeper problems of poverty and disengagement.

Taking a step back to look at the college in a global development context, it is clear that there is a mismatch between what the country needs from its teachers and what the Ministry, through colleges such as this, is capable of achieving. Five hundred students, motivated mainly by the prospect of a certificate, rather than a job, following a curriculum that bears the marks of one designed by frustrated academics rather than classroom practitioners, taught by tutors who feel abused by their employer, underpaid and under-valued, with little experience of the classroom and with few resources and dilapidated classrooms, are unlikely to become effective nor inspirational teachers.The extent to which this lack of motivation to excel pervades this college is seen in a number of ways: firstly, this two-year diploma course loses approximately three-quarters of its possible teaching time to other activities – meetings, holidays, late registration, or, like this week, a sports bonanza - all result in classes cancelled and students left to their own devices, but with neither access to quiet study space, books nor computers; secondly, tutors, who are timetabled to teach but three hours a week, can often leave the class, set work on the board or join classes together to deliver lectures. Of course, the syllabus is so content-rich that lectures are perhaps a more effective way of teaching.

Perhaps, most tellingly, and in stark contrast to a deep apathy in the classroom, is the college's response - both corporate and at a personal level - to extra-curricular activities. Excitement, bonhomie and a deep sense of community and shared experience often pervades the campus for such events. This week's sports bonanza is a simple competition between selected athletes from five colleges across this region; and yet, after fumbled attempts by the Principal to appear to be maintaining the taught timetable, within one hour of the start of the competition on Monday morning, tutors and students together had engineered a revolt and the timetable was cancelled. Over ninety percent of students and tutors moved to the athletics field just to cheer on their team. What happens every week-end in Europe – competitive matches in volleyball, basketball, netball, football and athletics – has consumed the energies of almost everyone here. An extra-ordinary briefing by one tutor to a hundred students resulted in whooping and cheering, chanting and dancing, as they proceeded to the touchline to shout and sing and beat their drums through the baking morning heat.It is easy, sometimes appealing, to look at what happens here and what doesn't happen and blame the lack of quality teaching on a benignly corrupt system which allows incompetent people to waste time and money; but that would be to overlook the deep-seated cultural context of authoritarianism which pervades most aspects of public life, to overlook the connection between authoritarianism and the consequent levels of disempowerment experienced by most public sector workers. The energy and commitment which has gone into preparing this sports bonanza is evidence for cynics, that if you give someone control of what they are doing, give them an opportunity to influence directly the outcome and make it relevant to their lives, their sense of personal satisfaction and the size of the contribution they are prepared to make is huge. If the teaching and learning in this college could mirror the energy and commitment shown on the sports field, the improvements could be very significant. For Tanzania to lift itself from poverty, it will need to think hard about how and why it educates its young people. Certainly a shift away from donor dependency is needed and with it a greater belief in its own capacity to change. But, for those international commentators who continue to use targets and measures as sticks with which to beat Africa, they should look more closely at governance and empowerment. I can see all around me the evidence of local action for local people. It starts in the family, but it quickly emanates to the street or the village. Once the straitjacket of the Ministry and its missives are put away, this college acts like an African village and enjoys life.

Sunday, 3 November 2013

Kelvin and Rashidi

We were delighted to accept an invitation last week to an impromptu party in honour of Kelvin's graduation from Form IV. Graduation is generally celebrated before the examinations as most students are not seen in school again once the examinations have finished; but on this occasion, the ceremony was cancelled, according to the school, on the grounds of cost; according to one inspector, because of ill-discipline. Whatever the reason, the Form IV students from Shangani Secondary, the school where I first taught some English classes when we arrived in 2010, were disappointed not to be dressing up for their very own graduation.Back in 2010 on one of our first trips down to the beach, we had been approached by two very confident young boys – one very tall and slim, the other short and squat; one, the tall one, deliberate and accurate in his English; the other, shy and nervous and with a weaker vocabulary. We had been warned of cheeky young boys approaching us and asking for money so we were on our guard. In fact, these two young boys were Kelvin and Muksini, Form I students at Shangani Secondary and Kelvin was to become a regular visitor and friend. Kelvin's mum and dad had separated some years earlier and Kelvin, for the sake of his education, was sent to Mtwara from Moshi to stay with his aunt. Over the years, I have talked to him about his anger and resentment at this state of affairs and only a few months ago had he been able to say how the relationship with his father had been repaired and how delighted he was that both his mum and dad would travel from Lushoto and Dar respectively to attend his graduation ceremony. In fact, his mum and aunt had arrived before they were told of the cancellation, but his dad cancelled the visit and Kelvin's disappointment was palpable. A small party was organised to be held in the garden of Kelvin's house in a poor but quiet district on the edge of Mtwara. We sat under the banana trees and ate a feast of pilau with chicken and beef, as Kelvin's friends regaled me with tales from school, their favourite teachers and how they liked to sing, "You are my sunshine". They were an impressive group of seventeen year olds; some of them a little shy, but each of them polite in conversation and hugely respectful of their host and at the same time, full of jokes and singing. It made for a wonderful evening.

Rashidi Saidi, is a short muscly man, with dark, dark skin with a bluish sheen. His eyes suggest a nervousness but when he smiles, his face relaxes into a warm openness. He has dark watery eyes, one of which is set aslant which adds to his timid appearance. He sits with Mwakibe on a wooden bench on Maibras' patio next to the rusty containers which were to be the chairman's 'Lite Bites Snack Bar'. Death brought those plans to an abrupt end and now the unfinished patio is used for our impromptu meetings while Gulshen, Maibras' widow, rests in the cooling breezes which swirl around the house. One of Maibras' legacies is the small micro loans scheme in operation throughout the small district of Kiangu of which Maibras was chairman and today Mwakibe and Rashidi are discussing how the business of selling soap, cosmetics and cheap jewellery is progressing.

Rashidi's family receives support from our small charity. Each month Mwakibe accompanies Mama Waliviu, Rashidi's wife, to the market to buy rice, flour, beans, soap, charcoal and any other basic household goods the family needs and the money will allow. Mama Waliviu has until recently earned a few thousand shillings as a street sweeper and now makes chappati and tea and braids hair on her baraza to make some more money. Rashidi used to work as a builder but jobs are scarce and he finds work where he can. In April, he will move to the villages near his family home where he can earn money milling maize, but that is seasonal work and right now, in the dry season the fields are empty and bare. If he and his brother could borrow the money to buy a milling machine they are convinced they could earn good money around the farms near their home at Nachingwea Rashidi was to have started a small goat rearing business but he remained unconvinced that anyone would buy his goat milk and instead persuaded me to make him a small loan to start this micro enterprise. Now, he traipses around dusty streets around the outlying districts and suburbs of sprawling Mtwara selling cheap Chinese trinkets from a plastic bowl which he holds deftly with one hand, swinging it down and round from shoulder to floor in one swift motion. His bowl is smartly packed with soaps, lotions, nose studs and hair dye. Starting with little more than a handful of cosmetics and jewellery two weeks ago, he now has stock and cash worth treble the initial capital; not yet a living that will support his family, but he is committed to trying. I will try and persuade him again to take on some goats as neither goats nor cosmetics alone are likely to provide him with the weekly income he needs. His two young boys are growing. One is already at school and the other will start soon. I've left Mwakibe to discuss the question of accounts with him. My Kiswahili still won't allow me to say or understand but a few words beyond greetings and ordering supplies in shops. Persuading Rashidi to keep rudimentary records is beyond both my language skills and the limits of my patience. His erratic ways disguises a willingness to work. Today I found him, digging a huge pit for a new toilet outside Gulshen's house. By evening, he had dug a whole, two metres wide and three metres deep and was half-way through lining it with stones and cement. He smiled up at me with a wide grin and upturned thumb. Mwakibe had asked him to produce some accounts but this was work and he couldn't refuse it.

Mwakibe is trying to revise his knowledge of mathematics. He has an interview and test next Saturday for a place at a technical training college. If he is not selected, he doesn't know what he will do. He has a Division 4 pass at Form IV which would make him eligible to apply for a certificate in primary school education or a nursing course, but he still needs to pass an entrance examination and pay the course fees.

This morning in Mass, we prayed especially for those students about to take their Form IV examinations. Sadly, this might yet be more effective than studying and revising. Education is the key to a prosperous future here. Education and a family that can afford to pay the fees and encourage you. So the time has come once again for the country to enter that annual national lottery which is the Form IV examination; thousands of young people sitting examinations, the courses for which have been, on the whole, badly taught and which will be marked both inconsistently and, on the whole, unfairly. We can only hope that this lottery which gave Mwakibe the lowest pass possible, failed Philibert's daughter completely and omitted Rashidi from its clutches altogether, will treat Kelvin more kindly.

Friday, 29 November 2013

All is rarely what it seems.

They stood for two hours in the baking sun, waiting for word from the office as to whether their demands were to be met. It started two weeks ago when a slight young man, Hildabrant, quiet and studious was taken to hospital, complaining of pains in his chest and difficulty breathing. No diagnosis was forthcoming and soon reports came out that his legs were now paralysed and that the pain was even more severe. After two weeks he was transferred in a ten hour journey by car to Dar es Salaam where he died two days later. Students were informed in a solemn announcement on the Sunday afternoon.

On Monday morning, as students should have been preparing for examinations, the campus resonated with haunting harmonies from four or five classrooms – Lutherans, Catholics, all denominations stood and prayed and sang. By Monday evening a small number of students were quietly pressing for the college to relax its decision that no delegation from this college would attend the funeral. By Tuesday mornings, there was a mood of anger around campus. Their fellow had died and they wanted to mourn him properly. The entire student body was taking direct strike action, had refused to eat porridge and was now refusing to enter the classrooms until their demands to see their fellow student mourned appropriately, were met in full. Tutors were adamant that it was unnecessary, that the students could not be trusted to go, that their motive was to take money for the fare.

By mid-morning, some students had spoken to me of the intimidation they faced from fellow students. Clearly there was a small group determined to see their collective action succeed. Some were threatened when they went for their breakfast; one man's porridge cup was knocked roughly from his hands as he was told,
"No-one is taking porridge this morning. We are together until the administration changes its mind."

And so they stood, in serried ranks, small groups occasionally attempting a feeble rendition of the college song; others perched on their haunches, an exercise book shielding their heads from the searing heat. Throughout this showdown, the student president, Oscar, only elected some two months earlier, stood impassively, looking on. Oscar is a tall man with a childlike face, a humble smile and an unctuous voice that I now know belies a scheming malevolence. Evidence was emerging that he and a small clique had distorted information regarding the arrangements for the funeral and that the bullying and intimidation was directed by him.

As the principal stood fiercely in the morning heat, resistance withered and students traipsed back to their desks. The crisis was over and now the ringleaders needed to be dealt with. It remained unclear, but Maskat had suggested that the whole episode was engineered by the president and one or two others for the sole purpose of levering the cost of bus fares from the college. Oscar still owed me an explanation as to what had happened to the TSH30,000 I gave him to buy seeds and fertiliser, so I was tempted to believe Maskat.

From the morbid to the sublime, there was to be a visit to a remote and beautiful beach. We invited a small group of friends to spend a day at perhaps the most beautiful beach in the world at Msimbati. For most local people, the name Msimbati is associated with gas, as it's off the coast at Msimbati that BG is extracting liquid natural gas and in the process provoking much local hostility. We were twenty-five sun-seekers, an eclectic group of old, young, African, European and American. Mwakibe had offered to organise a local bus to take us, but something told me to have him double-check that the bus he had ordered for the Saturday morning was in shape and ready. At four o'clock on Friday he phoned. I could see there was a problem as soon as the man spoke. Mwakibe's face fell as we realised we had only that evening to find another bus or risk disappointing the twenty-five friends booked to come with us on our 'Big Day Out'. There started a frantic hour of phoning, leaving messages, waiting nervously for calls to be returned Sister Tadea told me she was happy for us to use her big shiny new Montessori bus Mr Liwenga needed to find the driver. Liwenga, the college principal, less than dynamic, suggested I call him back at six-thirty to see if he'd found him. Not for the first time, my European habit of worrying to control rather than relaxing to see events unfurl, proved unhelpful. George called in to see Xavier the driver and confirmed he'd be there in the morning to take us all to Msimbati.

And he was, at seven, on the dot. We set off at eight and after a bumpy ride through dusty villages we arrived at a white beach in pouring rain. The sea looked murky for once, the beach seemed desolate under a grey sky but as we snorkelled, with rain beating down on our backs, we peered into a kaleidoscope of marine life, teeming with fish of every hue, darting in and out of the shimmering coral. After lunch we played cricket and football, lazed on wooden beds and sipped beer until it was time to leave. We'd done nothing, but the change of environment from bustling Mtwara on a Saturday, with its blaring speakers for weddings and football games, was enough to make it the most relaxing day out for a long, long time.

We and Mwakibe have been preparing to part for some time now. Having only the lowest pass mark at Form IV, there are few options open to him in education, but the technical training college is one such open route. He had completed a short course in electrical installation in August as a preparation for the full-time three year course due to start in January. It was expensive, but Mwakibe enjoyed it, particularly as he believed it was the useful step to successful application to the full-time course. However, after several futile cycle trips down to the college to collect his certificate, he was told by SMS that there would be no course in January. The college was not to accept admission in 2014, something they must have known when they accepted payment for the short course, but as tutors earn extra money, this was something they failed to share with the young men and women paying the course fees.

We began to look elsewhere; in particular, Ndanda, the Benedictine mission where, as well as a hospital, a nursing school, a printing press, a water bottling facility and a hydro-electric plant, there is also a vocational training college. It is small and offers high quality training, but there are very few places and competition is stiff. We began to prepare Mwakibe for the entrance examination, a simple test in literacy and numeracy and a short interview, after which we were told we would wait two weeks for the successful twelve candidates from the one hundred and twenty applicants to be informed. Earlier this week he received a phone call from a course tutor at Ndanda, informing him that he had been accepted. Mwakibe is thin and bony and I almost crushed him as we hugged and danced and whooped with excitement. We were leaving, but his future would be secure, at least for now. Five minutes later, he received another call, from another tutor, explaining gruffly that if he wanted his name to remain on the list he would have to pay TSH200,000 – a straight bribe of huge proportions as far as Mwakibe was concerned.

What to do! Mwakibe's disappointment was palpable. I could see the visions of his happy life in Ndanda disappearing from his fantasy. His face became contorted with stress and bitterness. He began to beat his forehead in anguish. He knows very well that he would never be able to persuade me to pay the bribe and his future was seeming to ebb away as quickly as it had emerged.

I needed to think carefully as to how we should react. If the man was genuine and had access to the list it would scotch Mwakibe's chances for good. If it was a bluff but he found out that Mwakibe knew it was a bluff, Mwakibe's days at the college could be miserable, as this tutor might exact some form of petty revenge. I phoned the principal, explained that I would be leaving soon and asked innocently if Mwakibe Kapinga had been admitted. Brother Sixtus confirmed that his name was on the list. With an SMS to confirm this I could relax; I was more confident than ever that the bribe was a simple corrupt opportunistic act from someone who had no control over the list but would use the two days between the list being prepared and the letters being posted out to extort money from the innocent young candidates.

Of course, few other candidates would have sponsors able to phone Brother Sixtus directly. I need a plan as to what to do about any of those potential victims. So, being a dish best served cold, we will wait until Mwakibe is registered, until he has moved to Ndanda, has started the course and established himself at the college. Only then will we see the perpetrator exposed. But we won't forget.

As we pack to leave, sell whatever useful household items we have acquired and say good-bye to friends and colleagues, it seems that these last few days have been more frenetic and more richly rewarding than usual. Is it that I am seeking some last drops of validity for our time here; or is it that my senses of what we will miss are heightened? When a woman with two scruffy children appeared on our porch looking for support, I knew exactly what to do. She was anxious that the older one could not go to school and the little one, at two years of age, had a medical condition for which she would need help. I was able immediately to refer to the principal social worker for school support, as no child of primary school age, can legally be denied a place; and Mwakibe within the hour had nipped round with the camera, photographed the family and had them registered for the community health scheme.

When I remember the youth who approached us two years ago for English lessons and I remember the times I have reprimanded him for laziness, for lateness and sometimes for simply being young, I see now a confident young man, able to use his own initiative and to whom many local people come to for assistance. Mwakibe is our own, some would say only, but nevertheless significant, success story in development.

Friday, 29 November 2013

Train to Mwanza

In the dimly lit shadows of the Dar railway station all shades and ages of Tanzanian life stood or hurried, squat on their haunches or leaned casually smoking a last cigarette. Ladies hurried carrying piles of empty buckets or armfuls of sliced bread or the ubiquitous nylon zipped back promoting Africa and all its wonders, perched atop their shawled heads. Small makeshift stalls sold water and nuts and cake and Fanta and brooches and everything you might need for a thirty-nine hour train ride to Mwanza.

We found our compartment easily because a notice board carried the hand written names of each of the occupants of each of the 1st and 2nd class compartments. This lumbering monster of a train that hadn't seen any paint, new light bulbs or even a good wash in perhaps thirty years was to be our home for the next two days. Our fan didn't work and the seats were grotty. After a swift negotiation with the lads next door we made the swap and then settled for the evening. They had just as many bugs and cockroaches as we did, so all was well. Nevertheless, the train left at 9.00 pm on the dot and we were soon served with cold beer followed by freshly cooked chicken and chips.

Our coaches had been built in the seventies and bore all the markings of that disco era, with salmon-coloured formica and other garish finishes. The windows were heavy and most needed a small section of timber inserting to prop them closed. The lower half of the window was opaque with forty years of salt and scratches and moisture. It meant that our relaxed viewing of the Tanzanian grasslands would have to be done standing with our necks craned. The upper bunk had been designed to be folded away but no-one had bothered to do that in a long time so we sat for the journey in a small den, the upper bunk above our heads, staring at an orange Formica wall, waiting for the cockroaches to scurry towards the ceiling. We became adept and smashing them with our shoes and the floor soon became littered with cockroach corpses.I took breakfast in the buffet car, where I was joined by Mr Mahsoodi, the train supervisor. An avuncular man with a shiny grey suit with the label still stitched to the outside of his cuff, Mahsoodi has been working this line since 1970. Once he knew I was British he spoke with pride of the diesel locomotive - British made - still working. Sure it needed more engineers on board to keep it going, and sure the stops were becoming longer and more frequent, but there are many more years in the engine yet.

I asked about the breakdown in the night and Mahsoodi said it was due to sloppy rails after the rain. Two guards spreading sand over the rails soon got the train moving again. There is an optimism about all the staff I've spoken to, epitomised in the electrician who came to fix the fan - yes there is an electrician on board- and seemed surprised when I asked about breakdowns,
"But of course, the train breaks down occasionally, but we have many engineers on board to fix it."
"What time do you expect we will arrive in Mwanza, Mr Mahsoodi?"

Some omelette dropped from his lip on to the cuff of his jacket and he deftly swept it away as he replied,
"Ah, Mr Adrian. It is too early to presume."
The idea of taking liberties with fate by presuming on an arrival time became a recurring theme in my conversations with train staff.

The train stops every hour or so and is greeted by hordes of women and young children selling fruit and vegetables, or baskets, or clay cookers or sugar beet or whatever local produce they have to sell.

Life on board the train is relaxed and slightly unreal - perhaps because it is so relaxed. The staff, nearly all male, work this line five or six days a week, every week. I asked one of the ticket guards Ambrose why he liked the work so much, as he's done this same job on this route now for ten years.
"I have two children and aged parents. Only a secure job like this will pay their school fees and feed my mum and dad."

We arrived at Morrogorro at about four in the morning. If we hadn't been woken by the jolts and the hawkers, the American missionaries who joined us would have seen to it that we were all awake. This middle aged couple, new to Tanzania, but very very fluent with the Bible, are here to bring the name of Jesus to those living 'in the bush' who have not heard His name. Although they speak no Kiswahili, they emulate many wazungu visitors by patronising everybody in a loud voice and comparing everything they see to familiar scenes 'back home'. Eventually I asked Jonathan whether or not his zeal would be better employed in urban America or Europe, because, as far as I could see, Christianity was thriving here in Tanzania and African priests are recruited to serve in ailing parishes in the developed world. His knowledge of Scripture was far too extensive for me as he was able to quote Chapter and Verse extensively to explain just why he and his wife were called.
"How long do you plan to stay?" I asked.
"Until The Lord calls us again," they replied.
Let's hope there are no "Network busy" issues when that does happen.

From Morrogorro to Dodoma, the landscape becomes brown and arid and dotted with flat-roofed mud houses. This region is notorious for the problems it has with water. At this time of the year, there is nothing growing and worryingly, I saw no signs of land having been prepared for rain. It's a desolate place where children minding some scrawny goats would stand and wave listlessly as the train ploughed on, belching its black plume.

There is a unique culture about the train. At each stop the guards and ticket collectors and the police (for the train is permanently staffed with six officers) greet their friends and contacts to buy or sell. There is a steady flow of young people in and out of the cabin next door, where Ambrose and his colleague conduct business, whatever that might be.

For two wazee (respectful term for old people) life on board is quite comfortable. Assuming you have nowhere to go in a hurry, no appointment to keep and you're happy reading and looking out of the window, then the daily routine beginning with breakfast of freshly cooked omelette with chai, lunch of rice and chicken and supper of chips and chicken, washed down with cold beer all served cheerily and promptly by kitchen steward Ayobu, is seductively comforting.

From Tabora to Shinyanga, we saw the effects of reliable rains. Not only was the landscape green and luscious, but the brown soil was tilled in long straight lines, awaiting planting. Judging the right time to plant maize - or rice - is critical. Too soon and the seeds will dry and perish; too late and the land will be too wet or you will lose critical growing time. From Tabora we saw an abundance of fruits and vegetables. We also saw many more goats and cattle. For the first time we saw donkeys used as beasts of burden. Everywhere, families would smile and wave as the train chugged by. Women stooped double would straighten and smile; children would race barefoot towards the train squealing and waving, shouting and jumping when thy caught sight of Caroline waving back. This train, the only train, only passes twice a week, so it's quite a feature in their lives.

There's time to chat with fellow travellers as the miles trundle by. Next door but one, on the other side of Ambrose and his business deals, is Mr Athumani, an elderly gentleman, travelling alone to his home near Shinyanga. As a retired accountant, I suggested he had no economic reason for travelling by train.
"No. You are right. But I am in no hurry and the buses are so dangerous."
We chatted as we chugged through the verdant countryside, fields of mango trees stretched into the distance and neatly ploughed fields with irrigation channels stood stiffly waiting for the rains. This is a fertile land and one can almost see the appreciation of such fecundity in the faces of the men and women on the land. When he got off the following afternoon, a man helped him with his luggage as well as each of the items he had bought - the cooker, the branch of green bananas, onions, spinach and a box of vegetable oil - each of them gifts for his family, a considerable number of which, old and young, greeted him as he alighted, with a curtsey and a kiss.

At the small station stop where Mr Athumani waved good-bye, the senior driver Ahmad, informed me that the engine oil was too thin and that they could either uncouple the goods wagons to lighten the load or have some more oil sent forward from Tabora. As the driver and engineers discussed this quandary, I tried to communicate telepathically my preferred option and sat on the grass and chatted with Windridge, the most confident, reflective and intelligent thirteen year old I have met for a long time. Home to stay with his grandmother while he awaits notice of his Standard 7 exam results and passage to secondary school, he was keen to question me about all aspects of my life and life in Europe,

"Tell me, sir. I read on the BBC website that an old person can die in your country and no-one know about it. Is this true?"

"Sadly, yes, Windridge. It has happened."

"I would like to visit England soon, but there must be no community there."

Thankfully my preference for uncoupling the goods wagons won the day and the driver within the hour had the goods wagons parked in an overgrown siding. I was unsure what goods were being carried but I suspect traders in Mwanza will remain disappointed for some weeks to come. The policemen, Ambrose, Ayobu and the rest of the staff began their farewells. The Texan missionary had locked a forlorn Muslim in the buffet car with a copy of the Bible and was explaining all about Isaac and Ishmael in a very loud voice. Fortunately this was drowned by the singing and harmonica playing of his wife, while the rest of the carriage looked on bemused.

As we began our final stage of the journey, the sun was dipping below the skyline in the west, flooding our carriage with light as we limped north towards Lake Victoria.

****

Part Three

Caroline and I travelled back to UK after this short visit to Lake Victoria. We stayed in a Capuchin monastery and then took a very old dirty and over-crowded bus through the Serengeti. Caroline saw the Ngorogoro crater and now it was time to go home. We travelled back to Dar by luxury coach from Arusha. With the help of Philibert I'd made good contact with the education offices in Masasi and was scheduled to return in March, but for now our adventure was over. We had learned far more than we'd given. We'd shared more from Africa than we could possibly have brought to them from Europe and we had been the clear winners in this unequal relationship.

I returned to southern Tanzania in February 2014 to conduct a short teaching programme in the town of Masasi, about a hundred miles west of Mtwara. It was funded by a private sponsor and organised by the District Education Office in Masasi.

Wednesday, 5 March 2014

Early days in Masasi
I groaned as I approached the small mini-bus leaving for Masasi. I'd thought I just felt the groan but it was heard by the young man selling nuts who flashed a broad white smile as he realised what I'd seen and said, "Jambo". I'd hoped for the larger Chinese 'Coaster' bus, high off the road, with wider seats and generally in better condition but luck had cast me forward to the creaking daladala which three men were trying to jump start as I negotiated the last space over the engine casing, facing backwards down the bus; eleven faces half smiling, half grinning as they watched this sweating white man perch close to the door. Mercifully, whether they took pity on me or I was considered a liability so close to the door, I was told to move to the front where a cushion had been placed next to the gear lever and I could squash my bum between the driver and the passenger seat. Things were looking up.

As we chugged away from the bus stand, leaving a thin trail of blue smoke hanging in the morning, I turned to my neighbour to greet him. He was a man of perhaps sixty, unshaven and with a lean weathered face and stern eyes. We greeted each other and he asked me in Kiswahili where I was going. I answered him, returned the question and he answered in English. From here a lively conversation followed in which I learned a great deal about farming, about land prices, about the Courts and about my fellow passenger, Paul.

He was a farmer, with ten acres, growing maize and breeding Nile perch. Although he had never attended secondary school and had never left the Ndanda area, he spoke excellent English using archaic vocabulary, indicating a superior education which had stayed with him for fifty years. We discussed the problems he had in getting his fish to market. If he had a refrigerated unit he could transport the catch to Mtwara where he could sell his fish for at least twice the price it got locally. If there were a cooperative to share transport costs, he and his family would be significantly better- off.

"Why then Paul is so much of the land around here uncultivated?" I asked, perhaps a little naively.

"You know Adrian. Poverty is not something you can count. It is in the mind."

Perhaps, I thought; but there is still much that the government and local development agencies could do to make the business of doing business much simpler and more profitable. Replacing a large culvert under the road between Ndanda and Masasi has for example taken nearly twelve months so far. In Europe it would take a week.

I was in Masasi to meet the education department. The senior officer had already told me that he would be in Mtwara for a seminar and that we should perhaps meet there. I declined and chose instead to meet his junior officers who in any case would be the ones doing the practical work of preparing my programme. The two 'Statistics officers' were there to meet me – Richard and Saidi. Richard runs a snacks shop; Saidi a phone repair shop. Both these businesses would prove very useful to me in the days to come; but first, the business of education and our first challenge. They reported that there was no budget to pay for tea and mandazi (a tasty doughnut eaten without sugar). I phoned Bushiru, the senior officer

"Am I interrupting your lunch Bushiru?"

"Don't worry, Mr Adrian. How can I help?"

"Well, whilst you're eating your rice and beans and meat and spinach which is provided to you by the government as part of the conditions of you attending your meeting, we are discussing our attempts to find five hundred shillings (40p) for each teacher attending my course to have a cup of tea and a snack. Can you help?"

He laughed so loudly down the phone, everyone could hear and they glanced at one another with knowing looks.

"I get your point Mr Adrian, but you know Tanzania is a very poor country and there is no budget."

"Mmm," I said. "I get your point too." And left it at that. Saidi was keen to distract me and reassure me that we could overcome these challenges.

We visited the school where my programme of teaching four weeks spoken English to teachers from across the district would be delivered. We sat in the staff room nibbling fried cassava roots and sipping hot sweet tea when my eye caught sight of a hand written notice in Kiswahili giving a timetable for the power cuts across Masasi. I had struggled with laptop and projector and cables on large bus, small bus, daladala and bajaj to get to this school, to find that on each and every day except Fridays, there is no electricity anywhere in Masasi for three months or until essential maintenance is completed. Essential maintenance like that culvert under the road had already taken a lot longer than three months but I was also quickly aware that others were not complaining; one teacher reminded us that once the essential maintenance was completed the power supply would be much more reliable. It reminded me of the story of the man who beat his own head on the ground because it felt so good when he stopped.

Against all these odds, the teaching programme started on time, in the chosen venue with all the teachers attending. On the first day, we had to switch the schedule to 'quiet discussion' from 'speech making', as we couldn't compete with the crashing and banging of rain and thunder overhead for over an hour but on the second day, tea and mandazi were served on paper plates and delicate white cups, thanks to Richard's snacks business. Saidi prefers to talk of challenges not problems and he's very good at overcoming them.

Tuesday, 11 March 2014

A varied diet

These days the mandazi arrive promptly at 10.45 in time for our tea break. Today, however, there was no water with which to wash our hands.

"How are we supposed to take tea if we cannot wash our hands?" asked Martha, who had already identified herself as a woman of strong opinions. I wanted to point out that there are as many germs in the water as might be lurking on her hands, but this is a strictly and universally observed Tanzanian custom and I said nothing. Many of the teachers have to travel by foot and by bus many miles to attend the course. Masasi district covers many hundreds of square miles of villages. Some teachers are unable to attend because they cannot travel daily and the District will not pay overnight accommodation. As it is, they receive a few shillings from me towards their transport costs and hope to receive a food allowance the next day from their headteacher. Not everyone is confident that the school will pay. Teachers are very appreciative of the lessons, though. When I came upon four of my class in a local bar, they offered to buy me a cold beer. I declined politely and immediately realised the offence I'd caused. To compensate I agreed to share a platter of fried pork and chillie. The pork is served in a separate eating area located behind the main bar, discreetly hidden from the gaze of Muslims or other non-pork eaters; and, crucially, being prepared in a separate kitchen. Simkoku, the teacher who had invited me, and who was on his third 'Safari', Tanzania's strongest lager, explained,"They will not serve pork in the main area – only goat and beef and chicken and fish."

"So you are not Muslim, Simsi, I must have misunderstood."

"Yes. I am Muslim, but I like pork. And beer."

Life with the Salvatorian Fathers is deeply peaceful, each day following the last in an ingrained pattern of prayer, food, work, food and finally prayer. There are Salvatorian priests spread across this region serving rural parishes. Here at the regional house, there are usually just three priests and two brothers.

We live in a small cluster of buildings huddled beneath the vast rocky outcrops that are emblematic of the Masasi landscape and surround the town. At this time of the year, following the rain and the thunder which shake the skies and scour the land each day, the rocky peaks are shrouded in heavy mist each morning. By midday, the great boulders strewn across the hillsides, like uninvited sentries, are visible once more, the lush vegetation suppliant at their feet, softening their fierceness.

I asked Brother Bogdan if someone might show me the way to climb one of these hills.

"Maybe," he said, after a long drag on his cigarette. He's fifty-four, moved here from his home of Krakow twenty-five years ago and has not kicked the habit. "But you should look out for leopards. Yes. I said leopards. The nightwatchman has reported hearing one quite a few times recently. He says it will come after the dogs. Leopards like dogs."

Apart from the sound of leopards which I might get to hear, it is very, very quiet here. Unlike Mtwara where the cacophony of noises was one of the biggest challenges of living there; here, at night, there is silence, only broken by the guava falling off the overhanging trees onto the tin roof of my lodge. Some of them fall and many are wrenched off by squirrels and bats. But it's still very quiet.

We eat together each evening chatting in a mixture of Kiswahili and English. After dinner they go to pray and I make my way back to my room.

"Take care with your flashlight Adrian as you go to bed. There was a puff adder waiting for me the other night."

Father James is full of practical advice for living in Tanzania. He has lived here for over forty years but retained the grin of the affable American who likes to share a joke. A septuagenarian, he has the look of a retired salesman and a sparkle in his eye like John Wayne. The swagger is more of a limp now, but he's tall with a commanding presence and has a pot belly which is more pot than belly, more deportment than fat. Now, almost bald, he sports a roguish moustache and a mischievous glint. He had been unwell.

"How have you been today Father?"

"Oh I slept for most of the day, you know, trying to shake off this cold, but they woke me this afternoon to go and shoot a baboon that had come down from the mountain and was stealing their seeds."

"And did you shoot it?"

"I did. One bullet and the creature fell tumbling from the rock; but, sad to say, it was a she and the baby she was holding now has no mother."

For a moment the glint receded as a glimmer of remorse softened his face, but it was back in a flash as he recounted those early days when he and the Sisters ate meat every day, thanks to his rifle.

"We lived on antelope, zebra and low cholesterol wart-hog."

Sunday, 16 March 2014

Moving around Masasi

This is the rainy season and here, nestled among these bulbous rocky outcrops, electric storms and torrential downpours are more dependable than the power supply. They arrive each afternoon, like clockwork, whereas the power cuts never stick to the timetable. The English classes are going well. Teachers attend and, by and large, attend punctually. I tried to impose discipline by requiring latecomers to give a full explanation and apology, but invariably the teachers' group listens attentively, asks one or two supportive questions and then offers sympathy for the defendant's plight and welcomes them to our group. Each morning there are at least six latecomers. Of these six, the reasons for lateness will be one or other of the following,
"The bus broke down."
"My child was sick and I took her to hospital."
"My headteacher required me to collect some papers."
"We were stopped by the police who told us we were overcrowded and so we had to wait for another bus."

One man had travelled some distance and had had to wait for a bus, once again, stuck in the mud; but, when I suggested that he should leave his home earlier, the group remonstrated, came to his defence and said,
"But it's far, sir. You must forgive him."
"But it's not as far as Edwin or Lucy have travelled and they arrived on time."
"No sir. Thank God, they were lucky."

Fate and the hand you're dealt plays such a large part in people's lives here. We discussed health issues today and the class was asked to share their good and bad experiences of hospitals, doctors and the healthcare system in general. Mama Nyoni started in one group,

"Well it's a good story and a bad story. I was five months pregnant and one morning had bad pains and was vomiting. I went to the doctor who told me that the baby was 'out of my stomach' and I should rest. For the next three months I went every day to see the doctor and then the baby was born dead."
"That's a very sad story Mama Nyoni. How is it a good story as well as bad?"
"Because I thought I was going to die and I didn't."

The honesty, the grim tales of harsh reality, the farcical mistakes and carelessness on the part of doctors, moved us and entertained us for the next hour. We heard from the boy who had influenza and was told to bring in a hen; the woman who was treated for one month for syphilis and was told the following month she had a simple fungal infection; and a woman who waited for six weeks by her baby's hospital bed only to watch her die as the hospital did nothing, once they had lost the X rays. We cheered when he heard from Angela who had had her baby delivered by Caesarian section by the light from a mobile phone during a power cut; and mother and child both survived. It was supposed to be an exchange of good and bad stories from our personal experience, but in reality it was a litany of horrific sadness contrasted with the odd tale of good fortune.

Small miracles seem commonplace in this forgotten region of one of the poorest countries in the world where eighty percent of the population exists on less than £1.00 a day. Brother Edward, a chubby man in his fifties, with a smile etched into the crow's feet round his gentle eyes, has started Masasi Radio. He started it in the sense that he built the steel broadcasting tower by hand, hauling each heavy steel strut into position himself. The station belongs to the Salvatorian Fathers and the equipment needed to open the station was a gift of £15,000 from the UK. Today there are four young trainees learning the craft of editing and production while five journalists move around the district interviewing farmers, covering the visit of a Deputy Minister and gathering news from across the region. Brother Edward proudly tells me that his mission is to keep remote communities connected. When there was trouble last year, sparked by a dispute over the price farmers were offered for their cashew nuts, Masasi Radio kept the farmers informed and united.

Masasi is a small, bustling town. Its sits at the crossroads where the roads to Newala, Tuunduru Nachingwea and Mtwara meet. Scores of villages use the town as their focal point for trade and shopping. Down the road, out of town, sit the same furniture shops - beds and coffins – you see all over Tanzania; the same guest houses, gaudily painted in pink or yellow; the same containers daubed in sky-blue paint, offering 'Spares' and 'Computa'. The market is full of the same tatty Chinese imported bric a brac – torches, watches and kiddies' toys. Shops dedicated to skin oil, hair pieces and soap; hand-made wooden tables, covered with plastic water bottles, filled with kerosene; and shop after shop of shirts, dresses, T-shirts and patterned cloth. Stalls selling second hand clothes – neatly washed and pressed and along the road, a display of blue jeans and shirts, suspended on hangers made from a twig, tied to the branch of a tree and swaying in the wind.

At the bus stand as the great buses from Dar spill a weary line of passengers, the bajaj and motorcycles wait for a fare, circling and heckling. The huge ancient buses, advertise wi-fi and air conditioning. In fact they have rust, bald tyres and a very loud TV, blaring *bongo fleva* videos continuously for ten hours. They sweep into town, where rickety stalls huddle round the muddy patch of earth called the bus stand. The drivers of these great beasts sit arrogantly chewing a stick, or calling their 'boy' to fetch a soda. They have driven at frightening speeds through villages and along dirt tracks to get here before dusk. Cars, mini buses and motorcycles scurry to the roadside as their blaring horns terrify all before them. Like some biblical beast they thunder through, leaving a demonic trail of dust or spray and scattered humans behind them.

Evance, a young candidate for the Brothers, made it as far as Masasi last night. His bus from Dar had waited for hours at a number of stages, whilst small cars, unable to ford the thick red bogs of mud, held up a long line of buses and lorries. He arrived at ten o'clock having been on the bus for seventeen hours.

"I'm very sorry, Brother," I sympathised.

"Oh we were lucky. There are many cars and buses that would spend the whole night in the mud. Only God and a Land Rover with a rope can help them."

Conclusion

This aspect of life in Tanzania has not changed in the three and half years we were there and nothing I've seen in southern Tanzania suggests that it will change any time soon. The same inefficiencies and petty corruptions; the same lack of ownership or purpose; the same sense of worthless in the face of gargantuan problems which only a super-State could overcome, continue to drag anyone with any enthusiasm for change or enterprise back to the ambient position of sloth and atrophy.

It seems a negative and pessimistic note on which to finish these entries. Readers might be surprised at the tone, having met such fortitude and optimism in many of the characters. And it is true, the resilience of individuals to make something of their own lives sits in stark contrast to the bewildering carelessness on the part of the State.

If my stay in Tanzania has taught me anything it is to have confidence in the individual and maintain deep scepticism towards anyone or any institution that tries to convince you that a more systemic approach can outdo the human spirit.

ABOUT THE AUTHOR

Adrian Strain lives and works in Leeds. Caroline and Adrian have five children and two grandchildren. Caroline and Adrian's experience in Mtwara led them to establish a small charity, Mtwaralinks (www.mtwaralinks.com) and the proceeds from the sale of this book will go to support its work.

Printed in Poland
by Amazon Fulfillment
Poland Sp. z o.o., Wrocław